国际经济法

INTERNATIONAL ECONOMIC LAW

（BILINGUAL COURSE）

主　编◎崔艺红

副主编◎王　卿　董临瑞

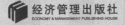

经济管理出版社

ECONOMY & MANAGEMENT PUBLISHING HOUSE

图书在版编目（CIP）数据

国际经济法：汉文、英文 / 崔艺红主编；王卿，
董临瑞副主编. -- 北京：经济管理出版社，2024.
ISBN 978-7-5243-0013-7

Ⅰ. D996

中国国家版本馆 CIP 数据核字第 2024NJ1550 号

组稿编辑：王　洋
责任编辑：高　娅
责任印制：张莉琼
责任校对：王淑卿

出版发行：经济管理出版社
　　　　　（北京市海淀区北蜂窝 8 号中雅大厦 A 座 11 层　100038）
网　　址：www. E-mp. com. cn
电　　话：（010）51915602
印　　刷：唐山玺诚印务有限公司
经　　销：新华书店
开　　本：720mm×1000mm/16
印　　张：15. 25
字　　数：307 千字
版　　次：2024 年 12 月第 1 版　　2024 年 12 月第 1 次印刷
书　　号：ISBN 978-7-5243-0013-7
定　　价：58. 00 元

前　言

当今世界正经历百年未有之大变局，法治在稳定国际秩序、规范国际关系、塑造国际规则、协调国际治理方面的作用越发凸显。习近平总书记审时度势，在构建"人类命运共同体"和共建"一带一路"倡议构想的基础上，又明确指出，"加快推进我国法域外适用的法律体系建设""要坚持统筹推进国内法治和涉外法治"，为我国涉外法治人才培养指明了方向。

"国际经济法"是教育部高等教育教学指导委员会审定的全国高等院校法学专业 16 门专业核心课之一，对我国涉外法治人才培养意义重大，但是目前国内图书市场有关该课程的"双语"教材仍然较少。

西安财经大学法学院法学专业是陕西省名牌专业、省级一流专业，2021 年获批"国家级一流专业"，而"国际经济法"课程的"双语教学"工作始于2005 年，积累了丰富的教学经验。

本教材立足于国家涉外法治人才培养在推进全面依法治国、涉外法治建设、参与全球治理中所具有的基础性、战略性、先导性地位和作用的客观实际，针对我国涉外法治人才储备不足的现实问题，直面国际经济贸易发展的客观需求，依据我国最新的对外经济贸易法律法规和相关的国际条约与公约，结合西安财经大学法学专业 20 年来"国际经济法""双语教学"的实践与经验，在西安财经大学"教材建设基金"的资助下成功出版，践行了"高校是法治人才培养第一阵地"的时代责任，切实服务于国家涉外法治建设和"一带一路"倡议的推进。

本教材包括八个部分，共 21 章。

第一部分为国际经济法的基础理论部分，即第 1 章国际经济法概述，包括国际经济法的概念与特征、法律渊源和基本原则，是学习和掌握国际经济法律规则的基础。

第二部分为国际经济主体法，包括第 2 章、第 3 章。第 2 章跨国公司的法律规范包括跨国公司的概念与组织结构、母公司对子公司的债务责任以及跨国公司与投资东道国、母国之间的冲突与管制。第 3 章国际经济组织法包括国际经济组织的概念、特征与类型，国际经济组织的法律规则与内部机构，以及国际货币基金组织（IMF）、国际复兴开发银行（IBRD）与世界贸易组织（WTO）三个全球性国际经济组织的法律制度。

第三部分为国际货物贸易法，包括第 4 章至第 6 章。第 4 章国际货物销售合同法包括联合国国际货物销售合同公约（CISG）概述，公约的结构与适用范围，合同的概念、形式与订立，合同生效与双方的义务，货物风险转移、违约救济和免责事由。第 5 章国际贸易术语解释通则包括国际贸易术语的概念与作用，2000 版国际贸易术语解释通则，传统与现代贸易术语的比较，国际贸易术语解释通则 2000 版、2010 版、2020 版之间的比较。第 6 章国际货物贸易管制法包括贸易管制的概念与特点、管制原则和管制措施。

第四部分为国际服务贸易法，包括第 7 章至第 10 章。第 7 章国际服务贸易法概述，聚焦于国际服务贸易的条约与公约、服务贸易总协定、国际海事服务贸易法和国际贸易金融服务法。第 8 章国际货物运输法包括国际货物运输方式、国际海上货物运输法、国际海上货物运输公约。第 9 章国际海运货物保险法包括海运保险的基础理论、国际海洋货物运输保险合同、承保范围、中国海运保险条款和代位求偿权。第 10 章国际货物贸易金融法包括国际贸易支付工具和支付方式的法律规范。

第五部分为国际知识产权贸易法，包括第 11 章、第 12 章。第 11 章国际知识产权贸易概述，内容涵盖国际知识产权贸易的概念、特点、法律体系。第 12 章国际知识产权交易的法律形式包括交易的具体法律形式、国际许可与国际特许经营的法律规制。

第六部分为国际投资法，包括第 13 章、第 14 章。第 13 章国际投资法包括国际投资概述、外资准入的行政管制制度、外资经营活动的管理和外国投资的保护与鼓励。第 14 章海外投资法包括海外投资的鼓励措施和管制措施、海外投资保险法律制度和我国的海外投资法。

第七部分为国际税法，包括第 15 章至第 17 章。第 15 章国际税法和国际税收管辖权包括国际税法的概念、特征与法律渊源以及国际税收管辖权的概念、类型与国际税收协定。第 16 章国际双重征税包括国际双重征税的概念与致因、国际双重征税问题的对策。第 17 章国际避税和逃税包括国际避税的概念与手段、国际逃税和避税的区别、国际逃税的主要方式与预防。

第八部分为国际经济争端解决法，包括第 18 章至第 21 章。第 18 章国际经济争端的主要解决途径包括概述、国际经济争端解决的法律途径与法律规则。第 19 章国际经济争端的外交解决途径包括外交解决途径的概念、特点与具体方法。第 20 章国际经济争端的国内司法解决包括国内法院的管辖权、法院及法律适用的选择条款。第 21 章国际经济争端的国际法解决途径包括国际法院争端解决机制、WTO 争端解决机制及国际投资争端解决中心争端解决机制。

本教材具有结构科学、内容新颖、创新性强、实用性强、实践性强等特点:

1. 结构科学

本教材遵循"法律是调整不同社会成员之间社会关系的行为规范"这一基本准则,按照"基础理论(概念、法律渊源、基本原则)""法律关系主体法(跨国公司法律管制、国际经济组织法)""国际经济行为法(国际货物贸易法、国际服务贸易法、国际知识产权贸易法、国际投资法)"和"国际经济行为调控法(国际贸易的法律管制、国际税法、国际经济争端解决法)"的逻辑,组织安排八个部分共 21 章的前后顺序,使本教材的逻辑结构更加符合法理和法律逻辑,更便于学习、理解和记忆,因而本教材的结构更加科学、合理。

尤其值得称道的是,在 1994 年《关税与贸易总协定》乌拉圭回合达成的"一揽子"协议中,明确了国际贸易除众所周知的传统货物贸易之外,还就两种新型的国际贸易形式,即国际服务贸易与国际知识产权贸易达成了《服务贸易总协定》(GATS)和《与贸易有关的知识产权协定》(TRIPs),确认了货物贸易、服务贸易、知识产权贸易"三分"国际贸易天下的客观现实。因此,本教材与时俱进,在第三、第四和第五部分分别将"国际货物贸易法""国际服务贸易法"和"国际知识产权贸易法"置于"国际经济行为法"体系之中,进一步强化了本教材体系的科学性。

2. 内容新颖

本教材以党中央、国务院最新的相关政策(2023 年习近平总书记在中共中央政治局第十次集体学习时强调,"加强涉外法治建设既是以中国式现代化全面推进强国建设、民族复兴伟业的长远所需,也是推进高水平对外开放、应对外部风险挑战的当务之急")和我国最新修订、制定的涉外经济法律法规(2020 年《外资企业法》、2021 年《民法典》、2022 年《对外贸易法》、2023 年《公司法》),以及最新的国际贸易惯例、国际公约与条约(国际贸易术语解释通则 2020 版、鹿特丹规则、视听表演北京条约等)为依据编撰完成,教材内容与时俱进,新颖性强。

3. 创新性强

我国已于 1988 年参加了《联合国国际货物销售合同公约》,其中关于合同订立步骤的规定,涉及"Invitation Offer(要约邀请)""Offer(要约)""Counter-offer(反要约)"与"Accept(承诺)"的英文汉译问题。由于既有汉译所用词汇令人费解,因而成为教学与科研工作的一大障碍。为此,本教材主编以英美法系的典型代表《英国合同法》为基础,结合《朗文字典(英文版)》及其公派留学英国一年对当地风土人情的切身体会,再结合中国传统文化与社会生活实践,将其分别汉译为"询价""报价""还价""成交"的本土生活语言,符合中国社会生活实际，言简意赅，直击本质，切实解决了中国加入该公约 30 余年来，关于"要约与承诺"这个事关合同是否订立的法律术语的汉译困惑，不仅为《民法典》"合同编"相关术语的修订提供了极具价值的参考，更为司法机关准确认定合同是否订立提供了简洁、直观的标准，因而极具创新性。

4. 实用性强

国际贸易术语是市场经济国家商人跨国贸易的传统习惯和做法，其并非制定法而是习惯法，并非法律规则，而是交易习惯。本教材第 5 章"国际贸易术语解释通则"是国际商会为统一国际商事交易中关于贸易术语的解释和适用所制定的。为了避免因疏漏而引致纠纷，国际商会不厌其烦地为每个术语做了条款烦琐的解释。本教材立足于法律视角，结合主编多年的教学和司法实践经验，从卖方义务维度总结出国际贸易术语的八大作用，如能确定卖方交货地点、交货方式、货物风险转移至买方的时刻、货物价格的构成成分、办理国际货运、货运保险的责任方以及办理货物进出口通关手续的责任方等，有效简化了国际贸易术语解释的规则，为学生准确理解、记忆和适用 2000 版解释通则中的 13 种贸易术语提供了新的视角，更为学生学习新版本的"解释通则"奠定了坚实基础，彰显了本教材的实用性。

5. 实践性强

本教材在重要章节和实践性强的部分（如合同缔结程序、买方义务、贸易术语、国际货运保险、国际贸易支付结算、国际投资等）设计了案例或问题思考，以引导学生深入思考、学以致用，强化学生的专业实践能力。此举不仅有助于强化学生对书本知识的理解和感悟，更有助于学生创新精神的培养，因此实践性强是本教材的又一特点。

鉴于西安财经大学法科学生的公共英语水平普遍达到四级或六级，本教材仅对新的专业术语和疑难句子，用脚注的方式予以中文解释。本教材既可作为国内普通高校法学专业学生的国际经济法教材，也可供从事国际贸易实务的专业人士使用，特别是还能作为涉外法律职业人员实务工作的参考书。

本教材作者分工如下：主编崔艺红教授负责本教材的结构设计、第一至第三部分（即第 1 章至第 6 章）内容的撰写以及全书的统稿，副主编王卿副教授负责第四与第五部分（即第 7 章至第 12 章）内容的撰写，副主编董临瑞老师负责第六至第八部分（即第 13 章至第 21 章）内容的撰写。在此，衷心感谢各位老师的辛苦劳动和默默付出。

本教材为西安财经大学校级规划教材。

目　录

Part Ⅰ　Basic Theory of International Economic Law

Part Ⅱ　International Economic Subject Law

Part Ⅳ　Law on International Trade in Services

Part Ⅵ International Investment Law

Part I Basic Theory of International Economic Law

The world today is undergoing profound changes unseen in a century. The rule of law plays an increasingly prominent role in stabilizing international order, regulating international relations, shaping international rules and coordinating international governance. The international economy and trade with market economy as its foundation need the rule of law to maintain its trading order of equality and voluntarism, equal value and compensation, honesty and trustworthiness, compliance with public order and good customs. International economic law is undoubtedly the inevitable result of the objective material life of the international economic market.

The contents of this part, chapter 1, mainly includes the concept and characteristics of international economic law, sources and basic principles of international economic law, which is the premise and foundation of learning and mastering international economic legal rules.

当今世界正经历百年未有之大变局，法治在稳定国际秩序、规范国际关系、塑造国际规则、协调国际治理方面的作用越发显著。以市场经济为基础的国际经济与贸易，更需要通过法治维护其平等自愿、等价有偿、诚实守信、尊重公序良俗的公平交易秩序，而国际经济法正是国际经济大市场客观物质生活现实需求的必然结果。

本部分即第 1 章的内容包括国际经济法的概念与特征、法律渊源以及基本原则，是学习和掌握国际经济法律规则的前提和基础。

Chapter 1   General Introduction

Section Ⅰ   Definition and Characteristics of IEL

Ⅰ. Definition

Due to the limited nature of the earth's natural resources, especially the uneven distribution of various resources in different countries and regions, it is the driving force for the sustainable development of international economy and trade since the beginning of the era of free capitalism. Therefore, international economic trade is one of the most effective ways to rationally allocate the limited resources of the earth on a global scale, and it is obviously essential for the economic development of countries and the improvement of people's quality of life.

In international economic trade practice, the transaction object[1] between two parties with places of business located in different countries needs to be transferred across the border, coupled with the conflicts and disputes caused by the distribution of interests between the two parties of the transaction. In order to protect and encourage their own international economic trade activities, sovereign states regulate their own foreign economic trade activities through laws and regulations, and even to sign international treaties or conventions with other relevant countries to coordinate their international economic trade relations based on common economic interests.

International Economic Law (IEL)[2] refers to the body of legal rules and norms that regulate the international economic relations resulted from international economic trade activities between private person, legal entity, state and international economic

---

[1]   交易标的。

[2]   For the sake of ease, we may use the abbreviated name IEL.

organization. Compared with the traditional international economic law, contemporary international economic law covers much more extensively, not only international trade of goods and trade in services, but also international technology transfer, international investment and international economic and trade dispute settlement.

II. Characteristics

(I) Diversity of subjects. Compared with subjects of domestic economic law, subjects of international economic law include not only nature person, legal entity and state, but also international economic organization, which is diverse.

A. Nature person. A natural person is a living individual born in a state of nature who has the qualification of civil subject on the basis of birth. ①To be a subject of IEL, nature person should be of full capacity for performing civil juristic act to enjoy civil rights and assume civil obligations independently by his/her own civil juristic act.

In western market economy countries, nature person engaging in international commercial transaction must be of full age and sound mind and must act without undue influence. In planned economy countries, nature person has not been permitted to engage in international commercial transaction. By Article 8 of the revised *Foreign Trade Law of China in 2016*, individuals with full capacity are allowed to engage in international trade and to be the so-called "foreign trade dealers" after November 7, 2016.

B. Legal entity. Legal entity is named juridical entity in Common Law, in Civil Law System it means the legal person created by national law. Article 57 of *China Civil Code* states, a legal person is a social organization with capacity for civil rights and capacity for civil conduct which independently enjoys civil rights and assumes civil obligations in accordance with law.

Legal entities can be either for-profit ones or non-profit ones. ② Legal entity here means just only the for-profit one. Article 76 of *China Civil Code* states, a legal person formed for the purpose of making profits and disturbing profits to its shareholders or other investors is a for-profit legal person. For-profit legal persons include limited liability companies, joint stock limited companies, and other enterprises legal persons. They

---

① 自然人是指在自然状态下出生并因其出生而具有民事主体资格的有生命的个体。

② Article 87 of *Civil Code of China*: A non-profit legal person is a legal person formed for the purpose of public welfare or any other non-profit purpose without distribution of profits to its investors, promoters, or members. Non-profit legal persons include but are not limited to public institutions, social groups, foundations, and social service organizations.

may be either an association of human beings or a property organized for a special purpose with the following characteristics:

(a) Be formed in accordance with the conditions and procedure stipulated by laws and regulations; (b) Having its own name, organs, domicile and property or funding; (c) With capacity for civil rights and civil conduct which independently enjoys civil rights and assumes civil obligations in accordance with law; (d) Independently assuming civil liability with all of its property which means the legal entity shall assume limited civil liability to all of its debt.

In west countries, the legal entity is free and active in international economic fields, especially in international commercial transactions. According to the legislation of China, only these legal entities registered with the authority of foreign trade under the State Council or its authorized bodies may engage in international trade. Nowadays, legal entities are the absolute majority subjects with its strong economic strength and good business reputation in international commercial transactions.

C. State. A state refers to a political unit with fixed territory, certain inhabitants, certain form of political power organization and sovereignty. ①Being the sovereignty, a state has the capacity to enjoy right and bear obligation according to the public international law and to conclude treaty or convention with other states or international organizations to regulate the economic relations between them. Each state has the ownership in its all wealth, natural resources and economic activities, and may sue or be sued in the international court to protect her sovereignty and interests.

In international economic field, sovereign state can be either one subject of horizontal international economic circulation relation or vertical international economic administrative relation. Being one party of horizontal relations, the state can directly sign a contract with foreigner. For example, in order to exploit natural resources or develop public facilities, a state may sign a special license agreement with the foreign investor. In such occasion, the state is immune from the jurisdiction of foreign courts when state engages in activities anywhere in the world that are unique to sovereigns. Meanwhile, being one party of vertical relations, a state has the power to make their foreign economic policy and laws to regulate the foreign economic relationships between national residents and foreigners.

D. International economic organization. International economic organization (here-

① 国家是指具有一定领土、一定居民、一定政权组织形式和主权的政治法律实体。

inafter referred to IEO）is the new subject appeared since World War Ⅱ. IEO refers to the economic alliances of two or more states or non-governmental organizations with a set of permanent organs established by signing agreements with the aim of pursuing common economic interests. ①

In today's international community with the growing economic conflicts, IEO plays a very important role in international commercial field. IEO may not only promote the conclusion of conventions between its member states, but also it may harmonize the legislation of member states. Meanwhile IEO may collect and disseminate information on international trade, investment or intellectual transfer for members, so as to promote the economic development of member countries.

（Ⅱ）Extensiveness of objects. The objects of IEL mean the various international economic relations resulted from economic activity beyond the legal boundary of states between subjects regulated by international economic law. According to the different legal status of the subjects, there can be two types of relations:

A. Vertical international economic control relations②. Relations of this type are named the international administrative relations resulted from the activities which states or international economic organizations regulate activities of international trade and investment according to national law or conventions. The foot of two subjects is not equal because one party is always a state or IEO who owns the sovereignty or the management authority from its members. Relations of taxation and the legal control of import and export are all this type.

B. Horizontal international commercial transaction relations③. They are also named international commercial circulation relations resulted from activities crossed the legal boundaries of states between different subjects. The foot of two subjects is equal. It's relation of international economic circulation and co-operation, such as relations of international trade and investments.

---

① 国际经济组织是指两个或两个以上国家或非政府组织之间为追求共同的经济利益，通过签订协议而建立的具有常设组织机构的经济联盟。

② 纵向的国际经济统制关系。

③ 横向的国际经济交易关系。

Section II   Sources of IEL

I . Definition

Sources in legal sense refer to the forms of expression and the sources of effect of law. In Common Law, sources are the evidence or content of law, such as a constitution, statute, treaty or Custom that provides authority for legislation and for judicial decisions.

II . Sources of IEL

According to different criteria, sources of international economic law are divided into domestic law and international law, substantive law and procedural law, compulsory law and arbitrary law.

(I) *National Law.* National law is usually the most extensive way of law-making, and one of the most important sources of international economic law. It refers to all rules and norms made by a state relating to the international economy. In China, national law includes both substantive law, such as *Civil Code of China*, *Foreign Trade Law*, *Foreign Capital Enterprise Law*, and procedure law, such as *Civil Procedure Law of China*, *Administrative procedure law of China.*

(II) *International Law.* International law is actually the equivalents of treaties and conventions. Treaties are legally binding agreements between two or more states. Conventions are also legally binding agreements between states but sponsored by international organization. [1]Economically, the most important conventions, belonging to the forced law, are *Hague Rules* in 1924, *CISG* in 1980, *GATS* in 1994.

(III) *International Model Law.* International model law refers to the rules and norms formulated and adopted by some international organizations as the model of certain legislation to reduce conflicts of laws between States and for individual state to voluntarily choose to apply. The most important ones are *Model Law on International Commercial Arbitration by the United Nations Commission on International Trade Law in 1985*, *Principles of International Commercial Contract by the International Institute for the Unifica-*

---

① ［美］Ray August. 国际商法［M］. 北京：高等教育出版社，2002：3.

tion of Private Law (*UNIDROIT PICC*) in 1994. The Preamble of PICC provides: "These Principles set forth general rules for international commercial contracts. They shall be applied when the parties have agreed that their contract be governed by them."

(IV) International commercial customs and usages. International commercial customs and usages refer to the general rules and practices in international commercial transaction that have been widely adopted by international community through invariable habits and common use. ① They are bound to the contracting parties only when they agreed to choose one of them in their contract. So they are laws of free choice.

International commercial customs and usages used to be oral rather than in writing. Years later, some NGOs complied them into written rules of which the most worldly recognized are *International Rules for the Interpretations of Trade Terms* (INCOTERMS) by International Chamber of Commerce (ICC), the *Uniform Customs and Practice for Commercial Documentary Credits* (UCP) by the International Chamber of Commerce.

Section Ⅲ Basic Principles of IEL

I. Definition

Basic principles of IEL are the guiding ideologies that embody the basic value of IEL and run throughout of the IEL, mainly including *Principle of National Economic Sovereignty*, *Principle of Equality and Mutual Benefit*, *Principle of International Cooperation and Development*.

II. Basic Principles of IEL

(I) Principle of National Economic Sovereignty. Being the primary principle of IEL, it's the core guiding ideology and the main spirit of all kinds of legal norms that run through the international economic law, which is the expression of national sovereignty principle in the field of international economic field. The Resolutions on Permanent Sovereignty over Natural Resources, the Charter of Economic Rights and Duties of States and other documents adopted by the UN General Assembly clearly declare that

---

① 国际商事惯例是指通过不变的习惯和共同的使用而被国际社会广泛接受和认可的国际商事交易普遍规则和实践做法。

every country has full and permanent sovereignty over its natural resources and all economic activities. It's manifested in the permanent sovereignty of the State over all natural resources within its territory, the right of the State to regulate and supervise foreign investors and their activities, and the right of the State to decide on measures to nationalize or expropriate foreign investments within its territory.

(II) Principle of Equality and Mutual Benefit. This principle means that all countries are equal in law and should participate in international economic activities with equal qualifications and share the fruits equally, which means all countries, big or small, strong or weak, are equal in legal status. Equality and mutual benefit is an inseparable whole and most-favored-nation treatment is a typical example of this principle.

(III) Principle of International Cooperation and Development. It refers to the gap of poor and rich countries should be gradually narrowed and eliminated through economic development of developing countries, and developed countries should cooperate with them in fields of economy, society, culture, science and technology to promote economic progress and social development of all countries, especially developing countries.

Part II International Economic Subject Law

As mentioned above, the subjects of international economic legal relations may be either natural persons and legal persons, or states and international economic organizations. Therefore, compared with the domestic economic legal relations, the subjects of international economic legal relations have the characteristics of diversity. The natural person and legal person are mentioned in civil law and commercial law of individual country, and the sovereign state, being the absolute subject of public international law, also has detailed provisions in public international law.

This part includes chapter 2 and chapter 3 which focuses on the two special subjects respectively—Transnational Corporation and International Economic Organization. Chapter 2 is the Legal Rules of Transnational Corporation, which consists of the basic theory of transnational corporation, the debt liability of parent company to its subsidiary, the conflict and regulation between transnational corporation and the host country and the home country of investment. Chapter 3 is the law of international economic organization which consists of concept, characteristics and types, the legal rules and internal structure of IEO, the legal systems of three famous global international economic organizations, namely IMF, IBRD and WTO.

如前文所述，国际经济法律关系的主体既可以是自然人、法人，也可以是国家和国际经济组织。与国内经济法律关系相较而言，国际经济法律关系的主体因而具有多样性特征。其中的自然人、法人主体在各国民法、商法中均已述及，而主权国家作为国际法的绝对主体，在国际公法中已有详尽的规定。

本部分包括第 2 章、第 3 章，分别聚焦于两个特殊主体——跨国公司与国际经济组织。其中第 2 章跨国公司的法律规范，内容包括跨国公司的基础理论、母公司对子公司的债务责任以及跨国公司与投资东道国、母国之间的冲突与管制等。第 3 章国际经济组织法包括国际经济组织的概念、特征与类型，国际经济组织的法律规则与组织机构以及三个全球性国际经济组织的法律制度，即国际货币基金组织、世界银行集团和世界贸易组织。

Chapter 2   Legal Rules on Transnational Corporation

Section Ⅰ   Introduction

Ⅰ. Definition and Characteristic

The Draft Code of Conduct for Transnational Corporations submitted in 1982 by the United Nations Economic and Social Council provides that the term transnational corporation means an enterprise consisting of entities located in two or more States, regardless of the legal form and scope of activities of those entities. The entities of an enterprise are linked by ownership or other factors, and one or more of them can exert a significant influence on the activities of others, in particular by sharing knowledge, resources and responsibilities with them. ① It can be seen that transnational corporation has the following characteristics:

(Ⅰ) Transnational of business organizations. The entities of transnational corporation may be different forms and natures, such as branch offices or head office, subsidiaries or parent company. They are distributed in many countries to engage in investment operation which show the transnational of business organizations.

(Ⅱ) Global strategy. When formulating strategies, transnational companies no longer focus on a branch or a region, but start from the interests of the whole company, take the world market as the competition goal, and consider the company's production,

---

① 本守则所用跨国公司一词，是指由分设在两个或两个以上国家的实体组成的企业，而无论这些实体的法律形式和活动范围如何。企业的各个实体由于所有制或别的因素相联系，其中一个或一个以上的实体能对其他实体的活动施加重要影响，尤其是可以同其他实体分享知识、资源以及分担责任——联合国经社理事会．跨国公司委员会特别会议的报告（中文版）[R]. 1983：15.

sales and expansion policies and strategies from the global scope so as to grab the maximum and long-term high profits.

(Ⅲ) Centralized unity of management. Benefit from the internal equity and non-equity structure arrangement, the global strategic decision-making power and the management power of each entity of transnational corporations are fully centralized and unified by the parent company.

(Ⅳ) The inter-connection of entities. A transnational corporation is an enterprise composed of its various entities distributed in various countries. The parent company may, through ownership control of an overseas subsidiary or contractual agreements, form a control relationship that enables the parent company or its entities to share knowledge, resources and responsibilities.

Ⅱ. Organizational Structure System

The organizational structure system of a transnational corporation refers to the organizational whole structure which consists of entities at home and abroad. ①

(Ⅰ) Branch (or branch office) and head office. Branch or branch office and head office are a pair of legal term. A branch is an office or business organ established by the head office at home or abroad, which has no independent legal status and has the nationality of the head office. The head office is directly responsible for the actions of its branches. Article 196 of *China Company Law* states, "The branch of a foreign company established within the territory of the People's Republic of China does not have the status of a legal person." Any company that has branches abroad is the head office. So the head office and the branch office are one legal entity and the same company.

(Ⅱ) Subsidiary and parent company. Subsidiary company is a legal term relative to parent company. A subsidiary is usually a company whose shares are wholly or majorly owned by its parent company or controlled by agreement with another company. ② It is established under the laws of host country and has an independent legal personality. It acts in its own name, not only its property is independent from that of the parent company, but also it independently assumes civil liability with all its own property. It may take

---

① 所谓跨国公司的组织体系是指由跨国公司海内外诸实体所构成的有机整体。
② 子公司是相对于母公司而言的一个法律术语。子公司通常是指其全部或多数股份被另一公司所拥有或通过协议方式受另一公司控制的公司。

the form of a limited liability company or joint stock limited company, according to laws of host country.

Any company holding a majority stock in a subsidiary company or exercising actual control over it by contract is the parent company which is independent legal person from its subsidiary. But they two are closely linked together by various control means and parent company is the core.

Ⅲ. Internal Control Relations between Entities

The entities of transnational corporation are organically connected through various complex control relations, mainly including two relations: Equity control and non-equity control.

(Ⅰ) Equity control. Among the various means of control, full or majority percentage of shares which a parent company owns in a subsidiary remains one of the most important means of exercising control. [1]

(Ⅱ) Non-equity arrangement control. Since 1970s, non-equity arrangements are increasingly used by transnational corporations which are not subject to equity investment. Such as from relatively simple licensing contracts, sales contracts, management contracts, to highly complex combinations of various provisions, even the combination of non-equity security and equity participation which allows for effective control of subsidiary company. Based on various means of control, the parent company occupies a dominant position in the entities of transnational corporations.

Ⅳ. Corporations Integration Development Based on Internal Control[2]

The internal control relations formed by the equity and non-equity structure arrangement between the parent and subsidiary companies enables the parent company to arrange the global production and operation activities of the entire multinational company according to its global strategy, so that each entity at home and abroad can comply with the development needs of the company's global strategy, and thus form internal integration. For example, in foreign investments, the parent company does not care of the

---

① 在各种控制手段中，母公司在子公司中持有全部或多数股份，仍然是行使控制权的一种最重要的手段。

② 基于内部控制关系的企业一体化发展。

profits of an individual subsidiary, but rather about the "contribution" it makes to the overall business plan of the multinational company.

Section II　Liability of Parent Company to It's Subsidiary

I . Interference and Damage by Parent Company to the Subsidiary

The parent company and its subsidiaries located in different countries are generally legally independent, but are economically linked to each other, which means their legal liabilities are separated from their economic ties. Since the parent company may instruct the subsidiary to make sacrifices based on the global strategy and interests of the group, according to the principle of limited liability of the legal person, the debt of the subsidiary is borne by the subsidiary itself, which has nothing to do with the parent company. Obviously, this will seriously damage the interests of its minority shareholders and creditors, and even the host country and the public. Therefore, the legal liability of the parent company to its subsidiaries attracts attention.

II . Liability of the Parent Company to the Subsidiary

The responsibility of the parent company to its subsidiary depends on the extent to which the subsidiary has been deprived of its independence.

(I) No responsibility of the parent company to its subsidiary. When the subsidiary has sufficient or necessary autonomy, it is an independent and autonomous body, which can independently make decisions to engage in various civil activities, and independently bear civil liabilities, the principle of limited liability shall prevail, and the parent company shall not be liable for the debts of the subsidiary. ①

(II) Bearing corresponding responsibility. When the subsidiary is deprived of its autonomy in certain matters due to the interference and domination of the parent company, such as wrong decisions or improper instructions of the parent company, and damages are caused to the subsidiary or its creditors, the parent company shall be liable for

---

① 当子公司具有足够的或必要的自主性，是独立自主的主体，能独立做出决定从事各种民事活动，独立对外承担民事责任时，有限责任的原则应占优势，母公司对子公司的债务不负责任。

specific damages resulting there from, not liable for the whole debt of the subsidary.

(Ⅲ) Bearing directly responsibility. When a subsidary loses its autonomy largely or completely as a result of the parent's control, the parent should be held directly responsible for the debts of the subsidary which is named the theory of Piercing the Corporate Veil or Corporate Personality Denial System, as the subsidary loses its independence and effectively has the status of a branch of the parent. Article 23 of the *China Company Law* stipulates that where a shareholder of a company abuses the independent status of a company legal person and the limited liability of a shareholder to evade debts and seriously damage the interests of creditors of the company, he shall bear joint and several liability for the debts of the company. [1]

Section Ⅲ   Conflicts and Control over Transnational Corporations

Ⅰ. Conflicts between Transnational Corporations and Host or Home Country

Due to the strong economic strength of transnational corporations and their pursuit of high profits world widely by their global strategy, there will be various contradictions and conflicts between either transnational corporations and host or home countries, or host and home countries, among which contradictions between transnational corporations and host countries are the most striking. For example, challenges of global strategy to national sovereignty, conflict between global strategies with the development goals of host country, transfer pricing to evade the tax and foreign exchange control of host country, which have adverse consequences on host country.

Meanwhile, the overseas investment of transnational corporations will reduce investment and employment opportunities in home country, which will affect the export of products, and cause problems such as technology outflow, tax evasion, and international balance of payments, which are manifested in contradictions and conflicts with home country.

---

① 我国《公司法》第二十三条规定，公司股东滥用公司法人独立地位和股东有限责任，逃避债务，严重损害公司债权人利益的，应当对公司债务承担连带责任。

In addition, conflicts between home and host countries based on personal and territorial jurisdiction to transnational corporations can lead to bad diplomatic relations of the two countries. For example, conflict between the nationalization of a foreign investment enterprise by host country and the exercise of the right of diplomatic protection by home country.

II. Control on Transnational Corporations

（Ⅰ）Regulation by host country. In order to give full play to the positive role of transnational corporation and to limit and avoid the negative role, all countries have promulgated some laws and regulations to supervise the investment activities of transnational corporations and to promote the development of national economy of host counties, such as Foreign Investment Law, Tax law, Foreign Exchange Control Regulations, which have two functions. One of which is to protect and encourage them by means of national treatment provision, protection legal rights and interests, tax incentives, investment profits and capital repatriation. The other one is to supervise or regulate investment activities that are detrimental to host country by means of the requirements of abiding by the host country's law, restrictions on entry and establishment of enterprises, or controls on repatriation of profits and principle, taxation and expropriation or nationalization of their property.

（Ⅱ）Regulation by home country. Transnational Corporations should also be regulated by home country. The relative laws and regulations include company law, securities law, tort liability law, labor Law, consumer protection law, anti-unfair competition law, accounting standards, tax law and insurance law of overseas investment, which also have two main aims. One is to protect and encourage transnational enterprise to invest overseas by means of tax incentives, financial subsidies, cash rewards, especially the overseas investment insurance system. The other one is to restrict or regulate the activities of them that are detrimental to the State by means of restrictions on export of technology and the outflow of investment capital, the elimination of tax incentives and so on.

（Ⅲ）International regulation. Since it is difficult for a single national law to effectively control the negative activities of transnational corporation, it is a common requirement of the international community, especially developing countries, to conduct international supervision through conventions. The aims of control by conventions are firstly to prevent and restrict negative activities of the corporation and secondly to stimulate them to play an active role in world economic development.

A. Washington convention. *Convention on the Settlement of Investment Disputes between States and Nationals of Other States* by IBRD in Washington, entered into force on October 14, 1966, is the first convention relating to the regulation of multinational enterprises in the world. More than 150 members, including China,① are members of the Convention. As stated in its preamble, the purpose of the Convention is to promote international economic cooperation and international private investment by establishing the International Centre for Settlement of Investment Disputes (ICSID) to deal with disputes of private international investments between member States and nationals of other members by means of mediation and arbitration, which will eliminate political and diplomatic interference to improve the investment climate.

B. United Nations Code of Conduct for Transnational Corporations. The second convention relating to regulation of multinational enterprises in the world is undoubtedly *United Nations Code of Conduct for Transnational Corporations (Draft)* in 1982. The draft contains six chapters of 71 articles including definition of transnational corporations and scope of application of the Code, the activities and treatment of multinational corporations, etc. Due to differences between developed and developing countries on host country jurisdiction, expropriation and nationalization compensation standards and other issues, the Code has not entered into force. Since 1982, China has participated in the drafting of the draft Code.

C. Agreement on Trade-related Investment Measures. *Agreement on Trade-Related Investment Measures* is abbreviated to TRIMs, which is one of the three new issues② in GATT Uruguay Round of multilateral trade negotiations and an integral part of the legal system of WTO. Binding on all member parties, TRIMs is the first global agreement on international direct investment measures formulated and implemented in the international community to date, and has had a significant impact on the growing prosperity of international investment. It integrates investment issues into the multilateral trading system of WTO and introduces the GATT principles of national treatment and the general abolition of quantitative restrictions into the field of international investment in the form of multilateral agreements. The basic principle of the agreement is that the implementation of trade-related investment measures by members shall not contravene the GATT principles of national treatment and the elimination of quantitative restrictions.

---

① On December 5, 2000, the 26th Meeting of the Standing Committee of the Seventh National People's Congress ratified the Convention, signed by Zhu Qizhen, representative of the Chinese Government, in Washington on February 9, 1990.

② The other two new topics are trade in services and trade-related aspects of intellectual property rights.

Chapter 3　Law of International Economic Organization

Section I　General Introduction

I. Definition

International Economic Organization, abbreviated to IEO, is the permanent nations-union by agreement of two or more states with the aim of pursuing common economic interests.

II. Characteristics

(i) Established by two or more states with common economic interests; (ii) With a set of permanent organs; (iii) The Charter including the aims and functions, principles and internal organs, resources, rights and duties of its members, right to vote, is drafted and adopted by all its member states; (iv) It's capacity or the juridical personality stipulated in its Charter, must be recognized by its members automatically while becoming member states; (v) Enjoy immunity from judicial process and other action.

III. Types

IEOs can be classified into different kinds according to different criterion.

(I) According to both general in scope and universal in its intended membership, there are two kinds of IEOs as follows.

A. Global economic organizations refer to the economic unions between countries with members coming from each continent on the earth, such as IMF, IBRD and WTO, the three pillars of the world economy.

B. Regional economic organizations, well known for EU, NAFTA, OECD and ASEAN,① are the economic unions between member states whose memberships are limited to a fixed certain area of the earth by their agreements.

(Ⅱ) According to the aim or function of IEO, there are two kinds as following.

A. The comprehensive IEO,② combines various functions which are not only economy, but also politics, culture, such as EU.

B. The professional IEO,③ mainly refers to an organization of exporting primary products④ and international commodity organizations. The first one refers to the union of states which can only produce some certain resources or primary products for export which are the lifeline of their national economy. Such as Organization of Petroleum Exporting Countries, Association of Natural Rubber Producing Countries, etc.⑤ International Commodity Organizations (ICOs) are established on multilateral agreements by governments of exporting and consuming countries of a certain commodity regarding the purchase, sales, and stable prices of the commodity. ICOs can play a role in reducing transaction costs between producer and consumer. Examples are the Joint Committee of Governments of Copper Exporting Countries and International Coffee Organization.

(Ⅲ) According to weather the governments represent their states to sign the treaty of establishment, there are also the following two kinds.

A. IGOs (Inter-governmental organizations), such as IMF, EU and ASEAN, are founded on basis of treaties negotiated by their central governments and approved voluntarily and adopted democratically by it's all member countries.

B. NGOs (Non-governmental Organizations) are voluntary and non-official organizations organized at the international level. NGOs can be either non-profit or for-profit one.

a. NPOs, as usually called Non-profit Organizations, serve as coordinating agencies for national private groups in international affairs. Examples are the International

---

① ASEAN: The Abbreviation of Association of Southeast Asian Nations.

② 综合性国际经济组织。

③ 专业性国际经济组织。

④ 初级产品出口组织。

⑤ 天然橡胶生产国联合会，以下简称 ANRPC，成立于 1970 年 10 月，秘书处设立在马来西亚的吉隆坡，11 个成员国包括中国、印度、印度尼西亚、马来西亚、巴布亚新几内亚、新加坡、斯里兰卡、泰国、越南、柬埔寨和菲律宾。联合会的目标是促进天然橡胶生产和消费合作，促进技术提升，稳定天然橡胶市场价格。

Chamber of Commerce (ICC), the International Air Transport Association.

b. FPOs, as usually called For-profit Organizations, also known as Transnational Corporations (TNCs) or Multinational Enterprises (MNEs), are businesses operating branches or subsidiaries or joint ventures in two or more countries[1].

In theoretical opinion, only NPOs are the international economic organizations here rather than the FPOs discussed in Chapter two.

IV. Roles

Since World War II, the number of IEOs has increased amazingly. In today's international community, IEOs also play a very important role in international commercial transaction: (i) They may enter into treaties and conventions with other states or IEOs; (ii) They may harmonize the legislation between members; (iii) They may collect and disseminate information of international trade, investment or intellectual property transfer; (iv) They may promote the economic development of member states.

Section II   Substantive and Procedural Rules for Accession of Members

A state seeking to get the membership or qualification, that's the legal status of a state to accept the rights and assume obligations in the Charter, should satisfy the essential rules of accession that is substantive and procedural requirements in the Charter.

I. Substantive Rules

(I) General requirement. Each IEO inevitably has the requirement for the state seeking to join to obey its purpose, compacts and charter and undertake member's obligations.

(II) Special requirement. Different IEO will have different special requirements which can be the following cases:

A. Regional IEO restricts the membership to a certain area of the earth, such as Economic Community of West African States whose members are developing countries of Caribbean area.

B. Professional IEO restricts membership to produce some certain resource or product for exporting, and these exported goods are their lifeline of national economy,

---

① Ray August. 国际商法 [M]. 北京: 高等教育出版社, 2002: 43.

such as the Organization of the Petroleum Exporting Countries (OPEC).

C. There are a few of IEOs, whose pr−requisite for joining is to join another IEO in advance which is relative to each other. For example, the membership of World Bank is limited to the member of IMF.

II. Procedure Rules

The legal procedures to join are different from each other, but generally including:

(I) Application, means a state seeking to join should apply for the accession with a statement of willing to undertake all the obligations in the charter.

(II) Examination, means the administrative arm of an IEO, the secretariat, is liable for reviewing if the application accords with the terms in the charter after acceptance the application.

(III) Negotiation, means the secretary−General of the IEO, heading up the secretariat, will inform all its members and set up a work term to negotiate with the applicant state.

(IV) Vote, means the work team will draft a protocol of joining and offer to the members to decide by vote after all the problems resolved. IEO generally requires a simple majority vote to admit new members, except an absolute majority vote.

Section III Organs of IEO

In order to achieve the strategic goals, IEO must set the internal organs to arrange the division of labor and cooperation. There are generally three agencies in an IEO: the authority organ, the executive organ and the administrative organ.

I. Authority Organ

It's a legislative body made up of representatives of all members, named the General Assembly or the parliament and the Board of Governors. Its function is to discuss any question or matter within the scope of the charter, formulate policies and make laws, examine and approve a budget, elect the representatives of executive organ and pass the draft resolutions.

II. Executive Organ

It's a usual practice that an executive organ is set up under the organ of Authority. It's commonly named the Council or committee of execution and the Board of Directors, and made up of the representatives of members or of the most important members. Its function is to carry out the draft resolutions, policies and laws. It's also the quasi—authority organ during the period after the annual meeting ending; so many powers of the Authority Organ have been delegated to the Executive Board during the remainder of the year, although certain other important matters remain the duties of the Authority Organ.

III. Administrative Organ

It's also named the administrative arm, liable for making reports and recommendations, handling with the daily work. It's the core of modern IEO. The Secretary—General, heading up the secretariat, is elected by the General Assembly.

Section IV   Global IEO

I. IMF

IMF is the abbreviation of International Monetary Fund which is a multilateral cooperation organization established by the United Nations specifically to promote international monetary and financial cooperation with the voluntary participation of sovereign states.

(I) Establishment. Because there isn't any international currency that can be spent around the world, foreign currency has to be converted into local currency. After the breaking down of the gold standard[1] in 1914 and the failure of the gold bullion standard[2] which came into being in 1920s before World War II, the currency exchange in world trade was very difficult. Meanwhile because of the deteriorating domestic economies, many countries had to maintain protectionist high tariffs rates and truculent international trade policies, which resulted in the Great Depression in 1930s and the outbreak of the World War II.

---

① 黄金本位制。
② 金块本位制。

From July 1 to 22, 1944, the United Nations convened a meeting, popularly known as the UN Monetary and Financial Conference in the small town of Breton Woods in New-Hampshire, US, to create a new international monetary system with the US dollar at its center and an international organization to oversee that system. Representations of 44 founding member countries attended, including the United States, Britain, China, the Soviet Union and France. At last, two agreements were drafted: One is *Articles of Agreement of the International Monetary Fund.* ①

On December 27, 1945, representatives of 29 countries, including China, formally signed the IMF Agreement, ② which announced the establishment of IMF. The organization itself began operations in May 1946 at headquarters in Washington. Its Membership has grown from the original 44 founding Members in 1945 to 190 Member States in 2023.

(II) Purpose and the critical missions. The purpose of IMF, directly stipulated in Article 1 of IMF Agreement by which Fund shall be guided in all its policies and decisions, is to work to achieve sustainable growth and prosperity for all of its 190 member countries by supporting economic policies that promote financial stability and monetary cooperation, which are essential to increase productivity, job creation, and economic well-being.

Thus, the critical missions of IMF are: (i) furthering international monetary cooperation; (ii) encouraging the expansion of trade and economic growth by providing loans③and developing capacity④; (iii) discouraging policies that would harm prosperity by Surveillance. ⑤

---

① Another One is the Articles of Agreement of the International Bank for Reconstruction and Development.

② Certainly Include the Articles of Agreement of International Bank for Reconstruction and Development.

③ Providing loans—Including emergency loans, is to help member countries experiencing actual or potential balance of payments problems to rebuild their international reserves, stabilize their currencies, continue paying for imports, and restore conditions for strong economic growth, while correcting underlying problems.

④ The IMF provides technical assistance and training to governments, including central banks, finance ministries, revenue administrations, and financial sector supervisory agencies. These capacity development efforts are centered on the IMF's core areas of expertise ranging from taxation through central bank operations to the reporting of macroeconomic data. Such training also helps countries tackle cross-cutting issues, such as income inequality, gender equality, corruption, and climate change.

⑤ The IMF monitors the international monetary system and global economic developments to identify risks and recommend policies for growth and financial stability. The fund also undertakes a regular health check of the economic and financial policies of its 190 member countries. In addition, the IMF identifies possible risks to the economic stability of its member countries and advises their governments on possible policy adjustments.

（Ⅲ）Quotas. Quotas are the amount of funds that a state is required to contribute when becoming the member of the Found, which is based broadly on the relative position of the member in the world economy. Members' quotas (expressed in SDR, Special Drawing Right) make up a pool of funds, named the IMF's resources. The quotas determine how much a contributing member can borrow from when they fall into financial difficulty and will receive the incremental interests. And quotas also determine the member's voting rights. ①

（Ⅳ）Organizations. The stipulation of article 12（1）of IMF Agreement states, the Fund shall have a Board of Governors, an Executive Board, a Managing Director and a staff.

A. The board of governors. At the top of its organizational structure is the Board of Governors. Being the highest authority and decision–making body, all powers of the Fund are vested in the Board of Governors. It consists of a Governor and an Alternate Governor appointed by each member. The Board of Governors shall select one of the Governors as Chairman.

B. The executive board. It's responsible for conducting the day–to–day business and shall exercise all the powers delegated to it by the Board of Governors. It's composed of 24 Directors, and 8 of which represent individual members: China, France, Germany, Japan, Saudi Arabia, the United Kingdom, and the United States, Russia. The other 16 Directors represent groupings of the remaining members. A Managing Director is appointed to be the Chairman for a term of 5 years and assisted by 4 Deputy Managing Directors. ② Decisions are made only when its members reach a consensus, a practice that minimizes confrontations on sensitive issues and that ensure full cooperation.

C. The administrative organ. It's composed by Managing Director and Staff. The Managing Director appointed by the Executive Board is not only the Chair of it but also the head of the staff of some 1700. By tradition, the person should be European. Kristalina Georgieva, born in Sofia of Bulgaria, currently serves as Managing Director. Unlike

---

① Under IMF rules, each member has 250 basic votes, which are then increased by one vote per 100000 SDR.

② In this tenure, Li Boa, one of 4 Deputy Managing Directors, is from China. He assumed the role of Deputy Managing Director at the IMF on August 23, 2021, responsible for the IMF's work on about 90 countries as well as on a wide range of policy issues. More information of Li Bo is available on the Internet of https: //www. imf. org/ en/ About/senior–officials/Bios/bo-li; https: //www. imf. org/en/About/senior–officials/Bios/bo-li, 2023–08-12.

the Executive Directors, who represent particular states or groups of states, the Managing Director and the staff are responsible to the members as a whole in carrying out the policies of the IMF.

(Ⅴ) Cooperation between China and IMF. Being one of the 27 founding members of IMF, due to special historical reasons, China didn't resume its legal seat in IMF until 1980. In 1991, the Representative Office of IMF in China① was established at the Unit 3612, China World Tower 2, No. 1 Jian Guo Men Wai Avenue, Beijing. ②

In 1996, China formally accepted Article Ⅷ of IMF Agreement and realized currency convertibility under the current account. On November 30, 2015, the Executive Board of IMF decided to include RMB in the Special Drawing Rights currency basket, which was expanded to five currencies, namely US dollar, Euro, RMB, Japanese Yen and British Pound. ③ The new SDR basket came into effect on October 1, 2016.

On January 27, 2016, IMF announced China has officially become the third largest shareholder of IMF behind the USA and Japan because the Amendment to the Reform of the Board of Directors has come into effect yesterday.

As China's cooperation with IMF continues to strengthen, the Chinese mainland's global financial competitiveness in 2022 ranked the 8th in the world, which shows the great power status of China. In May 2022, IMF announced the proportion of RMB in the SDR basket rose from 10.92% to 12.28%. It can be seen that the internationalization of RMB has made great progress in the past decade, but the international status of RMB still does not match the size of China's economy. The internationalization of RMB still has a lot of room for improvement.

Ⅱ. World Bank Group

World Bank Group is one of the world's largest sources of funding and knowledge for developing countries, established by United Nations after World War Ⅱ. It's the

---

① There is a reading room with a variety of fund publications in the IMF China Office. The reading room is open to the public from Monday to Friday, 9 a. m. to 12: 30 p. m. and 2 p. m. to 5 p. m.

② For more information please see articles of the Agreement between the Government of the People's Republic of China and the International Monetary Fund Concerning the Establishment of a Permanent Office of the International Monetary Fund in China in 1991 or search on https: //www. imf. org/zh/Countries/ResRep/CHN.

③ The weight of RMB in the SDR currency basket is 10.92% while the weights of the US dollar, Euro, Japanese Yen and British Pound are 41.73%, 30.93%, 8.33% and 8.09% respectively.

unique global partnership including five institutions①working for sustainable solutions that reduce poverty and build shared prosperity in developing countries.

（Ⅰ）IBRD, the abbreviation of International Bank for Reconstruction and Development, is a global development cooperative owned by 189 members. The Articles of Agreement of IBRD was drafted in July 1944 and formally signed on December 27, 1945, which announced the establishment of IBRD. It began operations on June 25, 1946 at Washington. Membership is restricted to the members of IMF.

The original purpose of IBRD was to help the European countries and Japan rebuild after World War Ⅱ. After they reached a certain level of per capital income, IBRD concentrates entirely on developing countries. Specifically speaking, IBRD supports the World Bank Group's mission by providing loans, guarantees, risk management products, and advisory services to middle-income and creditworthy low-income countries, as well as by coordinating responses to regional and global challenges.

IBRD raises most of its funds in the world's financial markets. IBRD has maintained a triple-A rating since 1959, which allows it to borrow at low cost and offer middle-income developing countries. IBRD earns income every year from the return on its equity and from the small margin it makes on lending. This pays for World Bank operating expenses, goes into reserves to strengthen the balance sheet, and provides an annual transfer of funds to IDA, the fund for the poorest countries.

Organs in IBRD consist of Board of Governors, Executive Directors, president and staff. The Board of Governors consist of one Governor and one Alternate Governor appointed by each member country. The office is usually held by the country's minister of finance, governor of its central bank, who serves for terms of five years and can be reappointed. All powers of the Bank are vested in the Board of Governors, the Bank's senior decision-making body according to the Articles of Agreement.

（Ⅱ）IDA. The full name of IDA is the International Development Agency. Being one of the five institutes of World Bank Group, IDA was established on September 24, 1960, based on the Agreement of IDA. IDA is the part of World Bank that helps 75 of the world's poorest countries or less developed countries which aims to reduce poverty by providing zero to low-interest loans (called "credits") and grants for programs that boost economic growth, reduce inequalities, and improve people's living conditions. IDA funds are allocated to the recipient countries in relation to their income levels

---

① The five member institutions are respectively IBRD, IDA, IFC, MIGA and ICSID.

and record of success in managing their economies and their ongoing IDA projects. Since 1960, IDA has provided $496 billion to 114 countries. ① IDA is overseen by its 174 shareholder countries, which comprise Board of Governors. Its day-to-day development work is managed by IBRD operational staff, governments and implementing agencies.

(Ⅲ) IFC. The full name of IFC is International Finance Corporation, established in 1956 based on the IFC Articles of Agreement. Owned by 186 member countries, it is the largest global development institution focused exclusively on the private sector. It helps developing countries improve the lives of people by investing in private sector growth of its member countries and providing advisory services to businesses and governments.

Although part of the World Bank Group, IFC is a separate legal entity. Membership in IFC is open only to members of IBRD. The President of the World Bank Group is also President of IFC. Programs and activities of IFC are guided by Board of Governors and Board of Directors which consisted of one governor and one alternate appointed by each member. Corporate powers are vested in the Board of Governors, which delegates most powers to a board of 25 directors.

60 years ago, IFC pioneered the idea of the private sector as a catalyst for progress in developing countries. ② For more than 60 years, IFC transformed this belief into reality throughout the developing world and has leveraged the power of the private sector for global good.

(Ⅳ) MIGA. The Multilateral Investment Guarantee Agency (MIGA) is the fifth and newest member of the World Bank Group. It provides political risk③ (non-commercial risk) insurance (guarantees) and credit enhancement for projects in a broad range of cross-border private sectors investors and lenders in developing members. On April 12,1988, MIGA was created by *Convention Establishing the Multilateral Investment Guarantee Agency* adopted in 1985,④ to promote foreign direct investment into developing countries to support economic growth, to reduce poverty and improve people's lives.

---

① https://idea.worldbank.org/en/what-is-ida, 2023-08-16.

② 60年前，国际金融公司率先提出了私营部门作为发展中国家进步催化剂的理念。

③ Risk arising from the adverse actions or inactions of governments, or wars, civil strife, and terrorism, as it's usually named "non-commercial risks".

④ Adopted at the Annual Meeting of the World Bank in Seoul on October 11, 1985 and entered into force on April 12, 1988. So the MIGA is also named the Seoul Convention.

The agency opened for business as a legally separate and financially independent entity. Membership was open to all IBRD members and Switzerland. On April 30, 1988, China became a non-original member. There are 182 members as of August 18, 2023, including 154 developing countries and 28 industrialized countries. ①

Organs in MIGA consists of the Council of Governors, the Board of Directors, the President and staff. The President of the World Bank Group is also the President of MIGA. MIGA only supports investments that are developmentally sound and meet high social and environmental standards. Product or coverage of political risk insurance/guarantees offered by MIGA includes Currency Convertibility and Transfer Restriction, Expropriation, Breach of Contract, War and Civil Disturbance and Non-Honoring of Financial Obligations②. No matter which insurance coverage, only eligible investments by eligible investors in eligible host country could be guaranteed.

（Ⅴ） ICSID. The International Centre for Settlement of Investment Disputes （ICSID） is established on Oct. 14, 1966 by the *Convention on the Settlement of Investment Disputes between States and Nationals of Other States* （the Washington Convention③） . The seat of the Centre shall be at the principal office of the IBRD. As at December 19, 2022, 158 countries have ratified the Convention to become Contracting States. China signed the Convention on February 9, 1990 and ratified it on February 6, 1993④ with the statement of "China will only consider submitting disputes over compensation arising from expropriation and nationalization to the jurisdiction of the 'Center'" .

After World War Ⅱ, the newly independent developing countries expropriated or nationalized foreign-funded enterprises involved in important natural resources and the lifeline of national economy, which caused the contradictions and disputes between developed and developing countries. Beginning in 1962, under the auspices of IBRD, the Washington Convention was drafted and officially adopted on March 18, 1965. On October 14, 1966, the Washington Convention entered into force and the ICSID became operational in Washington, DC. Finance of the Centre consists of charges for the use of its facilities, or other receipts （such as the fees and expenses of members of the Commis-

① https: //www. miga. org/member-countries, 2023-08-18.
② Non-Honoring of Financial Obligations, the new type of coverage in 2009, is one of substantial changes to the agency's operational regulations and the largest and most significant expansion of MIGA's business toolkit approved by MIGA's Board of Directors since 1988.
③ Done at Washington in English, French and Spanish Languages.
④ Member Countries （http: //www. worldbank. org）, 2023-08-22.

sion should be borne by two parties of dispute) and the subscriptions of IBRD offered by the Contracting States.

The purpose of the Centre shall be to provide facilities for conciliation and arbitration of investment disputes between Contracting States and nationals of other Contracting States in accordance with the provisions of this Convention. ① The Centre have an Administrative Council composed of one representative and one alternate representative of each member, and a Secretariat consisting of a Secretary-General, one or more Deputy Secretaries-General and staff, and maintain a Panel of Conciliators and a Panel of Arbitrators, ② each of which consists of qualified persons, who are willing to serve thereon.

Totally 14 persons with high moral character and recognized competence in the fields of law, commerce, industry or finance, which may be relied upon to exercise independent judgment, designated to serve on the Panels, for renewable periods of six years or both Panels. The steps of a Panel of conciliation or arbitration include request, registration, and formation of a conciliation or arbitration board, conciliation or arbitration.

No matter if the parties reach an agreement, the Conciliation Commission shall draw up a report noting the issues in dispute and recording the agreement reached by the parties or noting the submission of the dispute and recording the failure of the parties to reach agreement.

With regard to "arbitration", Article 42 of this Convention states, the Tribunal shall decide a dispute in accordance with such rules of law as may be agreed by the parties. In the absence of such agreement, the Tribunal shall apply the law of the Contracting State party to the dispute and such rules of international law as may be applicable and to decide questions in writing by a majority of the votes of all its members. The Secretary-General shall promptly dispatch certified copies of the award to the parties which is binding on the parties. Each Contracting State shall recognize an award rendered pursuant to this Convention as binding and enforce the pecuniary obligations imposed by that award within its territories as if it were a final judgment of a court in that State.

* **That's all for the five institutions of World Bank Group.** World Bank Group is committed to delivering results for developing countries and improving life for the poorest and most vulnerable. While the five institutions have their own country membership,

---

① Article 1 Sec. 1 (2) of the Washington Convention.

② 调解员小组和仲裁员小组。

governing boards, and articles of agreement, they work as one to serve their partner countries.

III. WTO

The World Trade Organization (WTO) is the only global international organization dealing with the rules of trade between member nations. At its heart is the WTO agreements, negotiated and signed by the member countries of GATT, the former body of WTO in 1994, and ratified in each of their parliaments. Its main function is to ensure that trade between member countries flows as smoothly, predictably and freely as possible. The goal is to help producers of goods and services, exporters, and importers conduct their business.

Over the past 60 years, WTO, which was established in 1995, and its predecessor organization the GATT have helped to create a strong and prosperous international trading system, thereby contributing to unprecedented global economic growth. WTO currently has 164 members, of which 117 are developing countries or separate customs territories. In order to understand WTO more clearly and accurately, we have to firstly focus on its former body—GATT.

(I) GATT. *The General Agreement on Tariffs and Trade* (abbreviated as GATT) is a multilateral international agreement concluded by member governments signed in 1947 in Geneva. Its purpose was to reduce tariffs and other non-tariff barriers, to promote international trade liberalization and fully utilize world resources.

A. Establishment. Due to the wave of protectionism and high tariff rates to keep foreign goods out from import in western of the world, which resulted from the Great Depression of the world economy in the 1930s, the World War II broke out. As part of the postwar examination, in order to early promote the "liberalization" of international trade, in Februray 1946 proposed by the US, the Preparatory Committee for the United Nations Conference on Trade and Employment, composed of 19 countries including US and UK, drafted the Charter of the United Nations International Trade Organization (ITO) at the London meeting.

Fearing a considerable amount of time would be required to complete the signature of ITO by members, the US proposed in November 1946 to launch, the negotiation of a "Multilateral Trade Agreement Embodying Tariff Concessions" among the principal trading nations. On 30 October, 1947, 23 contracting parties, including China, signed *the Final Act of the General Agreement on Tariffs and Trade* and its so-called

"Protocol of Provisional Application" (PPA) in Geneva.

Less than a month after GATT was signed, the Havana conference began on 21 November 1947 and the ITO Charter (or Havana Charter) was finally agreed in March 1948. But ratification in some national legislatures proved impossible, especially the US, because of the unsuccessfully eliminating the British imperial preferences in ITO Charter, thus the ITO and its Charter were effectively dead.

Representatives of contracting parties agreed to put principles of international trade in ITO Charter with the General Agreements on tariffs and Trade together, as a temporary measure to salvage the international Trade principles of the ITO Charter. On 30 June, 1948, the "PPA" came into effect, thereby committing to provisionally apply the GATT and its tariff concessions.

So, GATT became the only provisionally multilateral instrument governing international trade from 1948 to 1994. Throughout the 47 years, it was just a provisional agreement and organization only govern trade of goods, not trade in service and idea and was replaced by WTO in 1995.

B. 8 Rounds of Multilateral Discussion on Tariffs Concessions. After the implementation of GATT, global multilateral trade negotiations began and efforts to reduce tariffs further continued. In the past 47 years, GATT has hold totally 8 rounds of multilateral discussion on tariff concessions to reduce significantly the tariffs of the member countries and increase world trade of goods by more than ten times. The details of the 8 rounds are shown in Figure 3. 1.

Figure 3. 1   Eight Rounds of Multilateral Negotiation on Tariffs Concessions①

Round	Year	Place/Name	Subjects Covered	Participants
1	1947	Geneva	Tariffs	23
2	1949	Annecy (France)	Tariffs	13
3	1951	Toquay (England)	Tariffs	38
4	1956	Geneva	Tariffs	26

---

① The GATT Years: from Havana to Marrakesh, https://www.wto.org/english/thewto_e/whatis_e/tif_e/fact4_e.htm, 2023-08-28.

Round	Year	Place/Name	Subjects Covered	Participants
5	1960–1961	Geneva Dillon Round	Tariffs	26
6	1964–1967	Geneva Kennedy Round	Tariffs and anti–dumping measures	62
7	1973–1979	Geneva Tokyo Round	Tariffs, non–tariffs measures, "framework" agreements	102
8	1986–1994	Geneva Uruguay Round	Tariffs, non–tariff measures, services, IP, dispute settlement, textiles, agriculture, creation of WTO, etc.	123

C. The uruguay round. As history shows, the first seven rounds of GATT have greatly reduced the tariffs of the contracting parties and promoted international trade development. Since 1970s, protectionism, characterized by government subsidies, bilateral quantitative restrictions, market segmentation, and various non–tariffs, resurfaced. In order to contain protectionism, in September 1986, GATT ministers met in Punta del Este, [①] Uruguay, and agreed to launch the Uruguay Round.

The Uruguay Round took seven and a half years, almost twice the original schedule. As the last round of multilateral discussion in the history of GATT, the Uruguay Round was the longest lasting, most subjects covered and most participated in, and most effective and magnificent round of negotiations. So, this Round brought about the biggest reform of the world's trading system since GATT was created at the end of the World War II.

D. The achievements of the GATT year. From Havana in 1947 to Marrakesh in 1994, the era of GATT had made the great historic achievements mainly as followings:

a. Significant tariffs reductions. By 8 rounds of continual reductions in tariffs of trade in goods, the weighted average tariff rate of developed members fell from 47% in 1945 to 3.8% in 1994, and the tariff rate of developing members fell from 47% in 1945 to 12.3% in 1994.

b. A new set of agreements reached. In the early years, the GATT trade rounds concentrated on further reducing tariffs. Then, the Kennedy Round brought about a GATT Anti–Dumping Agreement and a section on development. The Tokyo Round was the first major attempt to tackle trade non–tariff barriers. The eighth, the Uruguay

---

① 埃斯特角城。

Round, was the most extensive of all which led to the Marrakesh Agreements reached with Severn main parts: An umbrella agreement (the Agreement Establishing the WTO); 4 agreements for each of the three broad areas of trade (goods, services and intellectual property) and another area of international investment that the WTO covers; dispute settlement; and reviews of governments' trade policies, which was known as the Marrakesh Agreements.

c. The jurisdiction expanded. Since GATT was only a multilateral international agreement on tariffs and trade of goods, which did not concern with trade in service and trade in idea, and in other respects. GATT had been found wanting because of agriculture, textiles, even GATT's institutional deficiencies and its leisurely pace of dispute settlement. As the new set of agreements was reached in 1994, the jurisdiction of GATT was expanded from then on to not only goods, services, but also intellectual property and international investment, especially to the dispute settlement system.

d. WTO created. Due to the Agreement of Establishing the World Trade Organization coming into effect on January 1, 1995, WTO was created, by which GATT was replaced on that day. The creation of WTO brought to reality, in an updated form, the failed attempt in 1948 to create an ITO.

e. Dispute settlement mechanism improved. Because the procedure for settling dispute under GATT has been criticized for its leisurely pace, the Uruguay Round agreement, called *Understanding on Rules and Procedures Governing the Settlement of Disputes*[1], underscores the rule of law, which makes the trading system more secure and predictable with timetables for completing a case. Now, rulings are automatically adopted unless there is a consensus to reject a ruling.

(Ⅱ) WTO.

A. Establishment. Due to the Agreement of Establishing the World Trade Organization coming into effect on January 1, 1995, which means WTO was created, and GATT was replaced by WTO on that day which headquartered in Geneva with 624 of Secretariat staff, and the Director-General is Ngozi Okonjo-Iweala[2] who took up appointment on 1 March, 2021. By the end of 2023, WTO had 164 members, accounting

① 《关于争端解决规则和程序的谅解》。

② On 15 February 2021, the WTO General Council convened an extraordinary session and appointed Okonjo to the post of WTO Director-General. Okonjo officially took office on March 1, and her term of office will expire on August 31, 2025. She is the seventh Director-General of WTO and the first woman and the first African to serve as Director-General. https://www.wto.org/english/thewto_e/dg_e/dg_e.htm, 2023-08-31.

for 98% of world trade and 25 government observers which were in the process of acceding to the WTO. ①

B. Objectives and main function. The overall objective of WTO is to help its members use trade as a means to raise living standards, create jobs and improve people's lives.

Main Function: Administering trade agreements; offering forum for trade negotiations; settling trade disputes; reviewing national trade policies; technical assistance and training for developing economies; cooperating with other international organizations.

C. Basic principles of international trade. The WTO agreements are lengthy and complex because they are legal texts covering a wide range of activities. But certain simple, fundamental principles run throughout all of these documents and form the foundations of the multilateral trading system.

a. Non-discrimination principle. This principle is named the foundation of GATT and WTO. It means member countries shouldn't discriminate between its trading partners and between its own and foreign products, services or nationals. It's embodied by the MFN and National Treatment principles.

(a) Most-favored-nation treatment principle (MFN). MFN principle requires that any trade advantage or privilege granted by one member to the goods of another member should be granted to all. Any tariff, tax, or other restriction on imports should be applied equally to products, without regard to origination. However, the MFN principle is not without exceptions, it does not apply to: the measures to counter dumping and subsidization; the creation of customs unions and free trade areas; restrictions that protect public health, safety, welfare, and national security.

(b) National Treatment principle. This principle means that imported products must not be regulated, taxed, or otherwise treated differently from domestic goods once they enter a nation's stream of commerce. It is the second manifestation of non-discrimination principle that appears in the GATT and WTO.

b. Opening trade. Opening trade refers to member states commit to negotiate to reduce tariffs and non-tariff measures that hinder international trade, making their markets more open and more conducive to the globalization and liberalization of trade between member states.

---

① https://www.wto.org/english/thewto_e/whatis_e/tif_e/org6_e.htm#observer, 2024-05-22.

c. Transparency. Transparency means the requirement that governments disclose to the public and other governments the rules, regulations, and practices they follow in their domestic trade systems. By notifying WTO about laws in force and measures adopted, all members must make their trade policies transparent and undergo periodic scrutiny of their trade policies and practices which provide assurance and stability for members' trade.

d. Tariff protection. Tariff protection principle refers to the fact that only tariffs are the legitimate means for member states to protect their own markets by the WTO agreements. And according to the opening trade principle, member countries commit to go on engage in regular negotiations designed to systematically reduce customs duties. So, the non-tariff barriers, such as quotas and quantitative restrictions to trade, should all be discouraged. The last but not least, the goal of multi-lateral negotiation on tariffs reduction is to achieve zero tariffs between members (in some cases, tariffs are being cut to zero).

e. Fair competition. Fair competition principle means discouraging "unfair" practices, such as export subsidies and dumping products at below normal value to gain market share. The issues are complex, and the rules try to establish what is fair or unfair, and how governments can respond, in particular by charging additional import duties calculated to compensate for damage caused by unfair trade.

f. Support for less developed countries. Over three-quarters of WTO members are developing economies or in transition to market economies. WTO agreements give them transition periods to adjust to WTO provisions and provide for practical support for implementation of the Trade Facilitation Agreement.

g. Protection of the environment. The WTO agreements permit members to take measures to protect not only public, animal and plant health, but also the environment. However, these measures must be applied in the same way to both national and foreign businesses: Members must not use environmental protection measures as a means of introducing discriminatory trade barriers.

D. Organizational structures. The internal organizations include the Ministerial Conference, the General Council, and the Secretariat.

a. The Ministerial Conference. The Ministerial Conference is the authority organ of WTO and the top-level decision-making body, which meets roughly every two years. It comprises all its members' ministers, with all of countries or customs unions that can take decisions on all matters under any of the multilateral trade agreements. The WTO is "member-driven", with decisions taken by consensus among all member governments, by which decisions are more acceptable to all members.

b. The General Council. Below the Ministerial Conference is the General Council, the executive organ of WTO, which normally comprises ambassadors and heads of delegation in Geneva of all members. It conducts the organization's business or act on behalf of the ministerial conference in the intervals between Ministerial Conferences and meets several times a year in the Geneva headquarters. The General Council also meets, under different rules, as the Trade Policy Review Body and the Dispute Settlement Body.

At the next level, specialized subsidiary bodies of the General Council, such as Councils, Committees, Sub-committees, also comprises all members, administer and monitor the implementation by members of the various WTO agreements. For example, the Goods Council, Services Council, Intellectual Property Council and Trade Negotiation Committee, report to the General Council. All WTO members may participate in all councils and committees, with the exceptions of the Appellate Body, Dispute Settlement Panels and Plural-lateral Committees.

c. The Secretariat. The WTO Secretariat is located in Geneva, with around 630 staff in divisions, and is headed by a Director-General, Ngozi Okonjo-Iweala, and the seventh Director-General of WTO.

E. Membership. All members have joined the system as a result of negotiation and therefore membership means a balance of rights and obligations. They enjoy the privileges that other members give to them and the security that the trading rules provide. In return, they have to make commitments to open their markets and to abide by the rules. Countries negotiating membership are WTO "observers".

F. Accession Process. Any state or customs territory having full autonomy in the conduct of its trade policies may join the WTO, but WTO members must agree on the terms. Broadly speaking, the WTO accessions go through four stages:

a. Application: The government applying for membership has to describe all aspects of its trade and economic policies that have a bearing on WTO agreements in a memorandum.

b. Bilateral negotiation: When the working party has made sufficient progress on principles and policies, parallel bilateral talks, covering tariff rates and specific market access commitments, and other policies in goods and services, begin between the prospective new member and individual countries. The new member's commitments are to apply equally to all WTO members under normal non-discrimination rules, even though they are negotiated bilaterally.

c. Membership terms drafted: Once the working party has completed its examination of the applicant's trade regime, and the parallel bilateral market access negotiations are completed, the working party finalizes the terms of accession which appear in a report, a draft membership treaty or protocol of accession and lists or schedules of the member-to-be commitments,[①] the final package, consisting of the report, protocol and lists of commitments, is presented to the WTO General Council or the Ministerial Conference.

d. Decision: If a two-thirds majority of WTO members vote in favor, the applicant is free to sign the protocol and to accede to the organization. In practices, the country's own parliament or legislature has to ratify the agreement before membership is completed.

(Ⅲ) China with GATT and WTO.

A. China and GATT. China is one of the 23 founding parties to GATT. On April 21 1948, the Chinese delegation signed *the Protocol of Provisional Application Agreement of the General Agreement on Tariffs and Trade* in Geneva. On May 21,1948, China became a founding party of GATT. Without the authorization of the sole legal Central Go-vernment of the People's Republic of China, Taiwan authorities notified the Secretary-General of UN on March 6, 1950, of their decision to withdraw from GATT. Although the Central Government of the People's Republic of China pointed out that the withdrawal decision was invalid, due to the constraints of domestic and overseas political and economic environment that time, China could not submit an application to resume the status of a member to GATT.

Since the implementation of the Reform and Opening-up Policy in 1978, China's economy has become increasingly closely linked with the world economy. On July 11, 1986, Qian Jiadong, Ambassador of the Chinese Mission in Geneva, made a formal application on behalf of the Chinese government to reinstate China's status as a founding party to the GATT. In March 1987, GATT established a "China Working Group" to begin negotiations on China's "re-entry". Until December 19, 1994, just before the establishment of WTO, negotiations between Chinese delegation with the Contracting parties on market access and the protocol in Geneva failed to reach an agreement. At the 19th Working Meeting of GATT China Working Group, Gu Yong-jiang, head of the

---

① 准会员的承诺。

Chinese government delegation and Vice Minister of Foreign Trade and Economic Cooperation, severely condemned a small number of contracting parties for asking inflated prices and obstructing without reason, resulting in the failure to reach an agreement on China's re-entry negotiations.

B. China and WTO. On January 1, 1995, WTO was established. On June 3, 1995, China became an observer of WTO and in November 1995, the Chinese government sent a note to WTO Director-General Ruggiero, changing the name of the Working Group on China's Customs Resumption into the Working Group on China's Accession to WTO. ① During the period from November 28, 1995, when the United States submitted the "Informal Document on China's Accession to WTO", to July 3, 2001, the members of WTO reached an agreement on the formal accession of China in November 2001, China successively completed bilateral market access negotiations with EU, Australia, Switzerland, America and other countries on China's accession to WTO.

On November 10, 2001, at the WTO Ministerial Conference held in Doha, the capital of Qatar, China was officially approved to join the WTO. The National People's Congress soon reviewed the Protocol on China's Accession to WTO (agreement text) and submitted it to the WTO for filing after approval. It officially took effect one month later, when the legal process for China's accession to the WTO was officially completed.

After entering the WTO, China enjoys mainly the following rights: (ⅰ) Enjoy MFN and National Treatment among its 142 members; (ⅱ) Enjoy most of the preferential and transitional arrangements of developing countries; (ⅲ) Use the WTO dispute settlement mechanism to resolve economic and trade frictions with other members; (ⅳ) Has decision-making power over international economic and trade rules in the WTO.

At the same time, China must undertake the following basic obligations: (ⅰ) Granting MFN and National Treatment to other members; (ⅱ) Expand market access for goods and services, reduce tariffs and standardize non-tariff measures; (ⅲ) Further regulate intellectual property protection in accordance with the Agreement on Intellectual Property Rights; (ⅳ) Increase the transparency of trade policies and regulations.

---

① 1995 年 11 月，中国政府照会时任世界贸易组织总干事鲁杰罗，把中国复关工作组更名为中国"入世"工作组。

Part III　Law of International Trade of Goods

International trade of goods refers to the transnational commercial transactions of tangible commodities between parties whose place of business in different countries. It is the main form of economic cooperation between countries in the world on the basis of international division of labor and one of the three modes of modern international trade[1].

This part consists of from chapter 4 to chapter 6. Chapter 4 is the Contract Law for the International Sale of Goods which includes the overview of the Convention of CISG, the structure and scope of application of CISG, the concept and form of contract, the formation of contract, the effectiveness of contract and obligations of the contracting parties, the time point when risk to goods transfer, remedies and excuses for nonperformance, etc. Chapter 5 is Rules of INCOTERMS which includes concept and function of trade terms, rules of INCOTERMS 2000, comparison between traditional and modern trade terms and between different INCOTERMS versions from 2000 to 2010 and 2020. Chapter 6 is Law of Government Control over Foreign Trade of Goods, including overview, principles and measures of control on foreign trade of goods.

国际货物贸易是指营业地位于不同国家的当事人之间以有形商品为标的进行的跨国商事交易活动,是世界各国在国际分工的基础上相互开展国际经济合作的主要形式,也是现代三大国际贸易形式[2]之一。

此部分包括第 4 章至第 6 章。第 4 章是国际货物销售合同法,内容包括联合国国际货物销售合同公约(CISG)概述,公约的结构与适用范围,合同的概念与形式,合同的订立,合同生效与双方的义务,货物风险转移时间、违约救济和免责事由等。第 5 章是国际贸易术语解释通则,包括国际贸易术语的概念与作

---

① International trade of goods, international trade in services and international trade in technology have been explicitly recognized in the agreements reached in the Uruguay Round of GATT negotiations in 1994.

② 国际货物贸易、国际服务贸易和国际技术贸易这三种现代国际贸易方式,业已被 1994 年关贸总协定乌拉圭回合谈判达成的协议所明文确认。

用，2000 版国际贸易术语解释通则的内容，传统与现代贸易术语的比较，国际贸易术语解释通则 2000 版、2010 版、2020 版之间的比较。第 6 章是政府对国际货物贸易的管制法，包括概述、管制的基本原则和管制措施。

Chapter 4 Contract Law on International Sale of Goods

Section Ⅰ General Introduction

Ⅰ. Introduction to CISG

Desiring to establish a uniform law on the international sale of goods, in July 1964, the International Institute for the Unification of Private Laws formulated two earlier conventions,① which had never been widely adopted because of the absence of the participation of the Third World and the Eastern bloc. ②

On April 11, 1980, the United Nations Commission on International Trade Law③ drafted and adopted *the United Nations Convention on Contracts for the International Sale of Goods* (CISG) . Then CISG came into force on January 1, 1988. Undoubtedly, CISG supersedes two earlier conventions, because it incorporates rules from all the major legal systems. China ratified CISG on December 11, 1988 and became one party of it. Translations of CISG are available in English, Chinese, Arabic, French, Russian, Spanish, and other languages.

The CISG is organized in four parts:

Part Ⅰ includes article 1 to 13, which consists of the general provisions, inclu-

---

① One is the Convention Relating to a Uniform Law on the International Sale of Goods (ULIS) and the other one is Convention Relating to a Uniform Law on the Formation of Contracts for the International Sale of Goods (ULFC) .

② Eastern Bloc: 东方阵营，指1947~1991年的美苏两个世界超级大国"冷战"时期，与以美国为首的西方国家阵营相对峙的以苏联为首的东欧国家阵营。

③ It consists of 36 representatives from nations in every region of the world and supported by a highly respected staff of lawyers, which is headquartered at the UN's Vienna International Center in Austria.

ding rules on the sphere of its applications and rules of interpretation.

Part Ⅱ is from articles 14 to 24, which governs the formation of contracts.

Part Ⅲ includes article 25 to 88, which provides rules of the obligations of buyer and seller.

Part Ⅳ is from article 89 to 101 which contains rules of ratification and entry into force of the Convention.

Ⅱ. Sphere of the Applicability of CISG

According to the provisions of Article 1, CISG applies if the following conditions are met:

(Ⅰ) This Convention applies to contracts of commercial sale of goods.

(Ⅱ) The contract is between parties whose places of business①are in different States.

(Ⅲ) The places of business of two contracting parties are located in Contracting States.

(Ⅳ) CISG may apply when the rules of private international law lead to the application of the law of a third Contracting State even if the buyer's and seller's places of business are not in the contracting state.

Ⅲ. Sales and Issues Excluded by CISG

According to Article 2 and 3 of CISG, this Convention doesn't apply to sales and issues as following: (i) Goods bought for personal, family, or household use; (ii) Goods bought by auction; (iii) Stocks, shares, investment securities, negotiable instruments, or mo-ney; (iv) Ships, vessels, hovercraft or aircraft; (v) Electricity; (vi) Assembly contracts for the supply of goods to be manufactured or produced wherein the buyer provides a "substantial part of the materials necessary for such manufacture or production"; (vii) Contracts that are in "preponderant part" for the supply of labor or other services; (viii) Liability of the seller for the death or personal injury caused by the goods sold by him; (ix) Contracts where the parties specifically agree to "opt out" of the convention or where they are willingly to choose to be bound by law of some other coun-

---

① 营业地。

try. ①

Recognized the sensitive matters of legality and competency reflect the mores and social value of particular cultures, to avoid a disagreement that might have harmed the adoption of CISG, these questions were left for settlement by domestic law.

Section II   Definition and Form of Contract

I. Contract Defined

Because there isn't the definition of contract or of sale of goods in CISG, we have to look for.

Article 2 of Sale of Goods Act 1979 of England states, "A contract of sale of goods is a contract by which the seller transfers or agrees to transfer the property in goods to the buyer for a money consideration, called the price".

Article 1 Sec. 1 of American Restatement (Second) of Contract (1981) states, "A contract is a promise or a set of promises, for the breach of which the law gives a remedy, or the performance of which the law in some way recognizes as a duty." Article 2 Sec. 1 further states, "A promise is a manifestation of intention to act or to refrain from acting in a specified way, so made as to justify a promisee in understanding that a commitment has been made". ②

Article 1101 of French Civil Code states, "Contract is a mutual assent by which one or several persons bind themselves, towards one or several others, to transfer, to do or not to do something to one person or more persons".

China Civil Code, Article 464 states, "a contract is an agreement on the establishment, modification, or termination of a civil juristic relationship between persons of civil law".

II. Form of Contract

Form of contract means how the terms of the contract are stated, in oral or writing

---

① [美] 雷·奥古斯特. 国际商法（英文版第 5 版）[M]. 高瑛玮，译注. 北京：机械工业出版社，2010：413-414.

② 美国法学会. 美国合同法重述（第二版）[M]. 徐文彬，译. 北京：中国政法大学出版社，2023：1.

or other form. Traditionally, many countries have required that a contract be in writing.

The civil law countries, for instance, France Civil Code, Article 1582 states, "A sale is an agreement by which one person binds himself to deliver a thing, and another to pay for it. It may be made by an authentic instrument or by an instrument under private signature".

Article 4 of England Sale of Goods Act 1979 states, "Subject to this and any other Act, a contract of sale may be made in writing (either with or without seal), or by word of mouth, or partly in writing and partly by word of mouth, or may be implied from the conduct of the parties".

Article 2-201 of American Uniform Commercial Code states, contract for sale of goods or $500 or that more must be in writing, otherwise, it has no enforceable effect.

Besides the writing and oral form of a contract, the other form of contract is created much more informally implied from conduct. For example, an offeror requires in the offer that the offeree should pre-pay 30% of the purchase price to indicate its acceptance of the offer. The act of pre-paying 30% of the price is the form of contract.

Under CISG, contracts for the sale of goods need not be in writing: (i) Article 11 states, "A contract of sale need not be concluded in or evidenced by writing and is not subject to any other requirement as to form. It may be proved by any means, including witnesses". (ii) However, Article 96 authorizes a contracting state "whose legislation requires contracts of sale to be concluded in or evidenced by writing" to make a declaration at the time of ratification that Article 11 (and some other provisions of the convention involving requirements of form) does not apply where any party has his place of business in that state.

Article 469 of China Civil Code states, "The parties may enter into a contract in written, oral or other forms", then China made a declaration at the time of ratification of CISG in 1986 and insisted that an international contract for sale of goods be in writing.

Section III   Formation of Contract

Formation of contract means the legal steps to make a contract. Contract is formed between buyer and seller by negotiation or bargaining, which consisted of invitation offer, offer, counter-offer or counter-offer again, then acceptance or refusal to the offer, in which offer and acceptance are the two integral steps to make a contract.

I. Invitation Offer

An invitation offer refers to an expression of intention to invite other one to make an offer. It generally takes the form of enquiry of a buyer or the advertisement of goods by a seller. An invitation offer is not capable of being turned into a contract by acceptance because there isn't any term of dealing in it.

In practice, invitation offer is an essential step for a rational businessman to obtain product information and understand market conditions, which can help him to decide to accept or refuse the offer. So, it can also initiate a potential transaction. Due to the fact that an invitation offer affects nothing of both parties, it isn't subject to legal regulation.

II. Offer

An offer is a proposal addressed to the offeree by the offeror to show that the offeror is willing to enter into a contract with the offeree in accordance with the trading terms fixed in the offer. Article 14 of CISG states, "A proposal is sufficient definite if it indicates the goods and expressly or implicitly fixes or makes provision for determining the quantity and price". The person sending the offer is the "offeror", the other one who accepts or refuses the offer is "offeree". In practice, either the buyer or seller may send an offer.

Validity of an offer means the offer becomes legally binding. CISG Article 15 (1) states, "an offer becomes effective when it reaches the offeree". ①The binding of an offer means who should be bound by the offer, the offeror or the offeree. Rules of binding of an offer are as following:

(I) An offer is binding on the offeror. Because it's a promise or a set of promises made by the offeror to the offeree, which during the period of validity of the offer, the offeror bears the obligation of keeping his promise and does not alter or revoke the offer.

(II) An offer is not binding on the offeree. In legal sense, by means of an offer, the offeree gets a right to accept or reject the offer as he pleases.

---

① Article 24 of CISG further provides, an offer "reaches" the addressee when it is made orally to him or delivered by any other means to him personally, to his place of business or mailing address or, if he does not have a place of business or mailing address, to his habitual residence.

An offer may be withdrawn by taking back of offeror before it reaches the offeree, so as to prevent the offer to be binding. Thus, offers, including offers that promise they are irrevocable, can be withdrawn prior to their reaching the offeree, stated in Article 15 of CISG.

An Offer may be revoked. Article 16 of CISG states: (ⅰ) Until a contract is concluded an offer may be revoked if the revocation reaches the offeree before an acceptance;① (ⅱ) However, an offer cannot be revoked, if: (a) it indicates, whether by stating a fixed time for acceptance or otherwise, that it is irrevocable or (b) it was reasonable for the offeree to rely on the offer as being irrevocable and the offeree has acted in reliance on the offer.

An offer lapse because of the following cases: (ⅰ) On the death either of the offeror or the offeree before acceptance. Death after acceptance does not affect the obligations from a contract unless they are of a personal nature. (ⅱ) By legal revocation before acceptance. (ⅲ) By rejection. (ⅳ) By no−acceptance within the time fixed for acceptance by the offeror. If no time for acceptance is prescribed, by no−acceptance within a reasonable time. (ⅴ) By a counter offer.

Ⅲ. Counter−offer

A counter−offer is a reply to an offer with the addition, limitation, or material modification to the terms of the offer. A seller, for example, who accepts a buyer's offer but informs the buyer that goods will be a different size or color, has made a counter−offer.

A counter−offer means the offeree doesn't agree with the trading terms in the offer. So, it's firstly a refusal to accept the offer and then a new offer with the changed trading terms made by the offeree, by which the original offer becomes null and void because of refusal.

Ⅳ. Acceptance

Article 18 (1) of CISG states: A statement made by or other conduct of the offeree indictating assent to an offer is an acceptace. Article 479 of China Civil Code states: Acceptance is the expression of the offeree's intention to agree to the offer. So, features

---

① However, the fact that an offeror may withdraw an offer does not mean that she/he is not liable for contracting negligence.

of acceptance are as following:

(I) An acceptance must be made by the offeree, acceptance by a third party is a new offer.

(II) The acceptance should reach the offeror within the time limit fixed by the offer, the late acceptance is just a new offer.

(III) An acceptance must be communicated to the offeror, which shows silence or inactivity does not, in and of itself, constitute acceptance.

(IV) An acceptance shouldn't alter the material terms in the offer,[1] which includes the price, payment, quality and quantity of goods, place and time of delivery, extent of one party's liability to the other, and settlement of disputes.

Article 19 (1) of CISG states, a reply to an offer which purports to be an acceptance but containing additional or different terms do materially alter the terms of an offer would constitute a rejection of the offer and a counter-offer. An acceptance containing new terms that do not materially alter the terms of an offer becomes a part of the contract, unless the offeror promptly objects to the change.

Article 488 of China Civil Code has the same stipulations that the contents of the acceptance shall correspondent to those of the offer. If the offeree makes a substantial modification to the contents of the offer, the acceptance will constitute a new offer.

A contract comes into existence at the time point an offer is accepted. So effectiveness of an acceptance means the contract is made. Under Common Law System, a contract is formed when the acceptance is dispatched by the offeree. In case of an acceptance sent by letter, the time of dispatch is the time the letter is put into the postal authorities. This is known as the "Mail-box rule". In Civil Law countries, the receipt theory is used, which means a contract comes into existence at the time point when acceptance reaches the offeror or the place of business of him. The difference between the two realities to the allocation of risk when an acceptance is lost or delayed is expressly.

Article 18 (2) of CISG opted for the receipt theory used in civil law countries. Article 2.6 (2) of UNIDROIT PICC and Article 481 of China Civil Code also adopted the receipt theory.

The form or mode in which an offeree expresses is unlimited in CISG, which means the acceptance can be sent to offeror by any means. It may take the form of a statement

---

① The traditional international sale of goods hold that an acceptance must match the terms of the offer exactly and unequivocally, this requirement is named the Mirror Image Rule (镜像原则).

or any other conduct by offeree that indicates the offeree's intention to be bound to the offer. If offeror asks for performance of an act rather than the indication of acceptance, the acceptance is effective at the moment the act is performed.

Rules of the time of an acceptance in article 18 (2) of CISG includes: (i) the acceptance must reach the offeror within the time period fixed in the offer. (ii) If no time period is given, acceptance must reach the offeror within a "reasonable" time. (iii) If the offer is oral, the acceptance must be made immediately, unless the circumstances indicate otherwise.

Because an acceptance is normally not effective until it arrives to the offeror, an offeree may withdraw his acceptance any time before or simultaneous with its receipt.

Refusal of an offer means that the offeree refuses to accept the terms of the offer. A rejection to an offer becomes effective when it reaches the offeror.

V. Case Study

Company A in China sent a message to Company B in Canada on February 9, 2024 showing that: "We can provide corn 15000 Kilo, $785/T CFR Ottawa, shipment in October with payment of confirmed Letter of Credit. Subject to your reply reach here within this month." On March 9, Company B in Canada sent back the reply to Company A stating that: "we are glad to accept the offer of you on February 9, you should provide us the certificate of commodity inspection of your nation besides documents fixed". Company A paid no attention to the reply, Company B claims for damages that Company A should undertake the obligations of breaching the contract. Please answer the following questions:

(I) Is the message on February 9, 2024 sent to Company B an offer? Why?

(II) Is the reply of Company B on March 9 to Company A an acceptance? Why?

(III) Is there any contract between Company A and Company B? Why?

(IV) Is the claim for damages of Company B legal? Why?

Section IV   Obligations of Contracting Parties

I. Validity of Contract

The obligations of the parties are based on the validity of the contract. In order to discuss the obligations of them two, we'd better firstly focus on the validity of the contract.

Under Common Law, a valid contract is an agreement that contains all of the essential elements of a contract as following: (ⅰ) A contract is an agreement between the parties entered into by their mutual assent. (ⅱ) The contract must be supported by legally sufficient consideration. (ⅲ) The parties must have legal capacity (not minors, legally incompetent or under the influence of drugs or alcohol). (ⅳ) The contract mustn't be for illegal purpose or to carry on an activity that is illegal or contrary to public policy. ①

The Civil Law countries have the similar stipulations as that of in Common Law, except for the legally sufficient consideration.

CISG only governs the formation of a contract and the obligations of seller and buyer, without any provision for determining whether a contract is valid, or a party to a contract is legally competent, or for determining whether a party is guilty of fraud or misrepresentation. These rules are left to individual state or national laws to govern.

Article 143 of China Civil Code states, a contract "satisfying all of the following conditions shall be valid: (ⅰ) The actors have corresponding capacity of civil conduct. (ⅱ) The wills expressed by the two parties are true. (ⅲ) The contract neither violates the imperative provisions of laws and administrative regulations, nor is contrary to public order and good moral. " (ⅳ) A contract that is subject to the formalities of approval shall not become effective until it is approved. ②

Ⅱ. Seller's Obligations

A seller is required to: (ⅰ) deliver goods; (ⅱ) hand over any documents relating to the goods, and (ⅲ) ensure that the goods conform with the contract; (ⅳ) assure the ownership of the Goods.

(Ⅰ) Deliver goods. The seller's primary obligation is to deliver goods fixed in the contract. Delivery may be either actual or symbolic delivery in international trade practice.

Delivery is symbolic when goods themselves are delivered to the carrier not to the buyer, but the documents relating to goods are delivered to the buyer. If goods and its

---

① If a contract is missing any one of these essential elements, it is a void contract and there is any obligation for neither the buyer nor the seller. It will not be enforced by the courts.

② Article 502 provides, with regard to contracts that are subject to approval as stipulated by relevant laws or administrative regulations, the provision thereof shall be followed.

documents are all delivered to the buyer or his agent, it is actual delivery which is seldom in international trade practice because of the long distance between the buyer and seller and the more expenses.

A. Place of delivery. Place of delivery is the place fixed in the contract, otherwise his obligation to deliver consists the followings:

a. if the contract of sale involves the carriage of goods, the seller is obliged to deliver goods to the first carrier for transmission to the buyer.

b. otherwise, the contract relates to specific goods, or unidentified goods to be drawn from a specific stock or to be manufactured or produced, and at the time of the conclusion of contract, the parties knew that the goods were at, or were to be manufactured or produced at a particular place, the seller is obliged to hand goods over to the buyer in placing goods at the buyer's disposal at that place.

c. Otherwise, in placing goods at the buyer's disposal at the place where the seller had his place of business at the time of conclusion of the contract.

B. Time for delivery. Article 33 of CISG states that: (i) if a date of delivery of the goods is fixed in the contract, the seller is bound to deliver the goods on that date; (ii) if a period of time is fixed in the contract, the seller may deliver the goods at any time within that period; (iii) if no date is fixed, within a reasonable time after the conclusion of the contract.

(II) Turn over the documents. Documents generally includes invoice of goods, bill of lading, insurance policy, certificate of origin, packing list, weighing list and something else relating to goods called for by contract.

CISG requires that: (i) at the time and place for delivery, a seller must turn over any documents relating to the goods that the contract requires. (ii) If he does so early, he has the right to cure any lack of conformity in the documents, so long as this does not cause the buyer unreasonable inconvenience or unreasonable expense.

(III) Conformity of goods. Article 35 of CISG states, goods delivered by the seller must be the same as the quantity, quality and description required by the contract. The rules for determining whether the goods conform with the contract are set in Article 35:

Except where the parties have agreed otherwise, the goods do not conform with the contract unless they (the goods delivered by the seller):

A. are fit for the purposes for which goods of the same description would ordinarily be used.

B. are fit for any particular purpose expressly or implicitly made known to the seller at the time of the conclusion of the contract, except where the circumstances show that the buyer did not rely, or that it was unreasonable for him to rely, on the seller's skill and judgment.

C. posses the qualities of goods the seller has held out to the buyer as a sample or model.

D. are contained or packaged in the same manner usual for such goods or, where there is no such manner, in a manner adequate to preserve and protect the goods.

(Ⅳ) Assurance the ownership of the goods. Article 41 of the CISG provides, the seller must deliver goods which are free from any right or claim of a third party, unless the buyer agreed to take the goods subject to that right or claim. Article 41 further states, the seller must deliver goods which are free from any right or claim of a third party based on industrial property or other intellectual property. Article 42 also states, the seller mustn't deliver goods which at the time of the conclusion of contract the seller knew or couldn't have been unaware that the right or claim is based on industrial property or other intellectual property by the third party.

Article 42.2 (a) and (b) of CISG states, the obligation of the seller under the preceding paragraph does not extend to cases where: (i) at the time of the conclusion of the contract the buyer knew or could not have been unaware of the right or claim; or (ii) the right or claim results from the seller's compliance with technical drawing, designs, formulas or other such specifications furnished by the buyer.

Ⅲ. Buyer's Obligations

A buyer is required to: (i) pay the price, and (ii) take delivery of the goods.

(Ⅰ) Pay for the price. Article 54 of CISG states, the buyer is obliged to take whatever preliminary steps necessary under the contract or any laws or regulations to enable payment to be made, such as asking the bank for the letter of credit or the foreign currency.

Buyer is to pay the price at the time and place specified in the contract. If no time or place for payment is fixed, he is to pay when goods or the documents controlling their disposition are delivered, at the place for the delivery of either goods or their controlling documents, nevertheless at the seller's place of business.

(Ⅱ) Take delivery. In connection with taking of delivery, the buyer is obliged to cooperate with the seller to facilitate the transfer and to actually "take over the goods", such as specifying the place of delivery.

Article 60 of CISG states, the buyer's obligation to take delivery consists in: (i) doing all the acts which could reasonably be expected of him in order to enable the seller to make delivery, and (ii) ta-king over the goods.

IV. Question

Why CISG provides taking delivery is the obligation but not the right of buyer?

Section V Time of Transfer of Risk to Goods

I. Introduction

Time of transfer of risk means the time point when the buyer becomes responsible for loss of risk to the goods in transit. In most cases, the loss will be covered by insurance. Even so, it is important to determine whether the buyer or the seller is responsible for procuring insurance.

CISG allows parties to allocate the time risk shifts between them and to specify when risks pass from the seller to the buyer by the use of trade term.

II. Principles of the Passing of Risk

Goods may be delivered by the seller to the buyer himself or his agent without a carrier (the actual delivery) or transported by a carrier to the buyer (the symbolic delivery). Because of the different modes of delivery, principles for the passing of risk are different as following:

(I) Actual delivery. When goods are delivered by the seller directly to the buyer or his agent, which means no shipping of goods, risks of loss to goods pass to the buyer when goods are delivered to the buyer or otherwise goods are put at the buyer's disposal. An example of such is one containing an "EXW" trade term.

(II) Symbolic delivery. Under circumstances of symbolic delivery, the time for transfer of risk of loss to goods should be allocated by considering the two cases: (i) Risk shifts to the buyer when goods pass over the ship's rail[1] or on board of the ship[2]

---

① In INCOTERMS 2000.
② In INCOTERMS 2010.

at the named port for shipment, under traditional trade terms.① (ⅱ) Risk passes to the buyer when goods are delivered to the carrier under modern trade terms.②

Section Ⅵ   Remedies

CISG provides for three types of remedies: (ⅰ) unique to the buyer; (ⅱ) unique to the seller, and (ⅲ) available to either party.

Ⅰ. Buyer's Remedies

Seller defaults, the buyer acquires unique remedies provided in article 45 to 52 of CISG as follows: (ⅰ) to compel specific performance; (ⅱ) to avoid the contract for fundamental breach or non-delivery; (ⅲ) to reduce the price; (ⅳ) to refuse early delivery; (ⅴ) to refuse excess quantities.

(Ⅰ) Specific performance. If goods delivered by the seller are nonconforming, article 46 of CISG states, a buyer can ask the seller to either deliver substitute goods, or make repair. In either case, the buyer must firstly notify the seller the goods are nonconforming. Also, the buyer can't have avoided the contract or resorted to some other inconsistent remedy.

(Ⅱ) Avoidance. Under aritcle 49 of CISG, the buyer may avoid a contract if either the seller commits a fundamental breach or the seller fails to or refuses to perform his obligations under contract or this convention within the additional period of time fixed by the buyer. During the additional period of time for performance, the seller is entitled to correct or cure the non-conformity at his own expense.

(Ⅲ) Reduction in Price. In article 50 of CISG, it means the remedy that allows a buyer to pay less for nonconforming goods in those cases where the buyer is not entitled to damages. That's to say, if the buyer is not entitled to damages when the seller delivers nonconforming goods, the buyer will be entitled to a reduction in price.

Principles of Application of Reduction in Price include: (ⅰ) a buyer must have

① Traditional trade terms refer to the oldest trade terms that are only applicable to marine transport of goods, which are formed along with the development of traditional modes of transport of goods by sea in the early international trade practices, such as FOB, CFR and CIF.

② Modern trade terms, such as FCA, CPT and CIP, are derived from traditional trade terms but can be applied to any mode of transport, including sea transport.

accepted goods of nonconforming; (ii) the seller must not be responsible for the non-conformity. Example of such a case is one where goods were damaged by "superior force", an event or effect that cannot be reasonably anticipated or controlled, or an act of nature.

(Ⅳ) Refusal early delivery and excess quantity. Article 52 of CISG states, if the seller either delivers goods early or delivers more than the quantity fixed in the contract, the buyer may accept or reject the goods or the excess part. If the buyer does accept, he must pay for the excess goods at the contract rate.

(Ⅴ) The effect of nonconformity in a part of the goods. If the seller agrees to sell the buyer 100 bag of corn, at the time of delivery, 10 bags are vermin infested and totally unusable. May the buyer reject the 10 bags and accept the balance or reject the entire contract? As to the defective part, CISG provides the buyer may seek specific performance, obtain a price reduction, or avoid that part of the contract. As for avoiding the whole contract, the buyer may do so only, if the partial delivery amounts to a fundamental breach of the whole[1].

Ⅱ. Seller's Remedies

Buyer defaults, remedies unique to the seller under CISG are to compel specific performance, to avoid contract for a fundamental breach or failure to cure a defect, and to obtain missing specifications.

(Ⅰ) Specific performance. If a buyer refuses to take delivery, article 62 of CISG states that the seller may require the buyer to take delivery and pay the contract price.

(Ⅱ) Avoidance. The seller may avoid the contract according to article 64 of CISG when there has been a fundamental breach or, the buyer refuses to perform his obligations or to cure any defect in his performance within an additional period of time given by the seller.

(Ⅲ) Obtaining missing specifications. If the buyer fails to specify the measurements needed by the seller by the date in the contract or within a reasonable time after the seller asks for them, article 65 of CISG allows the seller to ascertain them himself in accordance with the buyer's requirements that may be known to him, and the seller must inform the buyer of the details thereof and fix a reasonable time period for the buyer to make a different specification. If the buyer fails to respond within the fixed time

① Ray August. 国际商法 [M]. 北京：高等教育出版社, 2002: 577.

period, the seller's specifications become "binding".

III. Remedies Available to Both Parties

Remedies available to both parties are: (ⅰ) suspension of performance, (ⅱ) avoidance in anticipation of a fundamental breach, (ⅲ) avoidance of an installment contract, (ⅳ) damages.

(Ⅰ) Suspension of performance. Article 71 of CISG states a party may suspend the performance of his obligations if, after the conclusion of the contract, it becomes apparent that the other party will not perform a substantial part of his obligations as a result of:

A. A serious deficiency in his ability to perform or his creditworthiness.

B. His conduct in preparing to perform or in performing the contract shows that a serious deficiency in his ability to perform or his creditworthiness.

If the seller has already dispatched the goods before the grounds described in the preceding paragraph become evident, he may prevent the handing over of the goods to the buyer even though the buyer holds a document which entitles him to obtain them. A party suspending performance, whether before or after dispatch of the goods, must immediately give notice of the suspension to the other party and must continue with performance if the other party provides adequate assurance of his performance.

(Ⅱ) Anticipatory avoidance. Anticipatory avoidance in article 72 (1) of CISG means a remedy available to either party when it becomes clear that the other party will commit a fundamental breach. There seem to be only a few cases where this remedy can be invoked. These include: (ⅰ) the specific goods promised to the buyer are wrongfully sold to a third party; (ⅱ) the seller's only employee capable of producing the goods dies or is fired; (ⅲ) the seller's manufacturing plant is sold.

If a party opts to anticipatory avoid, article 72 (2) of CISG requires him, if time allows, notifying the other party so that the latter can provide adequate assurance of his performance. In practice, this is worth doing, both to comply with the convention's general requirement of "good faith" and to minimize any challenges to the use of the remedy. ①

(Ⅲ) Avoidance of installment contract. Rules of article 73 in CISG for avoiding installment contract uses the same logic found in its other avoidance provisions. For a

---

① Ray August. 国际商法 [M]. 北京: 高等教育出版社, 2002: 580.

particular installment, if there was a "fundamental breach with respect to that install-ment", then "the other party may declare the contract avoided in respect to that install-ment" . If the breach of one installment gives a party "good grounds" to conclude that a fundamental breach of future installments will occur, then those later installments may be anticipatory avoided. If the installments are interdependent, a fundamental breach of one will allow a party to avoid the entire contract, induding past and future install-ments.

(Ⅳ) Damages. Article 74 of CISG states, damages for breach of contract by one party consist of a sum equal to the loss, including loss of profit, suffered by the other party as a consequence of the breach. Such damages may not exceed the loss which the party in breach foresaw or ought to have foreseen at the time of the conclusion of the contract, in the light of the facts and matters of which he then knew or ought to have known, as possible consequence of the breach of contract. Calculation of the Damages:

A. Article 75 of CISG states, if the contract is avoided and if the buyer has bought goods in replacement or the seller has resold the goods, then damages are measured by the difference between contract price and price received in the substitute transaction.

B. Article 76 (1) of CISG states, if the party claiming damages did not enter into a substitute transaction, then the damages are calculated by taking the difference be-tween the contract price and the current price at the time of avoidance. The current price is defined in article 76 (2) of CISG as "the price prevailing at the place where deliver-y of the goods should have been made or, if there is not current price at that place, the price at such other places as serves as a reasonable substitute" .

C. No matter which of the two CISG damage rules applies, article 77 of CISG states that the party claiming dama-ges is under an obligation to take reasonable measures "to mitigate (obligation of a party claiming damages to keep the damages to a minimum) the loss" . If the claiming party fails to take such measure, the other may claim a pro-portionate reduction in the dama-ges.

Section Ⅶ Excuses for Nonperformance

Two excuses are provided in the CISG for a party's failure to perform. One is force majeure①, the other is "demurrer".

I. Force Majeure

Force majeure is also named the superior force, which means an event or effect that cannot be reasonably anticipated or controlled. Rules in the CISG:

(I) Article 79 (1) of CISG states, a party is not liable for any damages resulting from his failure to perform any of his obligations if he can prove: (i) that his failure was "due to an impediment beyond his control"; (ii) that the impediment was not something he could have reasonably taken into account at the time of contracting; (iii) that he remains unable to overcome the impediment or its consequences.

(II) It applies to situations, such as natural disasters, war, embargoes, strikes, breakdowns, and the bankruptcy of a supplier, that frustrate both the party attempting to perform and the party expecting performance. Because neither party is really at fault, the breaching party is excused from paying damages. ②

(III) A party seeking to use CISG's excuse of superior force is under some additional limitations: (i) He has a duty to promptly notify the other party of "the impediment and its effect on his ability to perform". (ii) If his claim is due to the failure of a third person to perform (such as a supplier), the third person must himself be able to claim the excuse. (iii) The excuse may be used only as long as the underlying impediment continues in existence. ③

II. Demurrer

Demurrer④ is based on a simple premise, directly stated in Article 80 of CISG: "A party may not rely on a failure of the other party to perform, to the extent that such failure was caused by the first party's act or omission". For example, if Company A promised to deliver goods at the warehouse of Company B, but Company B's warehouse was locked and inaccessible at the time that Company A is asked to deliver goods, Company B cannot claim that Company A failed to deliver on time.

---

① According to article 180 of China Civil Code, force majeure refers to objective circumstances that cannot be foreseen and avoided and cannot be resisted and overcome.

②③ Ray August. 国际商法 [M]. 北京: 高等教育出版社, 2002: 585.

④ Demurrer: 抗辩事由。

Chapter 5   International Rules for the Interpretation of Trade Terms

Section Ⅰ   Introduction

Ⅰ. Definition of International Trade Term

International trade terms, also known as price terms or standardized terms, are acronym of three English words used in sales contracts to describe the composition of the price of the goods, the place of delivery, the division of risks and liabilities of transport and insurance.

International trade terms originated from European trade practice in the early 19th century, expressed in form of abbreviated symbols, such as FOB or CIF, which permit parties to express their agreement quickly with little confusion and few language problems. So parties are always willing to incorporate a certain trade term in nearly each of their international contract for sale of goods.

Ⅱ. Role

Trade terms are very convenient for both parties to allocate their right and obligation in the sales contract. It can at least describe: (ⅰ) the place of delivery; (ⅱ) the manner of delivery; (ⅲ) the time point when risk of loss shifts from seller to buyer; (ⅳ) the composition of price of goods; (ⅴ) the party to arrange transport and bear the costs of fright; (ⅵ) the party procuring insurance of goods; (ⅶ) the party bearing the obligation of clearing up export or import.

Trade terms are neither national law nor treaty. Thus, it can't be "the governing law" of any contract. Instead, it is one form of custom and usage in international trade of goods, which can be, can often be expressly incorporated by parties to their international contract for sale of goods and become the rule for the division of contractual rights and obligations between the two parties.

III. Rules and Practices on International Trade Terms

To clear up the confusion of trade terms, some international commercial organizations drew up sets of rules or standard definitions as following.

(Ⅰ) Warsaw-Oxford Rules 1932. This rule was drafted by the Association of International Law in 1932. It contains 21 clauses, which only stipulate CIF contract, and the party bearing charges, risks and obligations.

(Ⅱ) Revised American Foreign Trade Definitions 1941. It was made out by nine American commercial organizations in 1941, a set of foreign trade terms which are considered obsolete, but still sometimes used in domestic US trade. It contains 6 trade terms which are EX (point of origin), FOB, FAS, C&F, CIF and EX DOCK.

(Ⅲ) International Rules for the Interpretation of Trade Terms. It has been commonly named INCOTERMS, an acronym for International Commercial TERMS, first published by the International Chamber of Commerce (ICC) in Paris in 1936 to develop trade terms and periodically revised in year of 1953, 1967, 1976, 1980, 1990, 2000, 2010 and 2020 because of not only changing modes of transport and the trade practice of document delivery, but also further harmonizing INCOTERMS with CISG and the Rotterdam Rules.

Because INCOTERMS 2000, coming into force on January 1, 2000, has the most trade terms and the most scientific grouping, we will take it as an example to introduce the 13 trade terms in it.

Section Ⅱ INCOTERMS 2000

Ⅰ. Structure of INCOTERMS 2000

The version of INCOTERMS 2000 includes thirteen trade terms which are classified into four different groups of E, F, C and D according to seller's responsibilities from small to large.

II. Rules of 13 Trade Terms in INCOTERMS 2000

(I) "E" Group. There is only one in "E" group, it's "EXW", the acronym for "Exchange at Works" which means "goods are Exchange (to the buyer or his agent) at Works of seller". It's the only trade term that buyer will take over the goods.

Seller's obligation is to make goods and documents available at his place of business. It's the unique term in the first group, also the first one of 13 trade terms. It means the seller assumes minimal obligations than others. On the other hand, it means the buyer bears the most obligations.

Rules of EXW are as following: (i) the place of delivery of goods is the seller's premises; (ii) the manner of delivery of goods is actual; (iii) risk of loss to goods shifts to the buyer when the seller deliver goods to the buyer; (iv) the price component of goods is just cost, no fright and insurance; (v) the buyer bears to arrange and pay for international fright and insurance of goods; (vi) the buyer has to clear up import and export of goods.

(II) "F" Group. F Group includes FCA (Free Carrier), FAS (Free Along-side Ship) and FOB (Free On Board), which the seller is bound to deliver goods to a carrier named by the buyer at the fixed time and place.

Seller's obligation is to: (i) deliver goods to a carrier named by the buyer at the fixed time and place by the contract; (ii) clear up export for the goods.

Rules of F group: (i) the seller should deliver goods to the carrier named by the buyer at the fixed time and place; (ii) the manner for delivery is symbolic; (iii) the risk of loss shifts from the seller to the buyer when the seller deliver goods to the carrier in FCA and FAS, or when goods pass over the ship's rail at the named port for shipment in FOB; (iv) the price component of goods doesn't contain costs of fright and insurance; (v) the buyer will bear costs of international fright and insurance of goods; (vi) the seller has to clear up export, while the buyer has to clear up import for goods.

(III) "C" Group. C Group includes CFR (Cost and Freight), CIF (Cost, Insurance and Freight), CPT (Carriage Paid To) and CIP (Carriage, Insurance Paid To). On the basis of the seller's liability in F Group, the seller's new liabilities are: (i) to arrange and pay for freight of goods; (ii) to procure and pay for insurance in CIP and CIF.

Seller's obligation is to: (i) deliver goods to carrier named by the seller at the fixed time, and at the place of the carrier's warehouse in CPT and CIP, or on board of a ship at the named port for shipment in CFR and CIF; (ii) bear the loss of risk before the delivery of goods to the carrier in CPT and CIP, or before the goods passed over the ship's rail at the named port for shipment in CFR and CIF; (iii) arrange and pay for transport of the goods; (iv) procure and pay for insurance in CIF and CIP; (v) clear export for goods.

Rules of C Group: (i) place for delivery of goods is at the carrier's warehouse in CPT and CIP, or on board of the ship at the named port for shipment in CFR and CIF; (ii) the manner for delivery is symbolic; (iii) the risk of loss shifts to the buyer at the point of time when the seller deliver goods to carrier in CPT and CIP, but at the point of time when the goods passed over the ship's rail at the named port for shipment in CFR and CIF; (iv) the price component of goods does contain cost and freight in CPT and CFR, but cost, fright and insurance in CIP and CIF; (v) the seller bears to arrange and pay for fright in this group, and to arrange and pay for insurance only in CIP and CIF; (vi) the seller has to clear up export while the buyer has to clear up import of goods.

(Ⅳ) "D" Group. "D" group includes DAF (Delivered AT Frontier), DES (Delivered EX Ship), DEQ (Delivered EX Quay), DDU (Delivered Duty Unpaid) and DDP (Delivered Duty Paid). The seller is responsible for all costs and risks associated with taking goods to destination fixed in the contract. D group means the seller bears the most obligations than the former three groups.

Seller is obliged to: (i) Deliver goods at the named frontier of his country in DAF, or at the named destination in terms of DES, DEQ, DDU and DDP and at the time fixed in the contract; (ii) Bear risk of loss to goods before goods are delivered to the car-rier; (iii) Arrange and pay for transport of goods to destination; (iv) Procure and pay for insurance to cover risks of loss to goods in transit to destination; (v) Clear goods for export, and also clear for import for goods in DDP.

Buyer is obliged to: (i) Handle import clearance for DAF, DES, DEQ and DDU goods; (ii) Bear the risk of loss after delivery of the goods to carrier.

Rules of D group: (i) the place for delivery is the place of destination fixed in the contract; (ii) the manner for delivery is symbolic; (iii) the risk of loss to goods shifts to the buyer when goods are delivered to carrier; (iv) the price components of goods do contain cost, fright and insurance of goods; (v) the seller bears the costs of fright and insurance; (vi) the seller bears to clear up export, and import in DDP.

Section Ⅲ Comparison between Traditional and Modern Trade Terms

Ⅰ. Traditional Trade Term

It refers to FOB, CFR and CIF which came into being and developed with and only used in the traditional marine transport of goods.

(Ⅰ) Similarities. (i) Places of delivery are all on board of a named ship at the named port for shipment; (ii) Modes for delivery of goods are all symbolic; (iii) when goods passed over the ship's rail at the named port for shipment, the risk of loss to goods passed from the seller to the buyer; (iv) Way of transport are marine; (v) The seller clears up export while the buyer clears up the import.

(Ⅱ) Differences. The price components is different from each other. FOB just includes the cost of the goods. CFR consists of the cost and freight of the goods, while CIF consists of cost, insurance and freight. The party obliged to arrange and pay for freight and insurance is different from each other: (i) In FOB, the buyer bears the two obligation; (ii) In CFR, the seller bears to arrange and pay for freight, the buyer is to procure and pay for insurance; (iii) In CIF, the seller bears two all.

Ⅱ. Modern Trade Term

It means FCA, CPT and CIP, derived from the traditional trade terms at the end of 20th century and used in all modes of transport to expand the application of trade terms to modern modes of transport.

(Ⅰ) Similarity. (i) Places of delivery are the warehouses of carrier; (ii) Modes for delivery of goods are symbolic; (iii) Suitable for all modes of transport, including marine, air and land transport even multi-modal transport; (iv) When goods are delivered to the carrier, risk of loss to goods shifts to the buyer; (v) The seller obliged to clear up export while the buyer clears up import of goods.

(Ⅱ) Differences. (i) The price components. FCA means the cost price without international freight and insurance of goods. CPT means cost and carriage without insurance of goods. So, actually CPT=FCA+Carriage. CIP means Cost, insurance and carriage of goods, so CIP = CPT+Insurance. (ii) The Party obliged to arrange and pay for carriage and insurance of goods. In FCA, the buyer is obliged to arrange carriage and insurance for goods sold by the seller. In CPT, the seller is obliged to arrange and pay for carriage of goods, but procuring insurance is the buyer's duty. In CIP, the seller bears to arrange and pay for carriage and insurance of goods.

III. Comparison between Traditional and Modern Trade Terms

(I) Similarities. (i) Due to modern trade terms are derived from the traditional trade terms, such as FCA from FOB, CPT from CFR and CIP from CIF, the basic principles of them two are relatively the same. (ii) Modes of delivery of goods are all symbolic delivery. (iii) Subjects bearing to arrange carriage and procure insurance are similar, for example, the same of FOB and FCA, CFR and CPT, CIF and CIP. (iv) Parties bearing obligation to clear up export and import are the same, the seller is to clear up export while the buyer is to clear up import.

(II) Differences. (i) The place of delivery: in traditional trade terms, the place of delivery is on board of a ship at the named port for shipment. In modern trade terms, the place of delivery is the warehouse of the carrier at the residence of seller. (ii) Mode for transportation of goods: Traditional trade terms are suita-ble only for marine transport, or inland waterway transport, while modern trade terms can be used to all kinds of transport, including marine transport and others. (iii) The time point when risk of loss to goods passes to the buyer: in traditional trade terms, risk of loss to goods shifts from the seller to the buyer when goods pass over the ship's rail. For modern trade terms, the time point is when goods are delivered to the carrier. (iv) Documents relating to Goods: In traditional trade terms, cargo documents are those relating to maritime transport, such as invoice of goods, bill of lading, insurance policy and others fixed in contract. In modern trade terms, there are not only documents relating to marine transport, but also documents relating to transport by air, by train or by multi-modal.

Section IV　Comparison of Different Versions of INCOTERMS

I . Comparison of INCOTERMS 2010 and 2000

(I) INCOTERMS 2010. INCOTERMS 2010 is the revised version of 2000 by ICC in light of the development of international trade of goods, published on September 27, 2010 and implemented globally on January 1, 2011. Compared with 2000 version, the INCOTERMS 2010 more accurately specify the liability of the parties to bear risks and costs of the carriage of goods, so that ship management companies can better understand the roles of the buyer and seller of goods in paying various charges, and help avoid the frequent terminal handling charges (THC) disputes.

New changes of 2010 version: (ⅰ) 13 trade terms become 11; (ⅱ) The classification of trade terms is changed from four to two categories; (ⅲ) The extension of the scope of use to domestic trade contracts; (ⅳ) Electronic means of communication are accorded full equivalent efficacy.

(Ⅱ) Comparison between INCOTERMS 2010 and 2000.

Similarities: Rules of trade terms in Group E, F and C remain unchanged.

Differences:

A. The number of trade terms. In 2000 version, there are 13 trade terms, while in 2010 version, 13 has been reduced to 11. Because DAF, DES, DEQ and DDU are actually replaced by DAT (Delivered At Terminal) and DAP (Delivered At Named Place).

B. The numbers of group and the classification method. In 2000 version, 13 trade terms are classified into four groups according to the seller's obligation from small to large. In 2010 version, 11 trade terms are divided into two distinct categories according to the applicable mode of transport. The first group consists of seven trade terms applicable to any mode of transport, including multi-modal transport, such as EXW, FCA, CPT, CIP, DAT, DAP and DDP. The second group actually contains four marine trade terms of FAS, FOB, CFR, and CIF, only applicable to sea or inland waterway transport.

C. The time point of risk of loss to goods transfer in 3 traditional trade terms. In 2010 version, the "ship's rail" principle, used in 2000 version, is abandoned and replaced by a transfer of risk "while the goods are loaded on board of ship", which undoubtedly is more in line with today's international trade realities.

D. The adjustment of extension of the scope of provisions use to domestic trade contracts caused by the expansion of the customs territory. Trade terms have traditionally been used in contracts for the international sale of goods across national borders. In recent years, the speed of economic integration has accelerated; the expansion of the tariff-free zone has rendered the existing border customs formalities meaningless. The subtitle of 2010 version therefore formally recognizes the applicability of these terms to both international and domestic contracts for the sale of goods, such as clearly stipulated in the instructions for the use of EXW that "applicable to domestic trade".

E. Give electronic records exactly the same efficacy as paper documents. INCO-TERMS 2010 now replaces EDI, an acronym of Electronic Data Interchange Information provided by Incoterms1990, with a new and broader term—Electronic record or procedure, and gives electronic records exactly the same efficacy as paper documents.

II. Comparison of INCOTERMS 2020 and 2010

(I) INCOTERMS 2020. ICC officially released INCOTERMS 2020 on September 10, 2019, which has come into effect on January 1, 2020. There are also two groups of total 11 trade terms as that of in 2010 version, except DAT is replaced by DPU in the first group.

(II) Comparison between INCOTERMS 2020 and 2010

Similarities:

A. The number of trade terms. There are totally 11 trade terms in both version 2010 and 2020.

B. The number of groups and the classification method. In 2020 version, 11 trade terms are classified into two distinct groups also according to criteria of the applicable mode of transport, the same as that of in 2010 version.

Differences:

A. One term changed. Term DAT (Delivered at Terminal) in 2010 version has been changed to DPU (Delivered at Place Unloaded) in version 2020 to clarify that the place of destination could be any place and not only a "terminal".

B. Amendment to FCA. FCA (Free Carrier) now provides the additional option to make an onboard notation on the Bill of Lading prior loading of the goods on a vessel. The new option about FCA in 2020 version means both parties to a transaction can agree buyer will instruct its carrier to issue and deliver the onboard notion on Bill of Lading to the seller before loading the goods on board of a vessel.

C. Insurance—related clauses in CIP and CIF. CIP now requires at least insurance with the minimum cover of the Institute Cargo Clause (A) (All risk, subject to itemized exclusions). CIF requires at least insurance with the minimum cover of the Institute Cargo Clause (C) (Number of listed risks, subject to itemized exclusions).

D. Goods may be carried by the seller's or buyer's own means of transportation.

FCA, DAP, DPU and DDP now take into account that goods may be carried by using its own means of transportation.

It should be emphasized that the implementation of the new version of INCOTERMS does not mean the invalidity of the old version. So, once you have selected a certain version of a trade term, attach the words "INCOTERMS 2010" or "INCOTERMS 2020".

III. Case Study

Company A in Shanghai China entered into a contract with Company B in New York USA for the sale of corn on CFR New York $100/Ton (of INCOTERMS 2000). On the fixed time for delivery, Company A delivered the goods on time. Please answer each of following questions:

(I) Where should Company A make the delivery?

(II) What's the mode of delivery? Is it symbolic or actual delivery?

(III) When the risk to the goods passed from Company A to Company B?

(IV) Who is bound to pay for the cost of shipment?

(V) Who is liable to procure insurance and pay for it?

(VI) Who is obliged to clean up the export?

(VII) Who is responsible for cleaning up the import?

(VIII) What's the component of the price of CFR New York $100/Ton?

Chapter 6   Law of Government Control over Foreign Trade of Goods

Section Ⅰ   Introduction

Ⅰ. Definition

In order to protect national security, national health and increase fiscal revenue, countries all over the world generally regulate their import and export of goods by government in accordance with the law, based on the principle of national sovereignty.

Law of government control over foreign trade of goods refers to the body of rules and norms on legal activities that the government, on behalf of the state, encourages, restricts or prohibits the import and export of goods.

Ⅱ. Feature

（Ⅰ）Legal control over foreign trade of goods is an administrative act. The essence of legal control over foreign trade of goods is an administrative act of direct intervention of the state in import and export trade, which creates, changes or eliminates the admini-strative legal relationship between state and a specific administrative counterpart,[①] which is the importer or exporter.

（Ⅱ）The objects of control including the imported and exported goods. It is the foreign trade of goods that should be regulated, including import control of foreign commodities and export control of domestic products, not foreign trade in serves or trade in intellectual property rights here. Since the later two should be regulated by different legal rules.

---

① A specific administrative counterpart: 特定的行政相对人。

（Ⅲ）The purpose of legal control is to serve the national interests. Generally speaking, the purpose of implementing import control on foreign goods is mainly based on the economic purpose of protecting the production and interests of the national industry and maintaining the balance of international payment. Of course, there is also the need to protect the national health, while the export control on domestic produc-cts is mainly based on the purpose of national security and foreign policy. ①

（Ⅳ）The means of control is by rules of law. Rules of law here mean not only national laws and regulations, but also treaties and conventions. National laws of controlling over foreign trade of goods mainly include laws and administrative regulations with the nature of public law,② such as foreign trade law, customs tax law, foreign exchange management law, etc. The international treaties and conventions concerning the control on foreign trade of goods are signed by one country and other contracting states to coordinate their economic relations based on common economic interests, such as CISG.

Section Ⅱ   Principles of Government Control on Foreign Trade of Goods

Ⅰ. Encourage Exports and Restrict Imports

Export encouragement means every country is willing to encourage the export of its products through preferential treatment such as exemption from export duties, granting of export credits and export tax rebates since exports could expand the international market share of domestic products and earn foreign exchange. Meanwhile, countries around the world restrict the import of foreign goods by imposing import tariffs and other non-tariff measures, because they worry that excessive import of foreign goods will exacerbate the imbalance of foreign exchange payments and that the domestic market will be crowded out by foreign imports with competitive advantages. ③However, it is important to remember that the practice of encouraging exports and restricting imports shouldn't

---

① 当然也有保护国民健康的需要，而对本国产品实施出口管制则多基于国家安全、外交政策方面的考量。

② 对外贸易法律管制的国内立法主要包括法律和具有公法性质的行政法规。

③ 国家担心外国商品进口过多会加剧外汇收支不平衡矛盾且本国市场会被有竞争优势的外国进口产品挤占。

violate treaties and conventions to which the country is a party.

II. Control by Rules of Law

Control by rules of law means the methods of control over foreign trade of goods is by legal rules. Rules of law here mean not only national laws and regulations, but also treaties and conventions signed between the countries concerned.

III. Tariffs Protection

The principle of tariffs protection means, according to the principle of non – discrimination and fair trade, the legal means for WTO members to restrict imports is to impose import tariffs on imported products, and the tariff rates must comply with the relevant provisions of tariff agreement. So, any non-tariff restriction on imported goods is ill-legal and should be prohibited, except legally permitted.

IV. No-violation to International Treaties and Conventions

As mentioned above, in international economic transaction, due to the need of resource exchange, countries often define each other's rights and obligations by signing international treaties or conventions. Therefore, while controlling import and export trade activities in accordance with relevant domestic laws and regulations, countries should also pay special attention to their obligations in international treaties and conventions, that is, the legal control of foreign trade by sovereign countries mustn't violate the provisions of treaties and conventions to which these countries are the parties.

Section III   Measures of Government Control over Foreign Trade of Goods

I. General Introduction

Although free trade is the dream and ultimate goal of human society, in the practice of international trade, as mentioned above, encouraging export and restricting import are the basic principles for countries to control their foreign trade. Therefore, government usually divides the country's import and export products into three categories for classified management: Free trade, restricted trade and prohibited trade of goods.

Among which, automatic licensing shall be applied to goods freely imported and exported. State applies quotas, licenses to goods whose import or export is restricted. Prohibited goods for foreign trade are not allowed to import or export, otherwise it will be investigated for illegal or criminal legal responsibility. Generally speaking, methods of government control mainly include tariff measures and non-tariff measures.

II. Tariffs

Tariffs are customs duties imposed on goods of restricted import or restricted export by government. Therefore, tariffs includes import duties and export duties.

(I) Import Duties. Import tariffs are imposed by importing country on foreign goods entering the customs which are the most important means to restrict the entry of foreign goods into the importing countries to protect their related industries. According to international practice, all imported goods are subject to import duty unless exempted by law. What is more, sometimes countries even restrict the import of certain foreign goods by imposing import taxes several times the value of the goods as a barrier, called the high tariff barriers. [1]

In international trade practice, the specific duty and advalorem duty are the two main tariffs levied on imported goods. The specific duty, or volume duty as it is sometimes called, refers to the method of levying duties by weight, capacity, length, area or quantity of imported goods. [2] Advalorem tax refers to the method of imposing a certain percentage of tariffs based on the value of imported goods. [3] According to the Principle of Tariffs Protection of WTO, the tariffs rate on imported products should be no more than the average tariff level 10% for developing members and 3% for developed members nowadays. [4]

(II) Export tariffs. Since it is normal for countries to encourage exports, only some certain kinds of goods restricted export will be levied on export tariffs. So, we may say exported goods are not subject to export duty unless otherwise stipulated by law. Thus, the exported goods not only enjoy the policy of exemption from export tax,

---

① 更有甚者，有时国家甚至以数倍于货物价值的高额进口税作为屏障，达到限制某些外国货物进口的目的，即所谓的高关税壁垒。

② 从量税是指按照进口商品的重量、容量、长度、面积和数量为单位征收关税的方法。

③ 从价税是指以进口商品的货值为税基征收一定比例关税的方法。

④ 目前，世界贸易组织成员的总体平均关税水平为6%，发展中国家为10%，发达国家为3%，我国约为15%。https://zhidao.baidu.com/question/590433596.html, 20240426.

but also could get other advantages such as export credit, export credit insurance, export tax rebate of exporting countries. ① Thus, the international competitiveness of exported products is enhanced.

III. Non-tariff Measure to Import

Non-tariff measure refers to all regulatory measures that hinder imports except tariffs. Because the lower tariff rate plays less of a role in restricting import, thus non-tariff barriers have already been the main means of import restriction, more than 1000 in the world. Since tariff measures are presented in an open manner in laws and regulations, it is clear if they comply with the duty of tariff reduction of WTO members, which is allowed by WTO. The non-tariff measures, unless complying with provisions of WTO, go against WTO principles of "fair trade" and "tariff protection", which are ill-legal and should be prohibited. ②

IV. Anti-dumping and Anti-subsidy

(I) Anti-dumping. Dumping refers to the exporter sells goods in foreign market at an abnormally low price which does harm to related products or industries of the dumped country. The purpose of which is mainly to seize the international market and expand the export of products. Because dumping violates the principle of fair market competition of WTO and damages the economic interests of importing countries. According to the WTO anti-dumping rules, the importing country may counter dumping by levying anti-dumping duties on dumped goods to offset the damage to their relevant industries. ③

(II) Anti-subsidy. Anti-subsidy or countervailing, refers to the legal activities that WTO members take necessary restrictive measures against subsidy on imported goods to protect the healthy development of their own economy, maintain the order of

---

① 出口货物不仅享受免交出口税的政策，而且还可以得到出口信贷、出口信用保险、出口退税等优惠待遇。

② 由于关税措施是以法律法规的公开方式呈现的，是否符合成员国关税削减的义务一目了然，所以在关税水平内的进口关税为 WTO 所允许。而非关税措施除非符合 WTO 的相关规定，否则均因违反 WTO 的"公平贸易原则"和"关税保护原则"而系非法措施，应被禁止。

③ 由于这种做法违背了公平的市场竞争原则，损害了相关国家的经济利益，根据 WTO 的《反倾销守则》，进口国有权对倾销的进口商品通过征收反倾销税的方式反击倾销，以抵消倾销给本国相关产业造成的损害。

fair competition. ①Subsidy prohibited by *Agreement on Subsidies and Countervailing Duties of WTO* is export subsidy, that's cash subsidy or financial concession from the government to its exported goods to encourage export. ② Cash subsidy is called direct subsidy, while financial concession refers to as indirect subsidies, including but not limited to refund or remission of domestic taxes, such as value-added tax, and income tax. ③

The export subsidies are often used as a means to stimulate exports or restrict imports which is harmful to importing countries and violates WTO principle of non-discrimination. According to the Agreement, importing countries may take countervailing mea-sures, including taking interim measures, making promise and imposing countervailing duties, against subsidized imported goods.

Based on the legality of anti-dumping and anti-subsidy, in recent years, some developed countries have abused the two measures on imported goods from developing countries which result in anti-dumping measures to have become a kind of non-tariff measures to limit imports which has attracted the attention of WTO and the international community, and worth further studying.

---

① 反补贴是指 WTO 成员国为了保护本国经济健康发展，维护公平竞争秩序，针对进口商品的补贴行为而采取必要限制措施的法律活动。

② 被 WTO《补贴与反补贴税协定》所禁止的是出口补贴，是政府为鼓励出口而对出口商品给予的现金补贴或财政优惠。

③ 现金补贴被称为直接补贴，而财政优惠被称为间接补贴，包括但不限于退还或减免出口商品所缴纳的销售税、消费税、增值税、所得税等国内税。

Part Ⅳ Law on International Trade in Services

As mentioned earlier, the agreement reached in Uruguay Round of the GATT shows that contemporary international trade is composed of three types of trade, including international trade in services. The ever-changing scientific and technological revolution nowadays has continuously limited the development space of traditional international trade of goods, but it has expanded the infinite possibilities for international trade in services, which has been widely concerned and valued by all countries worldwide.

This part includes from Chapter 7 to Chapter 10, which builds on the *General Agreement on Trade in Services* (*GATS*) negotiated in the Uruguay Round, and then focuses on international cargo transport law, international marine cargo insurance law and finance law of international trade of goods. Specifically speaking, Chapter 7 is Introduction to Law of International Trade in Services which includes treaties and conventions on international trade in services (GATS), international maritime services trade law and international trade financial services law. Chapter 8 is law on international carriage of goods which includes modes of international cargo transport, law of international carriage of goods by sea, and conventions for the unification of certain legal rules on international carriage of goods by sea. Chapter 9 is Law of International Marine Insurance, which includes the basic theory of marine insurance, contract of international marine cargo insurance, insured scope, marine insurance clauses, and subrogation. Chapter 10 is Financial Law of International Trade of Goods which includes rules of instruments and modes of international payment.

如前文所述，关贸总协定乌拉圭回合谈判达成的协议表明，尽管当代国际贸易是由包括国际服务贸易在内的三种贸易形态所共同构成，但是当代日新月异的科技革命不断限缩着传统国际货物贸易的发展空间，却为国际服务贸易拓展了无限可能，服务贸易因而受到了世界各国的普遍关注和重视。

本部分包括第 7 章至第 10 章，以乌拉圭回合谈判达成的《服务贸易总协定》

为基础，进而围绕国际货物运输法、国际货运保险法和国际贸易金融法逐一展开讲述。其中第 7 章国际服务贸易法概述包括国际服务贸易的条约与公约、GATS 协议、国际海事服务贸易法和国际贸易金融服务法。第 8 章国际货物运输法包括国际货物运输方式、国际海上货物运输法、统一国际海上货物运输某些法律规则的公约。第 9 章国际海运货物保险法包括海运保险的基础理论、国际海洋货物运输保险合同、承保范围、海运保险条款、仓对仓条款和代位求偿权。第 10 章国际货物贸易金融法则为国际贸易支付工具和支付方式的法律规范。

Chapter 7 Introduction to Law on International Trade in Services

Section I Introduction

I. Definition

(I) Definition of trade in services. Trade in services refers to the sale and delivery of an intangible product, called a service, between a producer and consumer. In international economic law, trade in services that takes place between producers and consumers based in different countries is called international trade in services. The narrowed meaning of international trade in services refers to the traditional intangible trade such as transportation, insurance, finance and tourism, which serve the international trade of goods. The broad meaning also includes new trade activities developed in modern times, except for services related to trade in goods, such as contracted labor services, satellite transmission, etc.

(II) Types of trade in services. GATS define the international trade in services as four modes:

Mode 1 Cross-Border Supply—which is defined as delivery of a service from *the territory of one country into the territory of another country*, e. g. remotely providing accounting services in one country for a company based in another country, or an airline flying between two international destinations.

Mode 2 Consumption Abroad—this mode covers supply of a service of one country to the service consumer of any other country, e. g. tourism, telemedicine, or study abroad.

Mode 3 Commercial Presence—this mode covers services provided by a service supplier of one country in the territory of any other country, e. g. a bank opening a physical branch or internet service provider offering internet services in another country.

Mode 4 Presence of Natural Persons—It covers services provided by a service supplier of one country through the presence of natural persons in the territory of any other country, e. g. a business transferring an employee from one country to another for work duties (doctors or architects traveling and working abroad).

II. Law on International Trade in Services

Law on International Trade in Services is a new branch of International Trade Law, which system and contents are still in an embryonic stage. It regulates international service trade relations, which consists of international legal norms and domestic legal norms. Firstly, the sources of international law on international trade in services include global legal norms of trade in services and regional legal norms of trade in services. The former mainly refers to GATS, and the latter mainly refers to RATS (Regional Trade Agreements in Services). Today, the domestic legal norms are still the mainly sources of law on international trade in service.

(I) GATS. The "Uruguay Round" negotiations in 1986 included trade in services into the negotiation agenda. Until the end of the "Uruguay Round" negotiations in December 1993, the General Agreement on Trade in Services was reached and entered into force in 1995.

GATS established a multilateral framework of principles and rules for trade in services with a view to the expansion of such trade under conditions of transparency and progressive liberalization and as a means of promoting the economic growth of all trading partners and the development of developing countries. GATS forms part of the Final Act rests on three pillars. The first is a Framework Agreement containing basic obligations which apply to all member countries. The second concerns national schedules of commitments containing specific further national commitments which will be the subject of a continuing process of liberalization. The third is a number of annexes addressing the special situations of individual services sectors.

(II) RATS (Regional Trade Agreements in Services). The makers of RATS are limited to specific countries in a certain region. The legal norms on trade in services in RATS are not signed as an independent legal document, but as an integral part of a broader multilateral agreement. For instance, in NAFTA, CPTPP, RCEP and other agreements, many clauses are related to trade in services.

For instance, RCEP has also made significant progress in the field of service trade openness compared to the WTO. RCEP member countries have committed to opening up over 100 service trade sectors, covering finance, telecommunications, transportation, tourism, research and development, etc. Cross border e-commerce, internet finance, online office, online education, online consultation, online trade fairs and other new formats and models will usher in greater development opportunities. They have stipulated market access commitments, national treatment, and most favored nation treatment for service trade among members. This regulation reduces restrictive and discriminatory measures that affect cross-border service trade, making it easier for the service industries of various economies in the region to enter each other's markets. It can be expected that RCEP will combine service trade with the digital economy and become a new regional economic growth point.

Section II General Agreements on Trade in Services

I. The Proposal and Negotiation Process of Services Trade Negotiations

As early as in the Tokyo Round of negotiations, the US government attempted to make service trade one of the topics of the round, and then some content on service trade in the customs valuation and government procurement agreements were included in the Tokyo Round. At first, the European Union had doubts about the proposal from the United States. But the European Union found that the EU export volume of service trade was higher than that of the United States, and instead strongly supported the United States. Although Japan was the largest importer of services trade and has a deficit situation, it had always supported the United States due to its surplus in international trade and the increasingly sharp trade friction between Japan and the United States. When the United States raised the issue of trade in services, the vast majority of developing countries firmly opposed the liberalization of trade in services. As developed countries gradually unified their understanding of trade in services negotiations, the stance of developing countries firmly resisting trade in services had changed. Firstly, some emerging developing countries and regions had already gained considerable advantages in certain services, and these countries hoped to expand their exports of advantageous services through negotiations. Secondly, most developing countries were under pressure from developed countries, and they realized that if they do not actively participate in negotiations on service trade, they would become passive recipients for the rules for service trade formulated by developed countries. Therefore, many developing countries also expressed their willingness to participate in service trade negotiations. On April 15, 1994, all member countries officially signed the General Agreement on Trade in Services in Marrakesh.

Ⅱ. Contents of the General Agreement on Trade in Services

There are totally six parts in GATS as following:

Part Ⅰ of the basic agreement defines its scope. Specifically, services supplied from the territory of one party to the territory of another; services supplied in the territory of one party to the consumers of any other (for example, tourism); services provided through the presence of service providing entities of one party in the territory of any other (for example, banking); and services provided by nationals of one party in the territory of any other (for example, construction projects or consultancies).

Part Ⅱ sets out general obligations and disciplines. A basic most-favored-nation (MFN) obligation states that each party "shall accord immediately and unconditionally to services and service providers of any other Party, treatment no less favorable than that it accords to like services and service providers of any other country". However, it is recognized that MFN treatment may not be possible for every service activity and, therefore, it is envisaged that parties may indicate specific MFN exemptions. Conditions for such exemptions are included as an annex and provide for reviews after five years and a normal limitation of 10 years on their duration.

Part Ⅲ contains provisions on market access and national treatment which would not be general obligations but would be commitments made in national schedules. Thus, in the case of market access, each party "shall accord services and service providers of other parties treatment no less favorable than that provided for under the terms, limitations and conditions agreed and specified in its schedule". The intention of the market-access provision is to progressively eliminate the following types of measures: limitations on numbers of service providers, on the total value of service transactions or on the total number of service operations or people employed.

Part Ⅳ of the agreement establishes the basis for progressive liberalization in the services area through successive rounds of negotiations and the development of national schedules. It also permits, after a period of three years, parties to withdraw or modify commitments made in their schedules. Where commitments are modified or withdrawn, negotiations should be undertaken with interested parties to agree on compensatory adjustments. Where agreement cannot be reached, compensation would be decided by arbitration.

Part V contains institutional provisions, including consultation and dispute settlement and the establishment of a Council on Services. The responsibilities of the Council are set out in a Ministerial Decision.

III. Meaning of General Agreement on Trade in Services

Firstly, GATS is the milestone of the liberalization on trade in services. It provides institutional arrangements and guarantees for the gradual liberalization. Secondly, it combines the general obligations and the flexibility rules, especially gives developing countries more flexibility choices. Thirdly, it's promoting the normalization of trade in services.

Section Ⅲ   International Maritime Service Trade Law

I. Domestic Legislation of International Maritime Service Trade

Different countries and regions also develop their own maritime regulations, such as Maritime Transport Law of the United States and Maritime Code of China. It is very important to comply with international and national maritime regulations in international maritime activities, which can effectively ensure the legality and stability of maritime activities.

Maritime Goods Act of the United States, also known as the Carriage of Goods by Sea Act (COGSA), is a regulation passed by the Federal government of the United States in 1936, which covers the provisions on the contract of carriage of goods by sea and the handling of transport accidents. On June 13, 2022, the United States House of Representatives passed the Ocean Shipping Reform Act of 2022.

British Maritime Law can be roughly divided into two parts: dry shipping and wet shipping. The former mainly includes the Maritime Carriage of Goods Law (including the Charter Party Law) and the Maritime Insurance Law, which adjust various types of maritime contract relationships. The latter is equivalent to China's maritime law, such as the Ship Collision Law, Maritime Rescue Law, Ship Oil Pollution Law, etc. The laws regulating various types of maritime contractual relationships in the UK include three parts. Firstly, English common law, which is also known as English case law; Secondly, legislation of the Parliament of the United Kingdom, such as the Carriage of Goods by Sea Act 1992, the Marine Insurance Act 1906 (part of which has been amended by the Insurance Act 2015), etc; Thirdly, international conventions implemented through legislation of the Parliament of the United Kingdom, such as The Hague/Visby Rules implemented through the Carriage of Goods by Sea Act 1971. The first part is the foundation, and the second and third parts are supplements.

II. International Legislation on International Maritime Service Trade of China

WTO regulations on trade in maritime services are contained in GATS concluded in the Uruguay Round. The gradual liberalization of maritime services under the GATS system is an effective way to balance the interests of developed and developing maritime countries. During the Uruguay Round negotiations, developed maritime countries included the maritime services industry in the scope of service trade negotiations, and in November 1990, the Annex to GATS (Draft) included maritime services. After the end of the Uruguay Round negotiations, all member countries continued negotiations on the opening of the maritime service industry.

III. Legal Norms on Maritime Service Trade of China

Since 1985, China has successively issued a series of laws and regulations, allowing foreign shipping companies to engage in normal business activities in China through joint ventures or sole proprietorships. Many foreign shipping companies have flooded into the Chinese market. The legal norms for the maritime service industry in China are mainly domestic law, supplemented by international law. In domestic law, administrative regulations and departmental rules are the main sources, while in practice, there are also guiding documents issued in the form of "methods", "opinions", "notices", etc.

Maritime Code of China has been in effect since July 1, 1993. What's more, China's International Maritime Transport Regulations (the latest revision in 2019) regulate the opening up of China's shipping market to the outside world through administrative regulations, which are in line with the provisions of Maritime Code of China and are conducive to improving the quality of maritime opening up. However, the Regulations have not yet made provisions on crew management and national support related to the maritime service industry.

Section IV   Law on International Trade in Financial Services

I. Domestic Legislation on International Trade in Financial Services

Financial service refers to the activity in which financial institutions use monetary trading methods to finance valuable goods and provide mutual benefits and satisfaction to participants and customers in financial activities. According to the WTO Annex, providers of financial services include the following types of institutions: insurance and related services, as well as all banking and other financial services (excluding insurance).

In the U. S. , the Financial Services Modernization Act of 1999 stipulates that financial institutions ensure the security and confidentiality of customer data, that data must be stored in hidden media, and that specific security measures must be taken to protect data storage and transmission security.

In U. K. , Financial Services and Markets Act 2000 ("FSMA") has taken effect on April 1, 2001. It changed the UK's financial regulatory system, from the "industry self-regulation within the statutory framework" established by the Financial Services Act of 1986 to the "Static Single Regulator" system. The Financial Services and Markets Act 2023 have been signed by King Charles III of the United Kingdom.

Japan's Financial Commodity Trading Law was officially implemented on September 30, 2007. The purpose of it is to improve the system of Japan's financial commodity trading law, in order to improve investor protection rules and investor convenience, ensure the transformation of market functions from savings to investment, and respond to the nationalization needs of the financial capital market.

II. International Legislation on International Trade in Financial Services

According to GATS of the WTO, by adhering to general obligations and disciplines such as most favored nation treatment and transparency, and making specific commitments such as market access and national treatment, WTO members practice the concept of gradual liberalization of trade in services.

In terms of financial services, WTO members have not only formulated the "Annex" and the "Second Annex on Financial Services" (hereinafter referred to as "Annex Ⅱ"), but also reached the "Understanding on Financial Services Commitment" (hereinafter referred to as "Understanding"). Among them, the Annex provides a comprehensive definition of financial services and specifically mentions the domestic regulatory issues and dispute resolution issues of WTO members regarding financial services. Annex 2 involves matters such as the addition and modification of existing exemptions and commitments by WTO members after the entry into force of the WTO Agreement. The Understanding provides more detailed provisions on the specific application of the third part of GATS, namely market access rules and national treatment rules, in financial services. According to the principle that special law is superior to general law, when disputes involving trade in financial services arise, they should first be resolved in accordance with the aforementioned annexes and understandings. Only when there are no provisions or vague provisions in the annexes or understandings can the relevant rules of GATS be referred to.

Ⅲ. Legal Norms on International Trade in Financial Services of China

To fulfill China's commitments in financial services, China has revised several laws and regulations in according to its specific commitments, such as the Commercial Bank Law, the Foreign Exchange Law, the Regulations on the Administration of Foreign Banks and their implementation rules, the Securities Law, and the Insurance Law.

As of March 2022, China has signed 19 free trade agreements with 26 countries and regions, among which positive list commitments are adopted for the opening of financial services. However, in multiple negative lists released independently, financial services have been opened. In April 2015, the State Council issued the "Foreign Investment Standards for Free Trade Pilot Zones". In the "Special Management Measures (Negative List)", 122 special management measures were listed for 15 categories. Among them, 14 Articles are related to the financial industry, involves the types, qualifications, stock ratios, and requirements for foreign stock ratios in the securities, futures, and insurance markets of banking shareholders. Since 2018, the National Development and Reform Commission and the Ministry of Commerce have issued a national version of the "Special Management Measures for Foreign Investment Access" every year (with negative effects).

In order to fulfill China's RCEP commitments and joining the CPTPP, China's financial services trade law should be aligned with it and gradually promote financial cooperation and openness. However, the financial regulation is also very important. In addition to applying the National Security Law and the Cyber security Law, China's regulation of cross-border flow of financial information data is also regulated by information protection clauses in relevant laws and regulations in the banking, insurance, and securities industries. For example, article 37 of the Cyber Security Law stipulates that information collected by infrastructure located within China should also be stored within the country, and data localization storage should be adhered to.

Chapter 8　Law on International Carriage of Goods

Section Ⅰ　Methods of International Cargo Transportation

Ⅰ. Cargo Transportation by Sea

The International Law on the Cargo Transportation by Sea regulates the various legal relationships between ships, their owners, and other relevant parties in international maritime transportation activities. International shipping law mainly involves international conventions, rules, regulations, and legal norms formulated by various countries in shipping. The content includes: the relationship between ships and crew members, the relationship between contracts for the carriage of goods by sea, the relationship between contracts for the carriage of passengers by sea, the relationship between contracts for towing at sea, the relationship between maritime salvage, the relationship between ships colliding, the relationship between oil pollution at sea, the relationship between general average, the relationship between the limitation of liability of ship owners, the relationship between marine insurance, the relationship between maritime dispute resolution, and so on. The various legal relationships mentioned above are within the scope of adjustment of international shipping regulations and maritime laws or shipping laws of various countries. The second section will elaborate in detail.

Ⅱ. Cargo Transportation by Railroad

Cargo transportation by railroad refers to the transportation of goods through railways that purposefully alter or displace their space or location. The railway, as the carrier, accepts the consignor's commission to transport the goods from the origin to the destination through the railway and deliver them to the consignee. According to the weight, volume, and shape of a batch of goods, it can be divided into whole vehicle cargo transportation, light load cargo transportation, and container cargo transportation. At present, there are treaties related to cargo transportation by railroad: Convention Concerning International Carriage of Goods by Rail (1961) and Agreement on International Railroad through Transport of Goods (1951).

The Convention Concerning International Carriage of Goods by Rail is the earliest international railway transportation rule drafted in the world and has been revised multiple times to be more perfect. If it is applicable to be shipped according to a combined waybill, the transportation distance shall pass through the territory of at least two contracting states. Agreement on International Railroad through Transport of Goods is a basic document jointly followed by the consignor, consignee, and transit handling of goods in the contracting countries. The Agreement consists of 8 chapters, 41 articles, and some annexes. The main content includes: "Scope of application" "Conclusion of transportation contract" "Obligations and rights of the shipper" "Rights and obligations of the carrier" "Compensation claims and statute of limitations", etc.

III. Cargo Transportation by Air

International air transportation refers to the use of aircraft, helicopters, and other aircraft to transport personnel, goods, and mail. The laws related to the transportation of air cargo mainly refer to treaties that unify air transportation rules. The treaty consists of eight documents, collectively known as the Warsaw System, mainly based on the Warsaw Convention, Montreal Protocol IV, and the Hague Protocol. Formally, the Warsaw Convention and the Hague Protocol constitute an inseparable and unified document. In actual use, these two treaties are the most commonly used.

The Warsaw Convention was signed in Warsaw by 23 European countries in October 1929 and came into effect on February 13, 1933. After multiple modifications and supplements, more than 130 countries have joined it. China joined this convention in 1958. This convention applies to air transportation where both the origin and destination specified in the transportation contract belong to member states, and also applies to air transportation where both the origin and destination are in one member state, but the aircraft stays in another country. In September 1955, the Hague Protocol did not make substantive modifications to the basic framework of the Warsaw Convention, but further unified and improved issues such as exemption from navigation negligence, limitation of liability, items of transport documents, and claim deadlines. China joined the Hague

Protocol in 1975.

International air cargo transportation mainly refers to transportation where the origin and destination of aircraft are located in two countries, or goods belonging to the same country but with an agreed stopping point for aircraft in another country. At the same time, the domestic segment of international air transportation is also applicable to the Warsaw system, rather than applying domestic air law, which is particularly noteworthy because there is a significant gap between domestic and international compensation.

IV. Multi-modal Transportation

United Nations Convention on International Multi-modal Transport of Goods defines international multi-modal transportation as the transportation of goods from a designated delivery point within the territory of one country to a designated delivery point within the territory of another country by at least two different modes of transportation. Maritime Law of China stipulates that there must be one method for domestic multi-modal transportation, which is sea freight.

Although multi-modal transportation involves two or more different modes of transportation, the shipper only establishes one contract with the multi-modal transport operator, obtains onemulti-modal transport document from the multi-modal transport operator, and only pays the freight to the multi-modal transport operator at one rate. This avoids the drawbacks of multiple transportation procedures and prone to errors in a single transportation method, and provides convenience for shippers to determine transportation costs and goods in transit time.

Section II   Law on International Carriage of Goods by Sea

I. Types of International Carriage of Goods by Sea

International Carriage of Goods by Sea includes liner transport, charter party, and other transport methods. The Liner Transport includes container ship transportation and bulk cargo ship transportation. The Charter Party is divided into the Voyage Charter, the time Charter and the Bare-boat Charter. Different types of transportation have different billing standards and require accounting based on actual needs.

(I) Liner transport. Liner Transport, also known as "bill of lading transportation", refers to the international maritime transportation of goods by the shipper who hands over a certain amount of goods to the shipping company as the carrier, and the shipping company stops at fixed ports along the route according to fixed shipping schedules and fixed freight rates. It is commonly used for goods with low transportation volume, high prices, and scattered delivery ports, and is the most widely used method in sea and sea freight transportation. The shipping company or its agent issues a bill of lading after accepting the delivery of the consigned goods, which is the form and evidence of a liner transport contract.

The characteristics of the Liner Transport:

A. Four "fixed": fixed routes, fixed ports, fixed shipping schedules, fixed freight rates.

B. Both the carrier and the shipper do not calculate demur-rage and dispatch fees.

C. The rights, obligations, and liability exemptions of both the liner companies and shipper are based on the terms of the bill of lading issued by the liner company.

(II) Charter party. A charter party refers to a written agreement signed by the ship owner to lease out all or part of the ship, and the charterer charter the ship to transport goods and pay the charter fee. It can be divided into three categories: Voyage Charter, Time Charter and Bare-boat Charter. These three types of charter parties for transporting goods have different rights and obligations in terms of chartering and using the ship.

A. Voyage charter. It refers to a written agreement signed between the ship owner and the charterer. The charterer hires a ship for a specified number of voyages and pays the freight to the ship owner. The operation of the ship is entirely the responsibility of the ship owner. The charterer is responsible to the responsible party for completing the voyage transportation task. Freight is calculated based on a lump sum fee or cargo tonnage. The rights and obligations of shippers and charterers are similar to those of time charter parties.

B. Time charter. It refers to a written agreement signed between the ship owner and the charterer. The charterer hires of a ship for a specified period. The charterer shall use the ship for the agreed purpose during the lease term and pay the rent. The ship owner is generally responsible for crew wages, crew meals, ship maintenance, ship insurance fees, materials, supplies, ship depreciation fees, and claims for partial cargo damage and difference, while the charterer is generally responsible for fuel costs, port usage fees, cabin cleaning fees, dunnage material fees, and is also responsible for partial cargo damage and difference claims.

C. Bare-boat charter. It refers to the leasing business method in which the ship owner provides a ship without crew members to the charterer, which is occupied, used and operated by the charterer within the agreed period, and the charterer pays rent according to the contract. Its characteristics are: The charterer is responsible for providing crew members, their salaries, and meals; the charterer shall bear the operating expenses of the ship, while the ship insurance and inspection fees may be agreed upon by which party to bear.

II. Bill of Lading

(I) Definition and functions of bill of lading. A bill of lading (sometimes abbreviated as B/L or BOL) is a document issued by a carrier (or their agent) to acknowledge receipt of cargo for shipment. Although the term historically related only to carriage by sea, a bill of lading may today be used for any type of carriage of goods. Bills of lading are the documents used in international trade to ensure that exporters receive payment and importers receive the merchandise.

A bill of lading must be transferable, and serves three main functions:

A. It is a conclusive receipt, i. e. an acknowledgement that the goods have been loaded.

B. It contains or evidences the terms of the contract of carriage.

C. It serves as a document of title to the goods.

(II) Types of Bill of Lading.

A. Bearer bill of lading, order bill of lading, straight bill of lading. A bearer bill of lading refers to a bill of lading that does not specify the name of the consignee on the front of the bill of lading. The consignee column of a bearer bill of lading is blank and does not include the words "holder" . In the case of issuing a bearer bill of lading, the carrier shall deliver the goods to the holder of the bill of lading. A straight bill of lading is used when payment has been made in advance of shipment and requires a carrier to deliver the merchandise to the appropriate party. An order bill of lading is used when shipping merchandise prior to payment, requiring a carrier to deliver the merchandise to the importer, and at the endorsement of the exporter the carrier may transfer title to the importer. Endorsed order bills of lading can be traded as a security or serve as collateral against debt obligations.

B. Clean and claused bill of lading. Clean Bill of Lading—A bill of lading bearing no findings of damage or shortage. A bill of lading indicates that there is no damage to or loss of the goods during transport. A bill of lading is a document in which the parties agree to ship a good to a certain location and also serves as the receipt upon arrival at the destination. Most banks or other institutions financing the shipment will only accept clean bills of lading.

A Claused Bill of Lading refers to a bill of lading indicates some damage to or loss of goods during transport. Most banks or other institutions financing the shipment refuse to accept or honor claused bills of lading, which mean that sellers often have difficulty receiving payment on them. It is also called a dirty bill of lading.

C. On-Board and received-for-shipment bill of lading. Bills of lading may take various forms, such as on-board and received-for-shipment. An on-board bill of lading denotes that merchandise has been physically loaded onto a shipping vessel, such as a freighter or cargo plane. A received-for-shipment bill of lading denotes that merchandise has been received, but is not guaranteed to have already been loaded onto a shipping vessel. (Typically, it will be issued by a freight-forwarder at a port or depot). Such bills can be converted upon being loaded.

(Ⅲ) Characteristics of bill of lading.

A. The proof of receipt of goods. The principal use of the bill of lading is as a receipt issued by the carrier once the goods have been loaded onto the vessel. This receipt can be used as proof of shipment for customs and insurance purposes, and also as commercial proof of completing a contractual obligation, especially under INCOTERMS such as CFR and FOB.

B. Evidence of the contract of carriage by sea. The bill of lading from carrier to the shipper can be used as an evidence of the contract of carriage by the fact that carrier has received the goods and upon the receipt the carrier would deliver the goods. In this case, the bill of lading would be used as a contract of carriage. In this case, the bill of lading can be used if shipper does not properly ship the goods then the shipper cannot receive the bill of lading from the carrier. Eventually, the shipper would have to deliver the bill of lading to the seller. In this case, the bill of lading is used as a contract of carriage between seller and carrier. However, when the bill of lading is negotiated to a bona fide third party then the bill of lading becomes conclusive evidence where no contradictory evidence can be introduced. It is because the third party cannot examine the actual shipment and can only pay attention to the document itself, not survey or examination of the shipment itself. However, the bill of lading will rarely be the contract itself, since the cargo space will have been booked previously, perhaps by telephone, email or letter. The preliminary contract will be acknowledged by both the shipper and carrier to incorporate the carrier's standard terms of business. If the Hague – Visby Rules apply, then all of the Rules will be automatically annexed to the bill of lading, thus forming a statutory contract.

C. The bill of lading as a document of title. When the bill of lading is used as a document of title, it is particularly related to the case of buyer. When the buyer is entitled to receive goods from the carrier, bill of lading in this case performs as document of title for the goods. There are two types of bill of lading that can perform as document of title. They are straight bill of lading and order bill of lading. Straight bill of lading is a bill of lading issued to a named consignee that is not negotiable. In this case, the bill of lading should be directed only to one specific consignee indicated on the bill of lading. Order bill of lading is the opposite from a straight bill of lading and there is no specific or named consignee. Therefore, an order bill of lading can be negotiated to a third party.

Simply, the bill of lading confers prima facie title over the goods to the named consignee or lawful holder. Under the "nemo dat quod non habet" rule ("no one gives what he doesn't have"), a seller cannot pass better title than he himself has; so if the goods are subject to an encumbrance (such as a mortgage, charge or hypothec), or even stolen, the bill of lading will not grant full title to the holder.

(Ⅳ) Transfer of property under a bill of lading. The bill of lading is not only a document of debt, but also a document of property or even a document of ownership. The delivery of a bill of lading based on the contract of sale of goods has the legal effect of transferring ownership of the goods under the bill of lading.

Business practices and laws express the rights on the bill of lading, endowing it with certain circulation functions, so that the transfer of the bill of lading and the transfer of goods under the bill of lading have the same property effect, and ultimately realized the "documentary transaction" of international trade.

(Ⅴ) Carrier's duties under a bill of lading.

A. The basic obligations of the carrier in bill of lading transportation.

a. Making the ship seaworthy.

b. Properly manning, equipping, and supplying the ship.

c. Making the holds, refrigerating, and cool chambers, and all other parts of the ship in which goods are carried, fit and safe for their reception, carriage, and preservation.

d. Properly and carefully loading, handling, stowing, carrying, keeping, caring for, and discharging (unloading) the goods carried.

B. Liability limits.

a. The Hague Rules of 1921 limits a carrier's liability to UK£100 per package or UK£100 per unit if the goods carried on the board lost or damaged.

b. The Hague—Visby Rules of 1968 set the limits at "10000 gold francs per package or unit, or thirty gold francs per kilo of the gross weight of the goods lost or damaged, whichever is the higher." This gold or francs is not a unit of currency, but rather an amount of gold. At current conversion rates, it is equivalent to approximately USMYM 1 or UK £0. 60.

C. Time limitations.

A claim for loss or damages must be instituted/started within 1 year after the goods were or should have been delivered. The claim may be initiated by filing suit or commencing an arbitration proceeding.

(Ⅵ) Frauds on bill of lading. Frauds on Bill of lading refers to the situation where one party uses methods such as anti-dating or advanced bill of lading in maritime transportation or activities related to maritime transportation, resulting in the fraudulent party having a wrong understanding and expressing their intention.

A. Antedated bill of lading. The Antedated Bill of Lading refers to a bill of lading issued earlier than the date of shipment of the goods. If the actual loading date is slightly later than the shipment date stipulated in the L/C, the carrier, sometimes, at the request of the shipper, will issue an anti-dated B/L so as to meet the requirements of the L/C. If the date shown on the B/L is later than the L/C stipulations, the bank will not accept such a bill of lading for negotiation, payment or acceptance. If the buyer finds this, he may refuse the goods or lodge a claim against the carrier or the seller.

B. Advanced bill of lading. Advanced bill of lading refers to the issuance of a bill of lading when the goods have not yet been fully loaded on board, or when the goods have been taken over by the carrier but have not yet started loading. All responsibilities arising from the pre borrowed bill of lading shall be borne by the issuer of the bill of lading.

C. Exchange the letter of guarantee for a clean bill of lading. In international goods sales, shippers often issue a Letter of Guarantee to the carrier and promise to bear all possible damages in exchange for a clean bill of lading in order to avoid the occurrence of bank refusal to pay due to obtaining an unclean bill of lading.

    D. Forged/Altered bill of lading. Forged/Altered bill of lading means that the shipper has not loaded the goods onto the ship, or the goods do not exist at all, or only a small amount of goods have been loaded, but the shipper has forged a bill of lading that appears to fully meet the requirements of the letter of credit to defraud the buyer of payment.

Section Ⅲ   International Conventions for the Unification of Certain Rules of Law Relating to Carriage of Goods by Sea

Ⅰ. Hague Rules

    (Ⅰ) Introduction. The official title of Hague Rules is the "International Convention for the Unification of Certain Rules of Law relating to Bills of Lading". On Aug. 25, 1924, it was signed in Brusselsof Belgium, and came into effect on June 2, 1931. It is an international agreement established to unify different legal provisions on bills of lading in various countries around the world and to determine the rights and obligations of carriers and shippers in the carriage of goods by sea.

    (Ⅱ) Carriers' duties. The duty of the carrier stipulated in the Hague Rules is minimal and only includes two mandatory obligations: Making the ship seaworthy and cargo management obligation. The liability system is an incomplete fault. The period of responsibility is from the loading of goods onto the ship to the completion of unloading.

    (Ⅲ) Exemption of the carriers. There are many provisions on the exemption of the carrier, including about 17 items: (i) the behavior, negligence, or failure to perform duties of the captain, crew member, pilot, or the carrier's employee in driving or managing the ship; (ii) Fire, except for those caused by the carrier's actual fault or personal conspiracy; (iii) Risks, dangers, or accidents at sea or other navigable waters; (iv) Natural disasters; (v) Acts of war; (vi) Public enemy behavior; (vii) The detention or detention of a monarch, ruler, or people, or the lawful seizure; (viii) Quarantine restrictions; (ix) The act or omission of the shipper or owner of the goods, their agents or representatives; (x) Partial or comprehensive strikes, lock downs, or labor restrictions caused by any reason; (xi) Riots and civil commotions; (xii) Rescue or attempt to rescue life or property at sea; (xiii) Loss of volume or weight, or any other loss or damage caused by inherent defects, properties, or defects of the goods; (xiv) Improper packaging; (xv) Unclear or inappropriate markings; (xvi) Potential defects that cannot be detected with due care; (xvii) Any other reason not caused by the actual fault or private conspiracy of the carrier, or the fault or negligence of the carrier's agent or employee.

Hague Rules, with many exemptions for the carriers which is unfair to the shipper, therefore, were modified and supplied by the Visby Rules.

II. Hague−Visby Rules

(I) History. The Hague−Visby Rules is a set of international rules for the international carriage of goods by sea. They are a slightly updated version of the original Hague Rules. The premise of the Hague−Visby Rules (and of the earlier English common law from which the Rules are drawn) was that a carrier typically has far greater bargaining power than the shipper, and that to protect the interests of the shipper/cargo−owner; the law should impose some minimum affreightment① obligations upon the carrier. However, Hague and Hague−Visby Rules were hardly a charter of new protections for cargo−owners; the English common law prior to 1924 provided more protection for cargo−owners, and imposed more liabilities upon "common carriers".

After being amended by the Brussels Amendments (officially the "Protocol to Amend the International Convention for the Unification of Certain Rules of Law Relating to Bills of Lading") in 1968, the Hague Rules became known colloquially as the Hague−Visby Rules. A final amendment was made in the SDR Protocol in 1979. Many countries declined to adopt the Hague−Visby Rules and stayed with the 1924 Hague Rules. Some other countries which upgraded to Hague−Visby subsequently failed to adopt the 1979 SDR protocol.

(II) Carriers' duties. Under the Rules, carrier's main duties are to "properly and carefully load, handle, stow, carry, keep, care for, and discharge the goods carried" and to "exercise due diligence to ... make the ship seaworthy" and to "... properly man, equip and supply the ship". It is implicit (from the common law) that the carrier must not deviate from the agreed route nor from the usual route; but Article IV (4) provides that "any deviation in saving or attempting to save life or property at sea or any reasonable deviation shall not be deemed to be an infringement or breach of these Rules".

---

① 租船货运。

The carrier's duties are not "strict", but require only a reasonable standard of professionalism and care; and Article Ⅳ allows the carrier a wide range of situations exempting them from liability on a cargo claim. These exemptions include destruction or damage to the cargo caused by: Fire, perils of the sea, Act of God, and act of war. A controversial provision exempts the carrier from liability for "neglect or default of the master... in the navigation or in the management of the ship". This provision is considered unfair to the shipper; and both the later Hamburg Rules (which require contracting states to denounce the Hague–Visby Rules) and Rotterdam Rules (which are not yet in force) refuse exemption for negligent navigation and management.

Also, whereas the Hague–Visby Rules require a ship to be seaworthy only "before and at the beginning" of the voyage, under the Rotterdam Rules the carrier will have to keep the ship seaworthy throughout the voyage (although this new duty will be to a reasonable standard that is subject to the circumstances of being at sea).

(Ⅲ) Shipper's duties. By contrast, the shipper has fewer obligations (mostly implicit), namely: (ⅰ) to pay freight; (ⅱ) to pack the goods sufficiently for the journey; (ⅲ) to describe the goods honestly and accurately; (ⅳ) not to ship dangerous cargoes (unless agreed by both parties); and (ⅴ) to have the goods ready for shipment as agreed; (q. v. "notice of readiness to load"). None of these shippers' obligations are enforceable under the Rules; instead they would give rise to a normal action in contract.

Ⅲ. Hamburg Rules

Hamburg Rules are a set of rules governing the international shipment of goods, resulting from the United Nations International Convention on the Carriage of Goods by Sea adopted in Hamburg on 31 March 1978. The Convention was an attempt to form a uniform legal base for the transportation of goods on oceangoing ships. A driving force behind the convention was the attempt of developing countries' to level the playing field. It came into force on 1 Nov. 1992.

(Ⅰ) History. In 1968, Hague Rules were updated to become the Hague–Visby Rules, but the changes were modest. The convention still covered only "tackle to tackle" carriage contracts, with no provision for multi-modal transport. The industry-changing phenomenon of containerization was barely acknowledged. The 1978 Hamburg Rules were introduced to provide a framework that was both more modern, and less biased in favor of ship-operators. Although the Hamburg Rules were readily adopted by developing countries, they were shunned by richer countries who stuck with Hague and Hague-Visby. It had been expected that a Hague/Hamburg compromise might arise, but instead of the more extensive Rotterdam Rules appeared.

(Ⅱ) Relation with other conventions. Article 31 of the Hamburg Convention covers its entry into force, coupled to denunciation of other Rules. Within five years after entry into force of the Hamburg Rules, ratifying states must denounce earlier conventions, specifically Hague and Hague-Visby Rules. A long-standing aim has been to have a uniform set of rules to govern carriage of goods, but there are now five different sets: Hague, Hague-Visby, Hague-Visby/SDR, Hamburg and Rotterdam.

(Ⅲ) Content. Hamburg Rules was divided into seven parts and 34 articles. The unreasonable provisions of the Hague Rules have been abolished, and the responsibilities and obligations of both the carrier and the shipper for the transportation of goods have been reasonably stipulated. There are provisions for cargo loading, combined transportation, carrier's liability, guarantees, claims, statute of limitations, arbitration, etc. The Hamburg Rules have made fundamental modifications to the Hague Rules, expanding the carrier's liability. The Hamburg Rules have significantly increased the carrier's liability limitations: Article 6 of the Hamburg Rules stipulates the carrier's liability limit for loss of or damage to goods, with a limit of 835 Special Drawing Rights (SDR) per piece or unit, or 2.5 SDR per kilogram of gross weight. When the two are inconsistent, choose the higher one.

Ⅳ. Rotterdam Rules

Rotterdam Rules 2008 (United Nations Convention on Contract for the International Carriage of Goods Wholly or Partly by Sea) are the culmination of the current international rules for the carriage of goods by sea. They involve not only multi-modal transport, including sea freight, and seek a new balance between the rights and obligations of both parties, but also introduce new content such as electronic transport documents, volume contracts, and control rights. In addition, the Convention specifically adds content on jurisdiction and arbitration. There are a total of 96 articles, with 88 substantive articles in this convention, which has not yet entered into force.

The Rotterdam Rules 2008 changed the provisions of the carrier's liability system, expanding the carrier's liability period, changing the carrier's liability basis, eliminating traditional carrier exemption matters, and increasing the carrier's liability limit. If this rule takes effect, it will greatly increase the carrier's liability.

Chapter 9　Law on International Marine Insurance

Section Ⅰ　Fundamental Theory

Ⅰ. Definition of Insurance

In international trade practice, the transportation of goods from the seller to the buyer is generally over a long distance by air, by land or by sea and has to go through the procedures of loading, unloading and storing. During this process, the potential for damages and loss to goods by sea, in comparison with land and air transportation, is tremendous. In order to protect the goods against possible loss in case of such perils the buyer or seller before the transportation of the goods usually applies to an insurance company for insurance covering the goods in transit. The trade terms the parties choose in their sales contract determine who is responsible for purchasing maritime insurance, and who will benefit from it.

Ⅱ. Basic Factors

The basic elements of insurance include the insurer, applicant, insured, object of insurance and insurable risks. An insurer is generally an insurance company that enters into an insurance contract with the applicant and is responsible for compensating or paying insurance benefits. The applicant refers to the person who enters into an insurance contract with the insurer and purchases insurance. Generally, the applicant is the insured. In international trade, the object of insurance is the property and related interests of the insured party. The insurable risks refer to specific risks that meet the underwriting conditions of the insurer. The existence of insurable risks, reasonable insurance rates, the formation of insurance contracts, and insurance claims and settlements are necessary conditions for the establishment of insurance.

III. Principles of Insurance

(I) Insurable interest. The principle of "insurable interest" is a fundamental principle in the insurance industry. The insurable interest principle refers to the legally recognized rights or interests of the applicant or insured in the object insured, such as the potential losses or lost benefits that may occur during an insurance accident.

(II) Utmost good faith. The principle of utmost good faith refers to the sincere and accurate disclosure of all important facts related to insurance by the parties to the other party, without any hypocrisy, deception, or concealment. Moreover, not only should this principle be adhered to when signing insurance contracts, but it is also required that the parties have "maximum integrity" throughout the entire validity period and performance of the contract.

(III) Proximate cause. The principle of proximate cause means that the insurer shall bear insurance liability for losses caused by insurance accidents within the scope of coverage as direct and closest causes, and shall not be liable for compensation for losses caused by reasons outside the scope of coverage.

(IV) Compensation for losses. The principle of compensation for losses is the core principle of property insurance. In property insurance, when an insurance accident causes economic losses to the insured, the insurance company provides compensation for economic losses to the insured, restoring them to the economic condition before the insurance accident.

Section II   Contract of International Marine Cargo Insurance

I . Definition

A contract of marine insurance is a contract whereby the insurer undertakes, as agreed, to indemnify the loss to the subject matter insured and the liability of the insured caused by perils covered by the insurance against the payment of an insurance premium by the insured.

The covered perils referred to in the preceding paragraph mean any maritime perils agreed upon between the insurer and the insured, including perils occurring in inland rivers or on land which is related to a maritime adventure.

A contract of marine insurance mainly includes: Name of the insurer; Name of the insured; Subject matter insured; Insured value; Insured amount; Perils insured against and perils excepted; Duration of insurance coverage; Insurance premium.

In exchange for an initial payment, known as the premium, the insurer promises to pay for loss caused by perils covered under the insurance contract. Insurance contracts are designed to meet specific needs and thus have many features not found in many other types of contracts. Since insurance contracts are standard forms, they feature boilerplate language which is similar across a wide variety of different types of insurance policies.

The insurance contract is generally an integrated contract, meaning that it includes all forms associated with the agreement between the insured and insurer. Oral agreements are subject to the *parole evidence rule*, and may not be considered part of the policy if the contract appears to be whole. Advertising materials and circulars are typically not part of a policy. Oral contracts pending the issuance of a written policy can occur.

II. General Features

(I) Contracts of adhesion. Insurance contracts are generally considered contracts of adhesion because the insurer draws up the contract and the insured has little or no ability to make material changes to it. This is interpreted that the insurer bears the burden if there is any ambiguity in any terms of the contract. Insurance policies are sold without the policyholder even seeing a copy of the contract.

(II) Uncertainty. Insurance contracts are aleatory in that the amounts exchanged by the insured and insurer are unequal and depend upon uncertain future events or risks. In contrast, ordinary non-insurance contracts are commutative in that the amounts (or values) exchanged is usually intended by the parties to be roughly equal. This distinction is particularly important in the context of exotic products such as finite risk insurance that contain "commutation" provisions.

(III) Unilateral. Insurance contracts are unilateral, meaning that only the insurer makes legally enforceable promises in the contract. The insured is not required to pay the premiums, but the insurer is required to pay the benefits under the contract if the insured has paid the premiums and met certain other basic provisions.

(IV) Utmost good faith. Insurance contracts are governed by the principle of utmost good faith, which requires both parties of the insurance contract to deal in good faith and in particular, imparts on the insured a duty to disclose all material facts that relate to the risk to be covered. In the United States, the insured can sue an insurer in tort for acting in bad faith.

Section Ⅲ   Insured Scope

Ⅰ. Insured Risks

Insured risks refer to the right of property to be insured. The risks of maritime cargo transportation are divided into Perils of the Sea and Extraneous Risks.

(Ⅰ) Perils of the sea. Perils of the Sea include natural calamities and fortuitous accidents.

A. Natural calamities. A natural calamity is a major adverse event resulting from natural processes of the Earth; examples include floods, lightning, storms, drifting ice, earthquakes, tsunamis, and other uncontrollable disaster.

B. Fortuitous accidents. They mainly include serious accidents with obvious marine characteristics, such as ship stranded, striking upon the rocks, ship sinking, ship collision, colliding with icebergs, fire, explosion, ship missing, etc.

(Ⅱ) Extraneous risks. Extraneous risks refer to various risks beyond maritime risks, divided into general extraneous risks and special extraneous risks.

A. General extraneous risks: Refer to theft, breakage, leakage, contamination, moisture and heat, odor, rust, hook damage, short term, fresh water and rain, etc.

B. Special extraneous risks: Mainly refer to the risks caused by military, political, and administrative laws and regulations, such as war, strikes, non delivery, rejection, etc.

Ⅱ. Insured Losses

Insured Loss is the injury or damage sustained by the insured in consequence of the happening of one or more of the accidents or misfortunes against which the insurer, in consideration of the premium, has undertaken to indemnify the insured. No loss, no compensation.

(Ⅰ) Total losses. The term total loss is understood in two different senses: Natural and legal. In its natural sense, it signifies the complete and absolute destruction of the thing inured. In its legal sense, it means, not merely the entire destruction or deprivation of the thing insured, but also such damage to it, though it specifically remain, as renders it of little or no value to the owner.

A. Actual total losses. In the transportation of goods by sea, the insured goods are completely lost or the goods have completely deteriorated. Such as sunken goods on the seabed, tobacco soaked in water and moldy. Some goods, although not completely damaged, are severely damaged and cannot be restored to their original state or utility, which also constitutes a total loss of goods. When an actual total loss occurs, the insured does not need any procedures and can demand total loss compensation from the insurer.

B. Constructive total losses. Constructive total losses refer to the actual total loss that cannot be avoided, or the residual value of the damaged goods. If the sum of the costs of rescue, organization, recovery, and transportation to the destination exceeds its value upon arrival at the destination, it is considered a total loss.

If the object of the insurance is presumed to have suffered a total loss and the insured requests the insurer to compensate for the total loss, the object of the insurance shall be abandoned to the insurer. The insurer may or may not accept abandonment, but shall notify the insured of the decision to accept or not to accept abandonment within a reasonable time.

(Ⅱ) Partial losses. A partial loss is any loss or damage short of, or not amounting to a total loss. Partial losses are sometimes denominated average losses, because they are often in the nature of those losses which are the subject of average contributions; and they are distinguished into general and particular averages.

A. General average. The law of general average is a principle of maritime law whereby all stakeholders in a sea venture proportionally share any losses resulting from a voluntary sacrifice of part of the ship or cargo to save the whole in an emergency. For instance, should the crew jettison some cargo overboard to lighten the ship in a storm, the loss would be shared pro rata by both the carrier and the cargo-owners.

In order to prove a general average claim, the claimant must show that:

a. the ship, cargo, and crew were threatened by a common danger.

b. the danger was real and substantial.

c. the cargo or ship was voluntarily sacrificed for the benefit of both, or extraordinary expenses were incurred to avert a common peril.

B. Particular average. It refers to insurance partial damage to or loss of a ship or its cargo affecting only the ship-owner or one cargo owner. It does not include damage voluntarily incurred, such as general average damage. In general, every kind of expense or damage, short of total loss which regards a particular concern, and which is to be borne by the proprietor of that concern alone. Between the insurer and insured, the term includes losses of this description, as far as the underwriter is liable. Particular average must not be understood as a total loss of a part; for these two kinds of losses are perfectly distinct from each other. A total loss of a part may be recovered, where a particular average would not be recoverable.

III. Insured Expenses

The expenses of insurance coverage refer to the compensation provided by the insurer (insurance company) for the loss of expenses incurred due to accidents within the scope of insurance liability. The insured expenses mainly include the following three types:

(I) Sue and labor expenses. Rescue expenses refer to the expenses incurred by the insured in taking all effective measures to prevent or reduce the loss of the insured in the event of a danger within the scope of insurance on the ship, which shall be compensated by the insurer.

(II) Salvage charge. Salvage expenses refer to the fees paid to a third party after the insured encounters a disaster or accident within the scope of insurance liability, and cannot escape the predicament by relying on the current round of force, and the third party takes rescue measures. This part of the cost is borne by the insurer.

(III) Reasonable expenses. Reasonable expenses mainly include reasonable legal defense costs and the cost of inspecting the bottom of the hold after grounding. Legal fees refer to the legal and arbitration fees incurred by the insured in claiming, suing, or arbitrating against a third party for damage to the insured vessel due to a collision accident or the fault of a third party. If no damage is found to the bottom of the ship during the inspection after grounding, the insurer shall still compensate for the inspection fee.

Section IV Insurance Clauses of China

Maritime Code of the People's Republic of China was drafted with reference to the Hamburg Rules and entered into force on July 1, 1993. Chapter X II "Contract of Marine Insurance" provided the Basic Principles, the Conclusion, Termination and Assignment of Contract, the Obligations of the Insured, the Liability of the Insurer, the Loss of and Damage to the Subject Matter Insured and Abandonment, and the Payment of Indemnity.

I. Basic Principles

A contract of marine insurance mainly includes: Name of the insurer; Name of the insured; Subject matter insured; Insured value; Insured amount; Perils insured against and perils excepted; Duration of insurance coverage; Insurance premium.

The following items may fall within the scope of marine insurance: Ship; Cargo; Income from the operation of the ship including freight, charter hire and passenger's fare; Expected profit on cargo; Crew's wages and other remuneration; Liabilities to a third person; Other property which may sustain loss from a maritime peril and the liability and expenses arising therefrom.

The insurer may re-insure the insurance of the subject matter enumerated in the preceding paragraph. Unless otherwise agreed in the contract, the original insured shall not be entitled to the benefit of the reinsurance. The insurable value of the subject matter insured shall be agreed upon between the insurer and the insured. Where no insurable value has been agreed upon between the insurer and the insured, the insurable value shall be calculated as follows:

(I) The insurable value of the ship shall be the value of the ship at the time when the insurance liability commences. This includes the total value of the ship's hull, machinery, equipment, fuel, stores, gear, provisions and fresh water on board, as well as the insurance premium.

(II) The insurable value of the cargo shall be the aggregate of the invoice value of the cargo or the actual value of the non-trade commodity at the place of shipment, plus freight and insurance premium when the insurance liability commences.

(III) The insurable value of the freight shall be the aggregate of the total amount of freight payable to the carrier and the insurance premium when the insurance liability commences.

(IV) The insurable value of other subject matter insured shall be the aggregate of the actual value of the subject matter insured and the insurance premium when the insurance liability commences.

The insured amount shall be agreed upon between the insurer and the insured. The insured amount shall not exceed the insured value. Where the insured amount exceeds the insured value, the portion in excess shall be null and void.

II. Conclusion, Termination and Assignment of Contract

(I) Conclusion of contract. A contract of marine insurance is concluded after the insured puts forth a proposal for insurance and the insurer agrees to accept the proposal and the insurer and the insured agree on the terms and conditions of the insu-rance. The insurer shall issue to the insured an insurance policy or other certificate of insurance in time, and the contents of the contract shall be contained therein.

Before the contract is concluded, the insured shall truthfully inform the insurer of the material circumstances which the insured has knowledge of or ought to have knowledge of in his ordinary business practice and which may have a bearing on the insurer in deciding the premium or whether be agrees to insure or not.

(II) Termination of contract. Prior to the commencement of the insurance liability, the insured may demand the termination of the insurance contract but shall pay the handling fees to the insurer, and the insurer shall refund the premium.

Unless otherwise agreed in the contract, neither the insurer nor the insured may terminate the contract after the commencement of the insurance liability.

Where the insurance contract provides that the contract may be terminated after the commencement of the liability, and the insured demands the termination of the contract, the insurer shall have the right to the premium payable from the day of the commencement of the insurance liability to the day of termination of the contract and refund the remaining portion. If it is the insurer who demands the termination of the contract, the unexpired premium from the day of the termination of the contract to the day of the expiration of the period of insurance shall be refunded to the insured.

Notwithstanding the stipulations in Article 227 of this Code, the insured may not demand termination of the contract for cargo insurance and voyage insurance on ship after the commencement of the insurance liability.

(III) Assignment of contract. A contract of marine insurance for the carriage of goods by sea may be assigned by the insured by endorsement or otherwise, and the rights and obligations under the contract are assigned accordingly. The insured and the assignee shall be jointly and severally liable for the payment of the premium if such premium remains unpaid up to the time of the assignment of the contract.

The consent of the insurer shall be obtained where the insurance contract is assigned in consequence of the transfer of the ownership of the ship insured. In the absence of such consent, the contract shall be terminated from the time of the transfer of the ownership of the ship. Where the transfer takes place during the voyage, the contract shall be terminated when the voyage ends.

Upon termination of the contract, the insurer shall refund the unexpired premium to the insured calculated from the day of the termination of the contract to the day of its expiration. The insured may conclude an open cover with the insurer for the goods to be shipped or received in batches within a given period. The open cover shall be evidenced by an open policy to be issued by the insurer. The insurer shall, at the request of the insured, issue insurance certificates separately for the cargo shipped in batches according to the open cover.

Where the contents of the insurance certificates issued by the insurer separately differ from those of the open policy, the insurance certificates issued separately shall prevail. The insured shall notify the insurer immediately on learning that the cargo insured under the open cover has been shipped or has arrived. The items to be notified of shall include the name of the carrying ship, the voyage, the value of the cargo and the insured amount.

III. Obligation of the Insured

Unless otherwise agreed in the insurance contract, the insured shall pay the premium immediately upon conclusion of the contract. The insurer may refuse to issue the insurance policy or other insurance certificate before the premium is paid by the insured. The insured shall notify the insurer in writing immediately where the insured has not complied with the warranties under the contract. The insurer may, upon receipt of the notice, terminate the contract or demand an amendment to the terms and conditions of the insurance coverage or an increase in the premium.

Upon the occurrence of the peril insured against, the insured shall notify the insurer immediately and shall take necessary and reasonable measures to avoid or minimize the loss. Where special instructions for the adoption of reasonable measures to avoid or minimize the loss are received from the insurer, the insured shall act according to such instructions. The insurer shall not be liable for the extended loss caused by the insured's breach of the provisions of the preceding paragraph.

IV. Liability of the Insurer

(I) Basic principle. The insurer shall indemnify the insured promptly after the loss from a peril insured against has occurred. The insurer's indemnification for the loss from the peril insured against shall be limited to the insured amount. Where the insured amount is lower than the insured value, the insurer shall indemnify in the proportion that the insured amount bears to the insured value.

The insurer shall be liable for the loss to the subject matter insured arising from several perils insured against during the period of the insurance even though the aggregate of the amounts of loss exceeds the insured amount. However, the insurer shall only be liable for the total loss where the total loss occurs after the partial loss which has not been repaired.

The insurer shall pay, in addition to the indemnification to be paid with regard to the subject matter insured, the necessary and reasonable expenses incurred by the insured for avoiding or minimizing the loss recoverable under the contract, the reasonable expenses for survey and assessment of the value for the purpose of ascertaining the nature and extent of the peril insured against and the expenses incurred for acting on the special instructions of the insurer.

The payment by the insurer of the expenses referred to in the preceding paragraph shall be limited to that equivalent to the insured amount. Where the insured amount is lower than the insured value, the insurer shall be liable for the expenses referred to in this Article in the proportion that the insured amount bears to the insured value, unless the contract provides otherwise. Where the insured amount is lower than the value for contribution under the general average, the insurer shall be liable for the general average contribution in the proportion that the insured amount bears to the value for contribution.

(Ⅱ) Exemptions. The insurer shall not be liable for the loss caused by the intentional act of the insured.

Unless otherwise agreed in the insurance contract, the insurer shall not be liable for the loss of or damage to the insured cargo arising from any of the following causes: (ⅰ) Delay in the voyage or in the delivery of cargo or change of market price; (ⅱ) Fair wear and tear, inherent vice or nature of the cargo; (ⅲ) Improper packing.

Unless otherwise agreed in the insurance contract, the insurer shall not be liable for the loss of or damage to the insured ship arising from any of the following causes: (ⅰ) Un-seaworthiness of the ship at the time of the commencement of the voyage, unless where under a time policy the insured has no knowledge thereof; (ⅱ) Wear and tear or corrosion of the ship.

V. Loss of or Damage to the Subject Matter Insured and Abandonment

(I) Actual total loss. Where after the occurrence of a peril insured against the subject matter insured is lost or is so seriously damaged that it is completely deprived of its original structure and usage or the insured is deprived of the possession thereof, it shall constitute an actual total loss.

Where a ship fails to arrive at its destination within a reasonable time from the place where it was last heard of, unless the contract provides otherwise, if it remains unheard of upon the expiry of two months, it shall constitute missing. Such missing shall be deemed to be an actual total loss.

(II) Constructive total loss. Where a ship's total loss is considered to be unavoidable after the occurrence of a peril insured against or the expenses necessary for avoiding the occurrence of an actual total loss would exceed the insured value, it shall constitute a constructive total loss.

Where an actual total loss is considered to be unavoidable after the cargo has suffered a peril insured against, or the expenses to be incurred for avoiding the total actual loss plus that for forwarding the cargo to its destination would exceed its insured value, it shall constitute a constructive total loss.

(III) Partial loss. Any loss other than an actual total loss or a constructive total loss is a partial loss.

(IV) Abandonment. Where the subject matter insured has become a constructive total loss and the insured demands indemnification from the insurer on the basis of a total loss, the subject matter insured shall be abandoned to the insurer. The insurer may accept the abandonment or choose not to, but shall inform the insured of his decision whether to accept the abandonment within a reasonable time. The abandonment shall not be attached with any conditions. Once the abandonment is accepted by the insurer, it shall not be withdrawn. Where the insurer has accepted the abandonment, all rights and obligations relating to the property abandoned are transferred to the insurer.

VI. Payment of Indemnity

After the occurrence of a peril insured against and before the payment of indemnity, the insurer may demand that the insured submit evidence and materials related to the ascertainment of the nature of the peril and the extent of the loss. Where the loss of or damage to the subject matter insured within the insurance coverage is caused by a third person, the right of the insured to demand compensation from the third person shall be subrogated to the insurer from the time the indemnity is paid. The insured shall furnish the insurer with necessary documents and information that should come to his knowledge and shall endeavor to assist the insurer in pursuing recovery from the third person. Where the insured waives his right of claim against the third person without the consent of the insurer or the insurer is unable to exercise the right of recourse due to the fault of the insured, the insurer may make a corresponding reduction from the amount of indemnity. In effecting payment of indemnity to the insured, the insurer may make a corresponding reduction therefrom of the amount already paid by a third person to the insured. Where the compensation obtained by the insurer from the third person exceeds the amount of indemnity paid by the insurer, the part in excess shall be returned to the insured.

After the occurrence of a peril insured against, the insurer is entitled to waive his right to the subject matter insured and pay the insured the amount in full to relieve himself of the obligations under the contract. In exercising the right prescribed in the preceding paragraph, the insurer shall notify the insured thereof within seven days from the day of the receipt of the notice from the insured regarding the indemnity. The insurer shall remain liable for the necessary and reasonable expenses paid by the insured for avoiding or minimizing the loss prior to his receipt of the said notice. Except as stipulated above, where a total loss occurs to the subject matter insured and the full insured amount is paid, the insurer shall acquire the full right to the subject matter insured. In the case of under-insurance, the insurer shall acquire the right to the subject matter insured in the proportion that the insured amount bears to the insured value.

VII. Practices of Marine Insurance in China

(I) Basic risk coverage.

A. FPA (Free of Particular Average Insurance) . It refers to marine cargo insurance that does not cover partial losses or partial damage unless caused by the vessel being sunk, stranded, burned, on fire, or in a collision. Under FPA, the insurance company will be responsible to pay claims for total or constructive total losses suffered by the whole lot of cargoes during transportation due to such natural calamities as vile weather, thunder and lighting, tidal wave, earthquakes, and floods, or for total or partial losses due to the ship or carrier being on fire, stranded, sinking, colliding or meeting other fortuitous accidents. This allows the insurer to only be liable for catastrophic losses resulting from transport; for example, the insurer will be liable if the ship sinks or all the products catch fire. It will not be liable if some of the products break in transit, up to a certain percentage of the total value.

B. WPA (With Particular Average Insurance) . It is a provision in maritime transport insurance stating that the insurer is responsible for partial losses on the value of the covered products. Depending on the amount of the deductible, the insurer of a WPA will be liable for losses if some of the products break in transit. For example, if one is transporting \$10,000 worth of goods over sea and \$2,000 in goods are washed overboard, the with-average policy covers the owner of the goods for \$2,000 (assuming no deductible) . This contrasts with a FPA, in which the insurer is generally only responsible for catastrophic losses. The cover of this insurance is more extensive. The insurer is liable, in addition to the total or constructive total losses covered by FPA insurance, also for the partial losses of the insured goods due to the risks caused by natural calamities mentioned under FPA insurance.

C. AR (All Risk Insurance) . An insurance policy that covers all possible claims not specifically excluded. All risk insurance covers most perils except strikes, riots, civil unrest, capture, war, seizure, civil war, piracy, loss of market, and inherent vice. Among the three kinds of basic insurance, under an "all risks" policy the goods are insured against all risks from natural calamities, fortuitous accidents at sea, or general extraneous risks, irrespective of percentage of loss, total or partial. What's more, a natural deterioration of perishable goods, delay, loss or damage caused by inherent vice or nature of the subject matter is not covered. All risk insurance is usually quite expensive.

(Ⅱ) Additional risks.

A. General additional risks. General Additional Risk covers goods loss caused by general external reasons, also known as ordinary additional insurance, and they are included in AS. If the AS is insured, the applicant need not apply general additional risk insurance. If FPA or WPA is insured, the insured shall choose one or more additional risks based on the characteristics of the goods and transportation conditions, and shall agree with the insurer to add insurance.

B. Special additional risks. Special Additional Risk is a type of insurance that covers certain government action risks that may cause damage to goods. It is not included in the scope of All Risks. Regardless of any basic insurance policies applied by the insured, in order to obtain insurance coverage for political risks such as government actions, the insurer must have a special agreement with the insurer and obtain special consent from the insurer. Otherwise, the insurer shall not be liable for this insurance. Special additional risk insurance can only be added to the coverage of FPA, WPA and AR.

Section V   Subrogation

I. Definition

If an insurance accident and damage is caused by a third party to the insured object, the insurer shall have the right to claim compensation for the damage to the third party from the date of compensating the insured for the insurance benefits. According to legal provisions, the actual payment of compensation insurance benefits should be the sole basis for determining whether and when the insurer has obtained the right to subrogation. The right of subrogation in maritime cargo insurance is a right granted to the insurer, and there are various ways for the insurer to exercise the right of subrogation, including negotiation, arbitration, and litigation.

II. Conditions for Insurers to Exercise Subrogation Rights

(I) Actual risk and loss. The accident that occurs must be a marine insurance accident, and the loss of the insured object must be within the scope of insurance liability assumed by the insurer as stipulated in the marine insurance contract, which is a necessary condition for the insurer to exercise insurance subrogation rights.

(II) Due to the third party. The occurrence of an insurance accident is caused by the actions of a third party, which must have caused damage to the insured object in order to have the right to subrogation. Here, the actions of third parties include infringement, breach of contract, general average, etc. Here, the marine insured has the right to claim compensation for damages against third parties. When a third party is legally liable, the insured only has the right to claim compensation, which is the possibility of transferring the right of claim to the insurer, that is, "no right of claim, no right of subrogation".

(III) Actually paid compensation. Before the insurer pays the insurance benefits to the insured, the insured can choose to request payment of the insurance benefits from the insurer or claim damages from a third party. At this time, the insurer's right of subrogation is manifested as the right of expectation. This expectation right can only be converted into a vested right after the insurer pays the insurance benefits.

(Ⅳ) Amount limitation. This element can serve as a limit condition for the exercise of subrogation rights in marine insurance. As an insurance contract serves as a compensation contract, the insurer is not allowed to profit from it. Therefore, the right of subrogation obtained by the insurer is limited to the actual amount paid by the insurer, and the excess amount should belong to the insured. The exercise of subrogation by a marine insurer shall not affect the other rights of the insured.

(Ⅴ) Time limitation. According to Chinese Maritime Law and relevant judicial interpretations, in case of international or coastal cargo transport, the insurer's subrogation claim should be issued in one year, which is calculated from the date on which the carrier delivers or should deliver the goods.

Chapter 10　Finance Law of International Trade of Goods

International trade finance is a comprehensive financial service provided by banks for cross-border trade in goods and services based on the debt relationship between both parties involved in the trade. It includes basic services such as trade settlement and trade financing, as well as value-added services such as credit guarantee, hedging, and financial management.

Section Ⅰ　Payment Instrument

Ⅰ. Definition and Characteristics of Negotiable Instruments

（Ⅰ）Definition. A negotiable instrument is a document that guarantees the payment of a specific amount of money, either on demand or at a set time, with the payer usually named on the document. More specifically, it is a document contemplated by or consisting of a contract, which promises the payment of money without condition, and may be paid either on demand or at a future date. The term has different meanings based on its usage in various legal contexts and the specific country in which it is applied.

（Ⅱ）Characteristics of negotiable instruments. A negotiable instrument can serve to convey value, which constitutes at least part of the performance of a contract. Although this may not be immediately obvious in the formation of a contract, it is inherent in the requisite offer and acceptance, as well as the conveyance of consideration. The underlying contract contemplates the right to hold and negotiate the instrument to a holder in due course. Payment on this instrument forms at least part of the performance of the contract to which the negotiable instrument is linked. The instrument records the following matters: (i) the power to demand payment; (ii) the right to be paid. The right can transfer, for example, in the case of a "bearer instrument", where the possession of the document itself confers the right to payment. However, there are certain exceptions, such as when the instrument is lost or stolen. In such cases, the possessor of the note may be a holder, but not necessarily a holder in due course. Negotiation requires a valid endorsement of the negotiable instrument.

The consideration constituted by a negotiable instrument is cognizable as the value given up to acquire it (benefit) and the consequent loss of value (detriment) to the prior holder; thus, no separate consideration is required to support an accompanying contract assignment. The instrument itself is understood as memorializing the right for, and power to demand, payment, and an obligation for payment evidenced by the instrument itself with possession as a holder in due course being the touchstone for the right to, and power to demand, payment. In some instances, the negotiable instrument can serve as the writing memorializing a contract, thus satisfying any applicable statute of frauds as to that contract.

II. Types of Bill

(I) Bill of exchange.

A. Definition and characteristic. A bill of exchange (or draft as it is sometimes called) is a written, drafted, and signed instrument that contains an unconditional order from the drawer that directs the drawee to pay a definite sum of money to a payee on demand or at a specified future date.

It is useful instrument because it allows one party (the drawer) to direct another (the drawee) to pay money either to himself, to his agent, or to a third party. Of cause, the order is valid only if the drawee has an underlying obligation to pay money to the drawer. This can arise in situations where the drawee is holding money on account for the drawer (the drawee is a bank), where the drawer lent money to a drawee (the drawee is a borrower), or where the drawer has sold goods to the drawee and drawee owes the sale price to the drawer (the drawee is a buyer) .

In the first of these situations (where the drawee is a bank), the bill involved is known as a check. In the second situation (where the drawee is a borrower), the bill of exchange is called a note. The bills referred to in the third situation (where the drawee is a buyer) are called trade acceptances.

Bills of exchange are important devices for facilitating international trade because they are negotiable instruments. A person properly holding a negotiable instrument takes it free of most claims or defenses that the drawer might have that the underlying contract was improperly performed or that the instrument was improperly made. This freedom from the so-called "equities" or "personal defenses" of the drawer makes bill of exchange more readily salable, and therefore financial tools for raising money.

B. Types. According to most of laws, the common types of bill of exchange are as following:

a. Clean bill and documentary bill. A bill of exchange is called a clean bill when no shipping documents are accompanied with it. If the bill of exchange is accompanied by shipping documents (chiefly bill of lading, invoice, insurance policy, etc), the bill is called a documentary bill. In international trade, most bills of exchange are documentary bill of exchange.

b. Sight (or demand) bill and time bill. According to the time of payment, a bill of exchange may be either a sight bill or a time bill. If the drawee is required to pay the bill on demand or at sight, the bill is called a sight bill. If the drawee is required to pay the bill at a later date, the bill is called a time bill. It requires acceptance before payment.

c. Commercial bill and banker's bill. If the drawer is a commercial firm the bill is called a commercial bill. When the drawer is a bank, the bill is called a banker's bill.

d. Commercial acceptance bill and banker's acceptance bill. In time commercial bills, when the drawer is a commercial firm and the drawee is another commercial firm, the bill after acceptance by the commercial firm or the drawee is called a commercial acceptance bill. When the drawer is a commercial firm or a bank and the drawee is a bank, the bill after acceptance by the bank or the drawee is called a banker's acceptance bill.

e. Straight bill, order bill and bearer bill. The Straight Bill refers to a bill of exchange where the drawer clearly records the name of the payee on the bill of exchange. The Straight Bill is beneficial for the safety of bills of exchange, but it may affect the frequency of bills of exchange. The bearer bill refers to the bill that the drawer made no any record on the bill of exchange. The bearer bills are not conducive to the exercise of the right of recourse by the holder, and their security is poor.

The Order Bill is a bill payable to a given person, or as such person shall direct by an endorsement he may make on it. Until the bill is so indorsed no other person can maintain an action on it.

(II) Promissory note.

A. Concept and nature. A promissory note, sometimes referred to as a note payable, is a legal instrument (more particularly, a financing instrument and a debt instrument), in which one party (the maker or issuer) promises in writing to pay a determinate sum of money to the other (the payee), either at a fixed or determinable future time or on demand of the payee, under specific terms.

The terms of a note usually include the principal amount, the interest rate if any, the parties, the date, the terms of repayment (which could include interest) and the maturity date. Sometimes, provisions are included concerning the payee's rights in the event of a default, which may include foreclosure of the maker's assets.

Although possibly non-negotiable, a promissory note may be a negotiable instrument if it is an unconditional promise in writing made by one person to another, signed by the maker, engaging to pay on demand to the payee, or at fixed or determinable future time, a sum certain in money, to order or to bearer. Bank notes are frequently referred to as promissory notes, a promissory note made by a bank and payable to bearer on demand.

B. Types and parties.

a. Registered promissory notes and anonymous promissory notes: based on whether the payee's name is stated on the face of the bill.

b. Fixed-term promissory notes and spot promissory notes: based on whether they have an expiration date or not.

The promissory note does not require acceptance, and the drawer is responsible for payment upon demand. The three basic parties to a promissory note are the drawer, payee, and holder.

C. Differences between bill of change and promissory note.

Promissory notes and bills of exchange are two primary types of negotiable instruments. The following chart shows the main differences (in Table 10.1).

Table 10.1 The main differences between promissory note and bill of change

	Promissory Note	Bill of Change
Subject	Unconditional order for the payment of the specified sum	Unconditional assumption of obligation for the payment of the specified sum
Drawee	The name of the person obliged to pay (drawee)	The name of the person obliged to acceptance (N/A)
Signature	The signature of the drawer	The signature of the issuer

The specification of the maturity, the place of payment, the payee and the issue date are specified on the bill or note.

(Ⅲ) Check.

A. Definition. Check is a document that orders a bank to pay a specific amount of money from a person's account to the person in whose name the check has been issued. The person writing the check, known as the drawer, has a transaction banking account (often called a current, check, checking account) where their money is held. The drawer writes the various details including the monetary amount, date, and a payee on the check, and signs it, ordering their bank, known as the drawee, to pay that person or company the amount of money stated.

B. Nature of a check. A check is a negotiable instrument instructing a financial institution to pay a specific amount of a specific currency from a specified transactional account held in the drawer's name with that institution. Both the drawer and payee may be natural persons or legal entities. Checks are order instruments, and are not in general payable simply to the bearer as bearer instruments are, but must be paid to the payee. In some countries, such as the US, the payee may endorse the check, allowing them to specify a third party to whom it should be paid.

Checks are a type of bill of exchange that was developed as a way to make payments without the need to carry large amounts of money. Paper money evolved from promissory notes, another form of negotiable instrument similar to checks in that they were originally a written order to pay the given amount to whoever had it in their possession (the "bearer").

Ⅲ. Legal Action of Bill

(Ⅰ) Issue. Issuing a bill refers to the act of the drawer in issuing a bill, which includes two actions: (i) Drawer prepare for the bill and sign it. (ii) Hand over the bill of exchange to the payee. The issuing of the bill is the foundation of the bill relationship. The drawer and payer must have a de facto financial or debt relationship.

(Ⅱ) Endorsement. Endorsement means placing one's signature on the back of a check or other negotiable instrument in order to transfer ownership to another. Endorsers warrant payment of the instrument unless they sign with the additional words "without recourse." If the endorser transfers the bill by endorsement, they are obligated to ensure that their subsequent parties can receive acceptance and payment.

(Ⅲ) Presentation. Presentation is the act of the payee or holder submitting a bill of exchange to the payer for payment or acceptance.

A. Prompt for acceptance: The holder presents the bill of exchange to the payer, requesting the payer to promise payment at maturity.

B. Prompt payment: The holder presents the bill of exchange to the payer or acceptor, requesting payment.

According to the Negotiable Instruments Law of China, bills of exchange payable at sight and periodically after sight shall be presented within one month from the date of issuance. A bill of exchange that is paid on a fixed date or periodically after the date of issue shall be presented for acceptance to the payer before the expiration date of the bill of exchange.

(Ⅳ) Acceptance. Acceptance of a bill is an engagement to pay it according to the terms. This engagement is usually made by writing the word "accepted" across the face of the bill.

(Ⅴ) Guarantee. Bill guarantee is a legal action in which a person other than the bill debtor guarantees the performance of the bill debt, with the aim of assuming the same content of the bill debt. Any person other than the guarantor, including other bill debtors, may become a guarantor.

The function of guarantee is to supplement the credit shortage of specific debtors, but in reality, the existence of guarantee often exposes the low credit level of the guaranteed party, which has a negative effect on the credit of the guaranteed party.

(Ⅵ) Payment. Payment refers to the payment made by the payer to the holder as recorded on the bill. A bill of exchange shall be paid within certain time or on a fixed date or at a fixed time. If the holder fails to present payment within the time limit specified, the acceptor or payer shall continue to be liable for payment to the holder after making an explanation. If the payment is presented to the payer through the entrusted receiving bank or through the bill exchange system, it shall be deemed that the holder has presented the payment.

Ⅳ. Rights on Negotiable Instruments

Rights on Negotiable Instruments refer to the right of the holder to request payment of the bill amount from the debtor, including payment request rights and recourse rights. The right to request payment, also known as the first request right, refers to the right of the holder to request payment of the bill amount against the main debtor of the bill (such as the acceptor of the bill of exchange, the drawer of the promissory note, the guarantor of the check, etc.) . The right of recourse refers to the right of the holder to request repayment of the bill of exchange against other payment obligors of the bill of exchange (such as the drawer of the bill of exchange or check, the guarantor of the bill of exchange or promissory note, the endorser of the bill, etc.) in the absence or inability to realize the first claim.

(I) Payment request. The constituent elements of the right to payment request:

A. The holder holds an instrument that is within validity period. If the instrument has passed this period, the holder's right to the instrument is lost.

B. The holder must present the original bill to the payer for payment.

C. The holder can only request the payer to pay the amount determined on the bill.

D. After receiving payment, the holder must hand over the bill to the payer.

E. After paying the bill amount, if the payer discovers that the bill has been forged or altered, they have the right to request the refund of the paid amount from the holder.

(II) Right of recourse. The right of recourse① is the second right of request, which is the re-exercise of the right to a negotiable instrument. The objects of recourse can include the drawer, endorser, guarantor, acceptor, and acceptor, depending on the type of bill. These individuals are joint debtors in the bill, and the holder may exercise the right of recourse against any one, several, or all of them, regardless of the order of the bill's debtors. If the holder has already made a claim against one or more of the debtors of the bill of exchange, they may still exercise the right of recourse against other debtors of the bill of exchange. After the defendant pays off the debt, they have the same rights as the holder.

(III) Feature. Rights on negotiable instruments are civil rights. Once this right arises, it is merged with the instrument as a security, and only by possessing the instrument can one obtain the right to the instrument. Rights on negotiable instruments are singular rights and special monetary claims. The debtor of the bill is required to unconditionally pay the face amount. Rights on negotiable instruments are secondary rights. The right holder may first exercise the right to request payment, and may also exercise the right of recourse when the right to request payment is frustrated. The holder shall not be liable for any consideration in realizing the rights of the bill, and the debtor of the bill shall bear the obligation to pay without consideration. The exercise of the right to a negotiable instrument is solely conditional on the presentation of the instrument.

(IV) Acquisition and loss of the rights. Without holding the instrument, anyone

---

① Right of Recourse: 追索权。

cannot exercise the right. Anyone who obtains the instrument in good faith also obtains the right to the instrument.

A. Acquisition of the rights. It must be obtained by endorsement or direct delivery; there was no malice or gross negligence in obtaining the bill; Pay the consideration.

B. Loss of rights. The record of the bill is unqualified or has expired; Exceed the deadline for preserving the right of the instrument.

Section II   Payment Method

I. Remittance

(I) Concept. Remittance is a business processing method in which the payer actively transfers funds to the payee through various settlement tools used by a third party (usually a bank). There are usually four basic parties involved in remittance business: remitter (i. e. payer), remitting bank, paying bank and payee.

(II) Types.

A. Mail Transfer (M/T). The remitter should apply for the remittance and mail the remittance to the remitting bank through a mail transfer authorization letter, and entrust it to pay to the payee.

B. Telegraphic Transfer (T/T). It refers to the process of notifying the foreign remitting bank by telegram or telex upon the application of the remitter, and entrusting them to pay the remittance to the designated recipient.

C. Demand Draft (D/D). The remitter shall apply for a bill of exchange to be issued by the remitter on behalf of the remitter, and shall deliver it to the remitter for mailing or carrying abroad, and then hand it over to the payee to collect the remittance from the remitting bank.

(III) Nature.

A. Remittance belongs to favorable exchange. The debtor or payer voluntarily deposits the funds with the bank and entrusts the bank to use a certain payment tool to pay a certain amount to foreign payees.

B. It's commercial credit. Whether payment is made depends on the importer (buyer) or service recipient, and there is no guarantee of payment.

II. Collection

(I) Definitionand natures.

A. Definition. Collection refers to a settlement method in international trade that the exporter issues a bill of exchange with the importer as the payer, and entrusts the exporter's bank to collect payment from the importer through its branch or agency in the importer. It includes D/P (documents against payment) and D/A (documents against acceptance) .

B. Nature. Under collection, the seller asks the buyer to pay the price through making instructions to the bank to present for acceptance or for payment a documentary bill. Because of this, we call collection "counter-remittance" .

Although there are two banks to get involved in the procedure of collection, banks do not advance money to the seller. The possibility of getting the purchase price for the seller entirely relies on the commercial credit of the buyer. So we call the collection commercial credit.

(II) Types.

A. Clean collection.

It means that the seller/exporter draws a bill of exchange without documents attached on the bill after the delivery of goods and asks the bank at the residence of the exporter to arrange for the acceptance or payment of the bill overseas, and the bank will carry out his task through its own branch office abroad or a correspondent bank.

B. Documentary collection.

a. Documents against Acceptance (D/A) . Documents against acceptance are an arrangement between importer and exporter, specifying that the importer is not to be given the documentation that confirms their ownership of the imported goods until the bill of exchange has been paid or an agreement to pay has been made.

In such a case, the URC 522 says that the importer accepts a time draft from the bank via the exporter and must sign, agreeing to pay the exporter (seller) at a future time. Once this has been accepted, ownership documentation is then turned over by the bank to the buyer.

This is rather danger to the seller if he knows nothing about the trustworthiness of the buyer.

Clearly, this mode of payment can be used only in the case where the seller knows the buyer well and the deal is small.

b. Documents against Payment（D/P）. Documents against payment are used to a similar end on the exporter's side. The documents are an agreement between the bank and the exporter, specifying that the importer is not to receive any of the paperwork confirming ownership of goods until the attached bill of exchange is paid or preparations for payment have been made.

The URC 522 says that the buyer（importer）should make full payment on goods once they are delivered, after which the documents confirming ownership can be handed over by the bank.

According to the different time of payment, it is divided into D/P at sight and D/P after sight.

（a）D/P at sight. The draft issued is demand draft. When the collecting bank makes presentation to the drawee（importer）, the latter should make payment upon presentation. The collecting bank will then deliver the documents to him.

（b）D/P after sight. Time draft is used in D/P after sight. When the collecting bank makes presentation, the buyer shall first make acceptance after checking the documents, and will make payment on the date of expiry of payment.

The common point between D/P at sight and D/P after sight is that the buyer shall not get documents without making payment. Therefore, the responsibilities and risks sustained by the seller are almost the same. Comparatively, this is a safe mode payment for the seller.

（Ⅲ）Parties and their legal relationship.

A. The relationship between the principal and the collecting bank. It is a principal-agent relationship. The collecting bank should strictly follow the collection instructions of the principal for collection business. According to URC522, the bank should act with good faith and reasonable caution. However, the collecting bank does not have any obligation to collect the collected funds.

B. The relationship between the collecting bank and the correspondent bank. It is a principal-agent relationship. The correspondent bank shall, in accordance with the instructions of the collecting bank, promptly make payment or acceptance presentation to the payer on the bill of exchange to collect the payment. If the correspondent bank violates the collection instructions and hands over the documents to the payer without payment, it violates the obligation of reasonable care and should be held liable for breach of contract by the collecting bank.

C. No direct contractual relationship between the principal and the correspondent bank.

D. No legal relationship between the collecting bank and the payer.

(Ⅳ) Operation process.

A. The seller (principal) issues a bill of exchange, applies for collection to the bank of the exporting country, and fills out a collection instruction letter.

B. After the export bank (collecting bank) accepts the application, it entrusts its correspondent bank in the import place to handle the collection matters on its behalf.

C. The correspondent bank shall make payment or acceptance presentation to the buyer (payer), and notify the collecting bank after the payer makes payment. The collecting bank shall immediately make payment to the seller. If the payer refuses to pay, the correspondent bank shall notify the collecting bank, which shall then notify the seller.

(Ⅴ) Uniform Rules on the Collection (URC522). It is the guidelines issued by the International Chamber of Commerce to govern collections. The Uniform Rules for Collections is a set of rules that help assist in the process of collecting debts or owed money or assets. The URCs were established-or proposed-by the International Chamber of Commerce (ICC), a worldwide organization that serves to promote and facilitate business interests and trade between nations. The last draft of the Uniform Rules for Collections, otherwise known as URC 522, sets out the need for the primary or remitting bank to draw up and attach a sheet that explicitly explains the purpose of, and the process that should be followed when, collecting debts. The Uniform Rules for Collections are an important protection for banks, traders, buyers, and sellers because they outline the responsibilities of each party when it comes to the collection of goods or money owed. The rules are particularly helpful to banks and other institutions that seek to collect money owed on a daily basis.

Ⅲ. Letter of Credit

(Ⅰ) Introduction to L/C. Letter of Credit is a document used to effect payment for internationally traded goods, usually as part of a contract for the sale of goods which ensures that the supplier receives prompt and guaranteed payment while the purchaser obtains a short-term CREDIT line. Under UCP600, Letter of Credit means any arrangement, however named or described, that is irrevocable and thereby constitutes a definite undertaking of the issuing bank to honor a complying presentation.

In brief, under this facility, a purchaser in country A of goods supplied by a firm in country B can arrange a letter of credit from his bank (the credit issuing bank) authorizing it to make payment to the supplier either through a branch of the bank in country B or, more usually, through a bank (the negotiating bank) holding the supplier's account.

Under a contract of sale of goods this will be done on the presentation to the negotiating bank of documents stipulated in the letter of credit, such as the bill of lading, insurance policy, certificate of origin, etc. In the case of certain letters of credit relating to particular transactions and customers located in heavily indebted countries, a secondary market has developed to offset political as well as commercial risk.

If the buyer fails to make payment, the bank will do so on his/her behalf. The buyer presents a letter of credit to the seller, which eliminates the risk that the seller will not be paid. Letters of credit have become very common in international commerce, as distance and other factors make it difficult for sellers to establish the creditworthiness of every buyer.

(Ⅱ) Governing Law: Uniform Customs and Practice for Documentary Credits (UCP600). The Uniform Customs and Practice for Documentary Credits (UCP) is a set of rules on the issuance and use of letters of credit. The UCP is utilized by bankers and commercial parties in more than 175 countries in trade finance. Some 11%~15% of international trade utilizes letters of credit, totaling over a trillion dollars (US) each year.

Historically, the commercial parties, particularly banks, have developed the techniques and methods for handling letters of credit in international trade finance. This practice has been standardized by the International Chamber of Commerce (ICC) by publishing the UCP in 1933 and subsequently updating it throughout the years. The ICC has developed and moulded the UCP by regular revisions. The result is the most successful international attempt at unifying rules ever, as the UCP has substantially universal effect. The latest revision was approved by the Banking Commission of the ICC at its meeting in Paris on 25 October 2006. This latest version, called the UCP 600, formally commenced on 1 July 2007.

The UCP600 remain the most successful set of private rules for trade ever developed. Where a credit is issued subject to UCP 600, the credit will be interpreted in accordance with the entire set of 39 articles contained in UCP 600. However, exceptions to the rules can be made by express modification or exclusion. For example, the parties to a credit may agree that the rest of the credit shall remain valid despite the beneficiary's failure to deliver an installment. In such case, the credit has to nullify the effect of article 32 of UCP 600, such as by wording the credit as: "The credit will continue to be available for the remaining installments notwithstanding the beneficiary's failure to present complied documents of an installment in accordance with the installment schedule."

(Ⅲ) Types.

A. Revocable L/C and Irrevocable L/C. Revocable L/C is a letter of credit that the granting bank or the letter holder (who is the buyer of some good) may cancel under some or any circumstances. This does not provide the seller with any extra assurance that he/she will be paid on time and in the correct amount. As a result they carry higher risk than irrevocable letters of credit.

Irrevocable L/C is a letter of credit that neither the bank granting it nor the letter holder (who is the buyer of some good) may cancel under any circumstances. This provides the seller with extra assurance that he/she will be paid on time and in the correct amount. Irrevocable letters of credit are most common in international commerce.

B. Confirmed L/C and Non-confirmed L/C. Confirmed Letter of Credit is a letter of credit which a bank other than the issuing bank agrees to honor as though they had themselves issued it. The letter of credit guaranteed by two banks. That is, a bank agrees to honor the letter of credit and make the required payment in case both the letter's holder and the original, issuing bank both fail to make payment. This reduces the risk of the letter of credit to an absolute minimum.

C. Sight L/C and Time L/C (Usance L/C). Sight L/C refers to a letter of credit made payable to a beneficiary immediately upon presentation to the issuing bank of conforming documents. Under a sight letter of credit, the beneficiary generally does not need to issue a draft, and the issuing or paying bank only pays against a complete set of qualified shipping documents. This type of letter of credit enables the exporter to quickly recover the payment and is the most common type of letter of credit in international trade.

Time L/C refers to a letter of credit requiring payment a certain number of days after the appropriate documents are presented. It is also called a usance letter of credit. Time L/C mainly includes acceptance letters of credit (Acceptance L/C) and deferred payment letters of credit (Deferred Payment L/C). When the issuing or paying bank receives the documents sent by the exporting bank, although the documents are verified to be in compliance, they do not make payment immediately, and wait until the maturity date of the long-term payment draft to fulfill the payment commitment.

In international trade practice, Time L/C is a means of financing for exporters and their banks to importers. But Time L/C has a higher risk than Sight L/C.

D. Transferable L/C and Un-transferable L/C. Transferable L/C is a document that allows the first beneficiary (an intermediary who accepts the letter of credit from the bank) on a standby bank assurance of funds to transfer all or part of the original letter of credit to a third party. In order for the letter of credit be transferable, the bank must be aware of the situation and agree to the transfer. This agreement allows the first beneficiary to transfer the letter of credit to the second beneficiary. A transferable letter of credit is relatively common for international transactions in the Far East. Only when the issuing bank indicates "transferable" in the letter of credit can the letter of credit be transferred. This letter of credit can only be transferred once. That is, it can only be transferred by the first beneficiary to the second beneficiary, and the second beneficiary cannot request the transfer of the letter of credit to a subsequent third beneficiary.

UN-transferable L/C refers to a letter of credit where the beneficiary cannot transfer the rights of the letter of credit to others. Any letter of credit that does not indicate "transferable" is considered non transferable.

E. Standby credit. It is an agreement that the bank promises to pay the seller if the buyer fails to pay. The standby credit is also known as guarantee letter of credit issued for the purpose of financing a loan or guaranteeing debt repayment, rather than settling the price of a commodity transaction. The beneficiary can receive reimbursement from the issuing bank by presenting a draft to the issuing bank in accordance with the provisions of the standby letter of credit, accompanied by a statement or proof of the applicant's failure to fulfill its obligations.

(Ⅳ) Principles of L/C.

A. Bank's credit. A letter of credit relies on the bank credit, which means that the bank guarantees payment with its own reputation and the issuing bank is the payer of the letter of credit. Even if the importer refuses or is unable to make the payment, the issuing bank must pay the beneficiary as long as the documents presented by the exporter comply with the provisions of the letter of credit.

B. Principle of independence. A credit by its nature is a separate transaction from the sale or other contract on which it may be based. Banks are in no way concerned with or bound by such contract, even if any reference whatsoever to it is included in the credit. Consequently, the undertaking of a bank to honor, to negotiate or to fulfill any other obligation under the credit is not subject to claims or defenses by the applicant resulting from its relationships with the issuing bank or the beneficiary. A beneficiary can in no case avail itself of the contractual relationships existing between banks or between the applicant and the issuing bank.

C. Rule of strict compliance. The letter of credit will set out the exact prerequisites to be met before the bank will issue payment. These usually include a particular time and place to present the original letter of credit and the exact documents that must accompany the letter. Some States still follow the old "strict compliance" rule holding that any deviation from the instructions, no matter how minor, will justify the bank in refusing to pay. Others follow a "substantial compliance" rule, so that minor typographical or syntax errors in the presenting documents will not justify nonpayment.

(Ⅴ) Parties and legal relationship.

A. Parties.

a. Applicant means the party on whose request the credit is issued.

b. Issuing bank means the bank that issues a credit at the request of an applicant or on its own behalf.

c. The beneficiary refers to the party in whose favor a letter of credit is issued.

d. Advising bank is the bank that will inform the Beneficiary or their Nominated Bank of the credit, send the original credit to the Beneficiary or their Nominated Bank, and provide the Beneficiary or their Nominated Bank with any amendments to the letter of credit.

e. Negotiation bank means the nominated bank that purchase the drafts and/or documents under a complying presentation, by advancing or agreeing to advance funds to the beneficiary on or before the banking day on which reimbursement is due to (to be paid the nominated bank) .

f. Confirming Bank is a bank other than the issuing bank that adds its confirmation to credit upon the issuing bank's authorization or request thus providing more security to the beneficiary.

B. Relationship.

a. The relationship between the applicant and the beneficiary is established based on the contract of sale.

b. The relationship between the applicant and the issuing bank is a principal-agent relationship which established based on the terms and conditions listed in the letter of application.

c. The relationship between the issuing bank and the advising bank is a principal-agent relationship, and both parties are bound by the letter of credit.

d. There is no legal relationship between the applicant and the advising bank.

(Ⅵ) Process of letter of credit transaction.

Typically, after a sales contract has been negotiated, and the buyer and seller have agreed that a letter of credit will be used as the method of payment, the Applicant will contact a bank to ask for a letter of credit to be issued. Once the issuing bank has assessed the buyer's credit risk—i. e. that the Applicant will be able to pay for the goods—It will issue the letter of credit, meaning that it will provide a promise to pay the seller upon presentation of certain documents. Once the Beneficiary (the seller) receives the letter of credit, it will check the terms to ensure that it matches with the contract and will either arrange for shipment of the goods or ask for an amendment to the letter of credit so that it meets with the terms of the contract. The letter of credit is limited in terms of time, the validity of credit, the last date of shipment, and in terms of how much late after shipment the documents may be presented to the Nominated Bank.

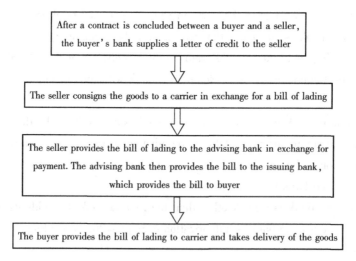

Figure 10. 1 Process of letter of credit transaction

Once the goods have been shipped, the Beneficiary will present the requested documents to the Nominated Bank. This bank will check the documents, and if they comply with the terms of the Letter of Credit, the issuing Bank is bound to honor the terms of the letter of credit by paying the Beneficiary.

(Ⅶ) Fraud and exemption. Letters of credit are sometimes used to defraud banks through presentment of false documentation indicating that goods were shipped when they actually were not. Letters of credit are also sometimes used as part of fraudulent investment schemes.

It is the issuing bank who bears the risk that is linked with non – payment of the buyer. This is advantageous because the issuing bank often has a personal banking relationship with the buyer. The whole commercial purpose for which the system of confirmed irrevocable documentary credits has been developed in international trade is to give to the seller an assured right to be paid before he parts with control of the goods under sale.

The only exception to this may be fraud. For example, a dishonest seller may present documents which comply with the letter of credit and receive payment, only for it to be later discovered that the documents are fraudulent and the goods are not in accordance with the contract. This would place the risk on the buyer, but it also means that the issuing bank must be stringent in assessing whether the presenting documents are legitimate.

IV. International Factoring

(I) Definition. International Factoring is a financial transaction and a type of debtor finance in which a business sells its accounts receivable (i. e. , invoices) to a third party (called a factor) at a discount. A business will sometimes factor its receivable assets to meet its present and immediate cash needs. Forfaiting is a factoring arrangement used in international trade finance by exporters who wish to sell their receivables to a forfaiter. Factoring is commonly referred to as accounts receivable factoring, invoice factoring, and sometimes accounts receivable financing. Accounts receivable financing is a term more accurately used to describe a form of asset based lending against accounts receivable.

(II) Obligations of the parties. There are three parties directly involved:

A. The factor who purchases the receivable. Accordingly, the receivable becomes the factor's asset, and the factor obtains the right to receive the payments made by the debtor for the invoice amount, and is free to pledge or exchange the receivable asset without unreasonable constraints or restrictions.

B. The one who sells the receivable. The seller sells the receivables at a discount to the third party, the specialized financial organization to obtain cash. The seller transfers the ownership of the receivable to the factor, indicating the factor obtains all of the rights associated with the receivables.

C. The debtor has a financial liability that requires him or her make a payment to the owner of the invoice. The receivable usually associated with an invoice for work performed or goods sold, is essentially a financial asset that gives the owner of the receivable the legal right to collect money from the debtor whose financial liability directly corresponds to the receivable asset.

(Ⅲ) Operation process. The factoring process can be divided into two key stages: The initial account setup and ongoing funding. Setting up a factoring account typically takes one to two weeks and involves submitting an application, a list of clients, an accounts receivable aging report and a sample invoice. The approval process involves detailed underwriting, during which time the factoring company can ask for additional documents, such as documents of incorporation, financial, and banks statements. If approved, the business will be set up with a maximum credit line from which they can draw. In the case of notification factoring, the arrangement is not confidential and approval is contingent upon successful notification; a process by which factoring companies send the business's client or account debtor a Notice of Assignment. The Notice of Assignment serves to inform debtors that a factoring company is managing all of the business's receivables; stake a claim on the financial rights for the receivables factored, and update the payment address—usually a bank lock box.

Once the account is set up, the business is ready to start funding invoices. Invoices are still approved on an individual basis, but most invoices can be funded in a business day or two, as long as they meet the factor's criteria. Receivables are funded in two parts. The first part is the "advance" and covers 80% to 85% of the invoice value. This is deposited directly to the business's bank account. The remaining 15% to 20% is rebated, less the factoring fees, as soon as the invoice is paid in full to the factoring company.

Part V　Law of International Trade in Intellectual Property Rights

Nowadays, the rapid development of a new round of scientific and technological revolution and industrial transformation has brought about profound adjustment of the international economic and trade pattern, and the position of intellectual property in the global value chain has become increasingly prominent, which has stimulated the rapid growth of intellectual property trade. Thus, among the three major trade forms in the world, the one with the greatest development potential and the most significant impact on the economic development of various countries is undoubtedly trade of international technology with intellectual property rights as the object of transaction.

Therefore, Part V is Trade Law of International Intellectual Property Rights, including chapter 11 and 12. Chapter 11 is introduction to international trade in intellectual property rights, covering the development and characteristics of international trade in intellectual property rights and the legal system of international trade in intellectual property right. Chapter 12 is legal forms of international intellectual property transfer, including an overview of legal forms of transfer, regulations on international licensing and international franchising.

当今世界，新一轮科技革命和产业变革的迅猛发展，带来了国际经济贸易格局的深度调整，知识产权在全球价值链中的地位日益凸显，激发了知识产权贸易的快速增长。因此，世界三大贸易形式中最具发展潜力、对各国经济发展影响最为重大的，无疑是以知识产权为交易标的的国际技术贸易。

本部分为国际知识产权贸易法，包括第 11 章、第 12 章。第 11 章国际知识产权贸易概述，内容涵盖国际知识产权贸易的概念、特点，国际知识产权贸易的法律体系以及国际知识产权组织的发展。第 12 章国际知识产权交易的法律形式，包括交易法律形式概述、国际许可的规制以及国际特许经营的法律规制。

Chapter 11   Introduction to International Trade in Intellectual Property Rights

Section I   Development of International Trade in Intellectual Property Rights

I. Definition of International Trade in Intellectual Property Rights

Intellectual Property Rights refer to the right of a person or company to exclusively use its own ideas, plans, and other intangible assets without competition, at least for a certain period of time. Examples of intellectual property include copyrights, trademarks, patents, and trade secrets. Intellectual property rights may be enforced by court through a lawsuit. The idea behind the protection of intellectual property is to encourage innovation without fear that a competitor may steal the idea and/or take credit for it.

According to the provisions of the TRIPS of the World Trade Organization, intellectual property includes the following Contents: Copyright, trademark, geographical indication, industrial design, patent, integrated circuit layout design, undisclosed information, etc. It is an important intangible property protected by specialized laws.

Trade of Intellectual Property Rights can be divided into broad and narrow senses:

In the narrow sense, intellectual property trade refers to trade with intellectual property as the subject matter, mainly including intellectual property licensing, intellectual property transfer, etc. , which refers to a trade behavior between enterprises, economic organizations, or individuals that sell or purchase intellectual property rights from the other party under general commercial conditions.

In a broad sense, intellectual property trade refers to the trade behavior of products containing intellectual property rights (intellectual property products, intellectual products), especially high-tech products with high added value attached to high-tech, such as integrated circuits, computer software, multimedia products, audio-visual products, literary works, etc.

II. The Current Situation and Prospects of International Intellectual Property Trade Development

With the deep adjustment of the international economic and trade pattern, the position of intellectual property in the global value chain is becoming increasingly prominent, driving the rapid growth of intellectual property trade. From 2002 to 2022, the total amount of intellectual property trade in China increased from 3.2 billion US dollars to 57.8 billion US dollars, with an average annual growth rate of about 15.5%. During the same period, the average annual growth rates of goods trade and service trade were 12.9% and 11.6%, respectively.

The early stages of global governance of intellectual property began with countries coordinating the trade needs of intellectual property rules, and ultimately took the international rules of intellectual property as the main manifestation of the global governance system. Intellectual property has become one of the focuses of international economic and trade relations. The Regional Comprehensive Economic Partnership Agreement (RCEP), which China actively participated in and signed, has a special chapter setting up intellectual property clauses with up to 83 articles.

Section II   Characteristics of International Trade in Intellectual Property Rights

I. Object of Sale: The Intangible

Intellectual property (IP) refers to creations of the mind, such as inventions; literary and artistic works; designs; and symbols, names and images used in commerce.

IP is protected in law by, for example, patents, copyright and trademarks, which enable people to earn recognition or financial benefit from what they invent or create. By striking the right balance between the interests of innovators and the wider public interest, the IP system aims to foster an environment in which creativity and innovation can flourish.

II. Transfer the Right of Use or Ownership

According to the types of intellectual property, intellectual property transfer includes four forms: Patent transfer, trademark transfer, copyright transfer, and other intellectual property transfer. Generally, the owner of intellectual property rights transfers the rights to the transferee, in accordance with laws and regulations and the transfer contract signed by both parties.

In the practice of intellectual property transfer, the vast majority of such transactions are paid transfers. As an intangible asset, the intellectual property has property value, which is a prerequisite for the paid nature of intellectual property transfer. On the other hand, from the perspective of intellectual property rights holders, obtaining transfer benefits through the transfer of intellectual property is an important purpose of intellectual property transfer. Therefore, the transfer of intellectual property rights is usually a paid act. The independent transfer of intellectual property rights and the improvement of the promotion and application efficiency of intellectual property rights have significant practical significance for intellectual property innovation, technological progress, and improving enterprise efficiency.

III. Target Price: Difficult to Estimate

Intellectual property is an intangible asset, and through the trading platform of a property exchange, its value and use value can not only be reflected, but also the transferor can obtain transfer benefits through the transfer of intellectual property. By transferring intellectual propertyrights, intellectual property rights holders can transform their monopoly advantage within a certain period of time into a competitive advantage in the market. This not only enables intellectual property rights holders to recover their scientific research investment, but also obtains excess property benefits.

The essence of intellectual property is still technological achievements, and as a property right, its value is easily influenced by technological, policy, and market changes, which will change with the aforementioned factors. With the development of technology in related fields and the variability of their intellectual property rights, expectations often deviate from the actual situation.

IV. Protection of Intellectual Property

Intellectual property protection is a complex system that involves fields such as patents, trademarks, copyrights, new plant varieties, and trade secrets. The content and boundaries of the rights protected by intellectual property have their own characteristics. The protection measures involve registration, review and authorization, administrative law enforcement, judicial adjudication, arbitration and mediation, and objectively require the construction of a work pattern for the protection of intellectual property rights.

Intellectual property protection has become a strategic point in the international economic order and one of the focal points of fierce competition among countries. The traditional intellectual property system is facing challenges, and the scope of intellectual property protection is constantly expanding.

Section Ⅲ　Legal System of International Trade in Intellectual Property Rights

Ⅰ. General Introduction

At present, in addition to TRIPS, there are 15 effective multilateral international rules for the international intellectual property protection system, 6 global protection system rules, and 4 classification system rules.

（Ⅰ）IP protection. Beijing Treaty on Audiovisual Performances,[①] Berne Convention, Brussels Convention, Madrid Agreement (Indications of Source), Marrakesh VIP Treaty, Nairobi Treaty, Paris Convention, Patent Law Treaty, Phonograms Convention, Rome Convention, Singapore Treaty on the Law of Trademarks, Trademark Law Treaty, Washington Treaty, WIPO Copyright Treaty (WCT), WIPO Performances and Phonograms Treaty (WPPT).

（Ⅱ）Global protection system. Budapest Treaty, Hague Agreement, Lisbon Agreement, Madrid Agreement (Marks), Madrid Protocol, Patent Cooperation Treaty

---

① Beijing Treaty on Audiovisual Performances （《视听表演北京条约》） adopted by the Diplomatic Conference on the Protection of Audiovisual Performances in Beijing, on June 24, 2012, which entered into force on April 26, 2020）. As the first international IP treaty signed in China and named after a Chinese city since the establishment of the United Nations, the Beijing Treaty on Audiovisual Performances is of great significance for improving the system of protection of the rights of international performers, promoting the healthy and prosperous development of cultural industries in various countries in the world, and promoting the development of Chinese culture and traditional folk performing arts.

（PCT）.

（Ⅲ）Classification. Locarno Agreement,① Nice Agreement, Strasbourg Agreement, Vienna Agreement.

Ⅱ. TRIPs

The Agreement on Trade-Related Aspects of Intellectual Property Rights （TRIPs） is an international legal agreement between all the member nations of the World Trade Organization. It establishes minimum standards for the regulation by national governments of different forms of intellectual property （IP） as applied to nationals of other WTO member nations. TRIPs was negotiated at the end of the Uruguay Round of the General Agreement on Tariffs and Trade （GATT） between 1989 and 1990 and is administered by the WTO.

The TRIPs agreement introduced intellectual property law into the multilateral trading system for the first time and remains the most comprehensive multilateral agreement on intellectual property to date. In 2001, developing countries, concerned that developed countries were insisting on an overly narrow reading of TRIPs, initiated a round of talks that resulted in the Doha Declaration. The Doha declaration is a WTO statement that clarifies the scope of TRIPs, stating for example that TRIPS can and should be interpreted in light of the goal "to promote access to medicines for all."

Specifically, TRIPs requires WTO members to provide copyright rights, covering authors and other copyright holders, as well as holders of related rights, namely performers, sound recording producers and broadcasting organizations; geographical indications; industrial designs; integrated circuit layout-designs; patents; new plant varieties; trademarks; trade names and undisclosed or confidential information. TRIPs also specify enforcement procedures, remedies, and dispute resolution procedures. Protection and enforcement of all intellectual property rights shall meet the objectives to contribute to the promotion of technological innovation and to the transfer and dissemination of technology, to the mutual advantage of producers and users of technological knowledge and in a manner conducive to social and economic welfare, and to a balance of rights and obligations.

---

① Locarno Agreement:《洛迦诺协定》是 "Locarno Agreement on Establishing an International Classification for Industrial Design"（《建立工业品外观设计国际分类洛迦诺协定》）的简称, 系巴黎联盟成员国于 1968 年 10 月 4 日在洛迦诺签订的专门协定之一, 1971 年起生效。

Chapter 12 Legal Forms of International Intellectual Property Transfer

Section I Introduction

I. Licensing

Licensing is the most common form of international intellectual property transactions. It includes licensing of intellectual property rights such as patents, trademarks, copyrights, etc. The licensor obtains license fees by signing a license agreement with the licensee, allowing them to use or exercise certain intellectual property rights within a certain period of time and territory. License agreements include various forms such as technology transfer, technology consulting services, and proprietary technology transfer.

II. Transfer

Transfer is another important international intellectual property transaction method. The transfer of intellectual property refers to the transfer of all or part of the intellectual property owned by the right owner to the transferee, in order to obtain transfer fees. The transferred intellectual property rights may include patents, trademarks, copyrights, etc. Unlike licensing, transfer means that the rights holder will no longer own the intellectual property, and the transferee will become the new rights owner.

III. Joint-exploration

Joint-exploration is a cross-border intellectual property transaction method that involves the cooperation of two or more companies or research institutions to jointly explore new products or technologies. Joint-exploration can promote technological exchange and cooperation between different countries or regions, and improve the efficiency of intellectual property utilization.

Ⅳ. Financing

Financing is also a way of international intellectual property transactions. It refers to financing intellectual property as an asset to obtain funds. For example, by issuing intellectual property securitization products, intellectual property can be converted into tradable securities to obtain funds. Financing can provide a new financing channel for intellectual property owners, as well as a new investment method for investors.

V. International Franchising

Commercial franchising refers to the business activities in which an enterprise with registered trademarks, corporate logos, patents, proprietary technologies and other business resources licenses its business resources to other operators in the form of a contract. The franchisee operates under a unified business model in accordance with the contract and pays franchise fees to the franchisor. The most prominent feature is that the commercial franchise contract requires the franchisee to follow a certain business model.

Section Ⅱ   Regulations on International Licensing

According to the different scope of authorized licenses, they can be divided into exclusive licenses (独占许可), sole licenses (排他许可), and ordinary licenses. According to whether the authorization license is voluntary or not, it can be divided into voluntary license and involuntary license, among which involuntary license includes statutory license in Copyright Law and mandatory license in Patent Law. According to the different types of authorized licenses, they can be divided into copyright licenses, patent licenses, trademark licenses, trade secret licenses, integrated circuit layout design exclusive rights licenses, plant new variety rights licenses, etc.

Ⅰ. Exclusive and Non-Exclusive License

Exclusive Licenses mean that no person or company other than the named licensee can exploit the relevant intellectual property rights. The licensor is also excluded from exploiting the intellectual property rights. If the licensor wishes to continue to conduct any activity covered by the intellectual property, or if the licensor has previously granted any rights in relation to the intellectual property, the exclusive license must explicitly state that it is exclusive.

Non-Exclusive Licenses grant to the licensee the right to use the intellectual property, but the licensor remains free to exploit the same intellectual property and to allow any other licensees to also exploit the same intellectual property.

When granting or receiving a license under intellectual property rights, the parties need to consider at the earliest stage the degree of exclusivity that will be granted. A license can also take a middle-ground between exclusive and non-exclusive. Such a license is sometimes known as a "co-exclusive" license and in which the licensor grants a license to more than one licensee, but agrees that it will only grant licenses to a limited group of other licensees. The group of licensees may be identified by name, description (a license will only be granted to licensees who meet certain criteria), or simply by number (a limited number of licenses will be granted by the licensor).

Whether a license is exclusive or non-exclusive has an impact on several other provisions of the license. The diligence obligations are likely to be more onerous in an exclusive license than in a non-exclusive license. An exclusive licensee is likely to have more rights regarding the prosecution, defense and enforcement of the intellectual property rights than a non-exclusive license. In UK, an exclusive licensee of a patent has an automatic right to enforce the patent unless the contract specifically provides otherwise.

When a license is stated to be "exclusive", but is limited to a particular territory or field of use, the parties should carefully consider the extent to which the licensee is permitted to prosecute, defend and enforce the intellectual property rights. Although the license is stated to be "exclusive", other licenses under the same intellectual property rights could be granted in other territories and/or fields. Such other licensees may want to be involved in the prosecution, defense and enforcement of the intellectual property rights as such activities are likely to impact on the value of their license. In this sense, a territory or field limited license is not equivalent to a fully exclusive license.

II. Exclusive License and Sole License

There's a distinction between an exclusive license and a sole license. In an exclusive license, only the licensee has the right to make use of the intellectual property. By contrast, in a sole license, the licensor agrees not to grant any additional licenses but retains the right to make use of the intellectual property. It would be preferable for them to explicitly state in the agreement the extent of the rights of each of the licensor and the licensee.

When working with US entities, a license may be expressed as "sole and exclusive". Given that these two terms do not necessarily mean the same thing, it is preferable to avoid expressing a license in this way. If one party insists on expressing the license in this way, it would be preferable for the agreement to explicitly state what is intended by the term.

Ⅲ. Voluntary License and Compulsory License

(Ⅰ) Voluntary license. Voluntary licensing refers to the legal act of authorizing others to use their intellectual property rights based on the wishes of the intellectual property owner. Generally speaking, most intellectual property licenses are voluntary, and users obtain permission from the intellectual property owner before using the intellectual property according to the agreed content.

The patent open license newly added to the Patent Law of the People's Republic of China (2020 Amendment), also known as "patent ex officio license", is actually a type of voluntary license. It refers to the patentee voluntarily declaring in writing to the State Council Patent Administration Department that they are willing to license any unit or individual to implement their patent, and clarifying the payment method and standards for licensing fees. If an open license declaration is filed for utility model or design patents, a patent right evaluation report shall be provided. If the patentee withdraws the open license declaration, it shall be submitted in writing and announced by the patent administration department of the State Council. If the open license statement is revoked by announcement, it does not affect the validity of the previously granted open license.

If any unit or individual is willing to implement an open license patent, they shall notify the patentee in writing and pay the license fee in accordance with the published payment method and standards, and then obtain a patent implementation license. During the implementation period of open license, the annual patent fee paid by the patentee shall be correspondingly reduced or exempted. The patentee who implements an open license may negotiate with the licensee on the licensing fee and grant a general license, but may not grant an exclusive or exclusive license for the patent.

(Ⅱ) Compulsory License. A compulsory license provides that the owner of a patent or copyright licenses the use of their rights against payment either set by law or determined through some form of adjudication or arbitration. Under a compulsory license, an individual or company seeking to use another's intellectual property can do so without seeking the rights holder's consent, and pays the rights holder a set fee for the license. This is an exception to the general rule under intellectual property laws that the intellectual property owner enjoys exclusive rights that it may license—or decline to license—to others.

Article 11 (2) and Article 13 (1) of Berne Convention for the Protection of Literary and Artistic Works provide the legal basis for compulsory licensing at the international level. Berne Convention provides that member states are free to determine the conditions under which certain exclusive rights may be exercised in their national laws. They also provide for the minimum requirements to be set when compulsory licenses are applied, such as that they must not prejudice the author's right to fair compensation.

In addition to the exclusive rights mentioned in Article 11 (1) and 13 (1), the Berne Convention also provides that members may determine or impose such conditions for the exercise of exclusive rights in cases where an exclusive right is not provided as remuneration right and not as an exclusive right of authorization. Members to the Berne Convention may also determine or impose such conditions where the restriction of an exclusive right to the mere right to remuneration is allowed.

Many patent law systems provide for the granting of compulsory licenses in a variety of situations. The Paris Convention of 1883 provides that each contracting State may take legislative measures for the grant of compulsory licenses. Article 5A (2) of the Paris Convention: Each country of the Union shall have the right to take legislative measures providing for the grant of compulsory licenses to prevent the abuses which might result from the exercise of the exclusive rights conferred by the patent, for example, failure to work.

Patent Law of the People's Republic of China provides the Compulsory License for exploitation of patent (Article 48–55). The requirements include:

A. Reasonable Request. Where any entity which is qualified to exploit the invention or utility model has made requests for authorization from the patentee of an invention or utility model to exploit its or his patent on reasonable terms and conditions and such efforts have not been successful within a reasonable period of time, the Patent Administration Department Under the State Council may, upon the request of that entity, grant a compulsory license to exploit the patent for invention or utility model.

B. Public Interest Requires. Where a national emergency or any extraordinary state of affairs occurs, or where the public interest so requires, the Patent Administration

Department under the State Council may grant a compulsory license to exploit the patent for invention or utility model.

C. Important Technical Advance. Where the invention or utility model for which the patent right has been granted involves important technical advance of considerable economic significance in relation to another invention or utility model for which a patent right has been granted earlier and the exploitation of the later invention or utility model depends on the exploitation of the earlier invention or utility model, the patent administration department under the State Council may, upon the request of the later patentee, grant a compulsory license to exploit the earlier invention or utility model.

Where, according to the preceding paragraph, a compulsory license is granted, the Patent Administration Department Under the State Council may, upon the request of the earlier patentee, also grant a compulsory license to exploit the later invention or utility model.

D. Procedural Requirements. The entity or individual requesting, in accordance with the provisions of this Law, a compulsory license for exploitation shall furnish proof that it or he has not been able to conclude with the patentee a license contract for exploitation on reasonable terms and conditions.

The decision made by the patent administration department under the State Council granting a compulsory license for exploitation shall be notified promptly to the patentee concerned, and shall be registered and announced, and the scope and duration of the exploitation shall be specified on the basis of the reasons justifying the grant.

If and when the circumstances which led to such compulsory license cease to exist and are unlikely to recur, the patent administration department under the State Council may, upon the request of the patentee, terminate the compulsory license.

E. Result. Any entity or individual that is granted a compulsory license for exploitation shall not have an exclusive right to exploit and shall not have the right to authorize exploitation by any others. The entity or individual that is granted a compulsory license for exploitation shall pay to the patentee a reasonable exploitation fee, the amount of which shall be fixed by both parties in consultations. Where the parties fail to reach an agreement, the Patent Administration Department under the State Council shall adjudicate.

Section Ⅲ　Regulations on International Franchising

International Franchising is based on a marketing concept which can be adopted by an organization as a strategy for transnational business expansion. Where implemented, a franchisor licenses its know-how, procedures, intellectual property, use of its business model, brand, and rights to sell its branded products and services to a franchisee. In return the franchisee pays certain fees and agrees to comply with certain obligations, typically set out in a Franchise Agreement. Franchising is not an equal partnership, especially due to the legal advantages the franchisor has over the franchisee. But under specific circumstances like transparency, favorable legal conditions, financial means and proper market research, franchising can be a vehicle of success for both franchisor and franchisee.

Ⅰ. Characteristics of International Franchise Contracts

The franchisor and franchisee have a contractual relationship;

The franchisor shall provide the franchisee with registered trademarks, corporate logos, patents, proprietary technologies and other business resources, and provide business guidance and assistance;

Engaging in business activities under a unified operating system (i. e. the franchisee obeys the franchisor's control);

The franchisee pays remuneration to the franchisor;

The two parties are independent operators, and the franchisee operates based on their own capital, but it does not exclude the franchisor's financial support.

Ⅱ. Obligations of the Parties

Each party to a franchise has several interests to protect.

(Ⅰ) Obligations of the franchisor. This mainly includes information disclosure, providing business manuals, conducting business training, providing start-up assistanceand ongoing support. Due to the unequal actual status between the franchisor and the franchisee, these obligations are crucial for franchising.

The franchisor is involved in securing protection for the trademark, controlling the business concept and securing know-how. The franchisee must be seen as an independent merchant. It must be protected by the franchisor from any trademark infringement by third parties.

The franchisor must provide adequate training period and the costs of which are in great part covered by the initial fee. Many franchisors have set up corporate universities to train staff online.

(II) Obligations of the franchisee. The obligations of the franchisee include development plans, cost payments, compliance with quality control requirements, adherence to business models, confidentiality, etc. Due to the fact that the franchisor and the franchisee are legally independent enterprises, the franchise agreement generally requires the franchisee to purchase relevant insurance and third-party liability insurance on their own.

The franchisee is obligated to carry out the services for which the trademark has been made prominent or famous. There is a great deal of standardization required. The place of service has to bear the franchisor's signs, logos and trademark in a prominent place. The uniforms worn by the staff of the franchisee have to be of a particular design and color. The service has to be in accordance with the pattern followed by the franchisor in the successful franchise operations. Thus, franchisees are not in full control of the business, as they would be in retailing. A service can be successful if equipment and supplies are purchased at a fair price from the franchisor or sources recommended by the franchisor.

The franchisee must carefully negotiate the license and must develop a marketing or business plan with the franchisor. The fees must be fully disclosed and there should not be any hidden fees. The start-up costs and working capital must be known before the license is granted. There must be assurance that additional licensees will not crowd the "territory" if the franchise is worked according to plan.

Also, franchise agreements carry no guarantees or warranties and the franchisee has little or no recourse to legal intervention in the event of a dispute. Franchise contracts tend to be unilateral and favor of the franchisor, who is generally protected from lawsuits from their franchisees because of the non-negotiable contracts that franchisees are required to acknowledge.

III. Regulations of China

Previous legislation (1997) made no specific inclusion of foreign investors. On February 6, 2007, State Council Order No. 485 issued the "Regulations on the Administration of Commercial Franchise" (effective from May 1, 2007), which is currently the highest level normative document specifically regulating franchising in China. The laws are applicable if there are transactions involving registered trademarks, corporate logos, patents, know-how combined with payments with many obligations on the franchisor.

(I) Obligations of Franchisor.

A. FIE (foreign-invested enterprise) franchisor must be registered by the regulator.

B. The franchisor (or its subsidiary) must have operated at least two company-owned franchises in China (revised to "anywhere") for more than 12 months.

C. The franchisor must disclose any information requested by the franchisee. The disclosure must take place 30 days in advance.

D. Cross-border franchising with some caveats is possible.

E. The franchisor must meet a list of requirements for registration, among which are:

a. The standard franchise agreement, working manual and working capital requirements.

b. A track-record of operations, and ample ability to supply materials.

c. The ability to train the Chinese personnel and provide long-term operational guidance.

d. The franchise agreement must have a minimum three-year term.

(II) Obligations of Franchisee.

A. Without the consent of franchisor, franchisee shall not transfer franchise right to others.

B. The franchisee shall not disclose or allow others to use the franchisee's trade secrets they hold to others. The franchisee's confidentiality obligations continue indefinitely after termination or expiration of the franchise agreement.

C. If the franchisee has paid a deposit to the franchisor, it must be refunded on termination of the franchise agreement; upon termination, the franchisee is prohibited from continuing to use the franchisor's marks, patent, logos, etc.

Part Ⅵ International Investment Law

International trade and international investment are two different kinds of international economic activities. Although they are completely different from each other, they are both reasonable flows and transfers of production factors in the world. Therefore, they are concrete ways of international economic cooperation. Since international investment involves the outflow and inflow of capital, technology, and management experience, which should be subject to the double control by the laws of the home country and the host country, and international investment includes both the attraction of foreign investment and the overseas investment of the home country, international investment law is therefore complicated.

This part is the International Investment Law, including chapter 13 and 14. Chapter 13, Legal Rules on Foreign Investments, includes the overview of international investment, the administrative system of foreign capital admission, the management of foreign capital business activities, and the protection and encouragement of foreign investment. Chapter 14 is Overseas Investment Law including encouragement and management of overseas investment, overseas investment insurance system and China's Foreign Investment Law.

国际投资和国际贸易是两种不同的国际经济活动，尽管二者的性质完全相异，但本质上都是生产要素在国际间的合理流动和转移，都是国际经济合作的具体方式。由于国际投资涉及资本、技术和管理经验的输出和输入，因而要受到母国和东道国法律的双重管制，加之国际投资包括外国投资的引进和本国企业的海外投资两个方面，因而国际投资法更具有复杂性。

本部分国际投资法包括第 13 章、第 14 章。其中第 13 章国际投资的法律规范包括国际投资概述、外资准入的行政管理制度、外资经营活动的管理和外国投资的保护与鼓励。第 14 章海外投资法，内容包括海外投资的鼓励措施和管理措施、海外投资保险法律制度和我国的海外投资法。

Chapter 13　Legal Rules on Foreign Investments

Section Ⅰ　General Introduction to Foreign Investment

Ⅰ. Foreign Investment

(Ⅰ) Definition of foreign investment. Investment means every asset that an investor owns or controls, directly or indirectly, that has the characteristics of an investment. Foreign investment involves capital flows from one country to another, granting the foreign investors extensive ownership stakes in domestic companies and assets. Foreign investment denotes that foreigners have an active role in management as a part of their investment or an equity stake large enough to enable the foreign investor to influence business strategy. A modern trend leans toward globalization, where multinational firms have investments in various of countries.

Foreign investment is primarily seen as a catalyst for economic growth in the future. Foreign investments can be made by individuals, but are most often endeavors pursued by companies and corporations with substantial assets looking to expand their reach.

(Ⅱ) Types of foreign investment. Foreign investments can be classified in two ways: Direct and indirect. Foreign direct investments (FDIS) are the physical investments and purchases made by a company in a foreign country, typically by opening plants and buying buildings, machines, factories, and other equipment in the foreign country. These types of investments find a far greater deal of favor, as they are generally considered long-term investments and help bolster the foreign country's economy.

Foreign indirect investments involve corporations, financial institutions, and private investors buying stakes or positions in foreign companies that trade on a foreign stock exchange. In general, this form of foreign investment is less favorable, as the domestic company can easily sell off its investment very quickly, sometimes within days of the purchase. This type of investment is also sometimes referred to as a foreign portfolio investment (FPI). Indirect investments include not only equity instruments such as stocks, but also debt instruments such as bonds.

The main distinction between direct investment and indirect investment lies in whether the investors participate in the management of the invested enterprises or whether the investors remain effective control over the enterprises.

II. Foreign Direct Investment

Foreign direct investment (FDI) plays a pivotal role in economic development. It can bring with it firm-specific knowledge and must be beneficial to both the host nation and the investing entity for it to be sustainable.

(I) Definition of FDI. Foreign direct investment is an ownership stake in a foreign company or project made by an investor, company, or government from another country. FDI is a flow of long-term capital based on long-term profit considerations, it is associated with a significant degree of influence or control by the investor in the management of the enterprise.

Generally, the term is used to describe a business decision to acquire a substantial stake in a foreign business or to buy it outright to expand operations to a new region. The term is usually not used to describe a stock investment in a foreign company alone. FDI is a key element in international economic integration because it creates stable and long-lasting links between economies.

(II) Types of FDI. FDI are commonly categorized as horizontal, vertical, or conglomerate.

With a horizontal FDI, a company establishes the same type of business operation in a foreign country as it operates in its home country. A U. S. -based cellphone provider buying a chain of phone stores in China is an example.

In a vertical FDI, a business acquires a complementary business in another country. For example, a U.S. manufacturer might acquire an interest in a foreign company that supplies it with the raw materials it needs.

In a conglomerate FDI, a company invests in a foreign business that is unrelated to its core business. Because the investing company has no prior experience in the foreign company's area of expertise, this often takes the form of a joint venture.

(III) Advantages and disadvantages of FDI. FDI can foster and maintain economic growth, in both the recipient country and the country making the investment. On one hand, developing countries have encouraged FDI as a means of financing the construction of new infrastructure and the creation of jobs for their local workers. On the other hand, multinational companies benefit from FDI as a means of expanding their footprints into international markets. A disadvantage of FDI, however, is that it involves the regulation and oversight of multiple governments, leading to a higher level of political risk.

III. Sources of the FDI

The sources of international investment law include domestic law and international law.

(I) Foreign investment law of the capital importing country. The Foreign Investment Law is the general term of the legal norms regulating the relationship of foreign private direct investment in the capital importing country, and its main content is to stipulate the rights and obligations of the government of the capital importing country foreign investors and foreign investment enterprises in relation to investment. It usually includes provisions on access and investment of foreign capital, legal status of foreign investors and foreign-invested enterprises, taxation and preferential treatment, remittance of legal income such as original and profit, expropriation, nationalization and compensation, protection of enterprise autonomy and settlement of investment disputes. The forms and systems of laws used to regulate foreign investment in countries around the world are different. Some formulate uniform investment codes, some promulgate special regulations, and some only apply general domestic laws. The laws of capital importing countries on foreign investment are an important source of international investment law.

(II) Foreign investment laws of capital exporting countries. In order to protect their own economic interests, capital exporting countries usually formulate laws on foreign investment, the most important of which is the overseas investment insurance law. In addition, some capital exporting countries also have legal provisions on controlling or encouraging overseas private investment.

(III) The international treaties relating to FDI. The international treaties that regulate the rights of States in relation to international investment include bilateral treaties and multilateral treaties, which are important sources of international investment law.

A. Bilateral investment treaty. In order to promote and protect mutual investment, the bilateral investment treaty concluded between two countries occupies an important position in international investment. There are three main forms of the treaty of friendship, trade and navigation, investment guarantee agreement, and mutual promotion and protection of investment agreement.

B. Multilateral treaties. There are regional multilateral treaties and universal multilateral conventions on international investment. Regional multilateral treaties are multilateral treaties signed by regional countries in order to regulate the foreign investment laws of member countries.

The world's multilateral conventions on international investment include the Convention on Settlement of Investment Disputes between States and private Parties of other countries, the Multilateral Investment Guarantee Agency Convention and the Agreement on Trade-related Investment Measures under the WTO system, the General Agreement on Trade in Services Agreement on Subsidies and Countervailing Measures.

IV. Subjects of International Investment

(I) Natural person. As the subject of international investment law, natural persons should have the general legal capacity and the legal capacity to engage in international investment activities.

(II) Legal person. legal person is an organization established in accordance with legal procedures, with a certain organizational structure and independent property, with capacity for civil rights and civil conduct, and independently enjoying civil rights and bearing civil obligations according to law.

Whether a legal person can be the subject of international investment law depends on the scope of its rights. The scope of the legal person's capacity is determined by the relevant law and the legal person's constitution. Some national laws restrict the qualifications of legal persons engaged in foreign economic cooperation. As for the general capacity of legal persons, the international community has always believed that the legal person's personal law should be determined.

(III) Transnational corporation. A Transnational Corporation is an enterprise composed of entities located in two or more States, regardless of the legal form and scope of activities of those entities. The operations of such enterprises are carried out through one or more decision-making centers in accordance with a system of decision-making and, as a result, have consistent policies and common strategies in which one or more entities can exert a significant influence on the activities of other entities, in particular by sharing knowledge, resources, and responsibilities with them.

Transnational corporations have no special status in domestic law. They have the same status as business organizations in the host country. The parent or head office of a transnational corporation in its home country, like other commercial companies, is incorporated under the laws of the home country and its legal capacity is determined by the laws of the home country. An entity of a transnational corporation in the host country, or a subsidiary company established under the law of the host country and controlled by the parent company, on the same footing as other companies in the host country; Or as a branch registered in the host country, its status is still a foreign company. Whether these entities of TNCS are domestic or foreign, there is no difference in legal status between them and other commercial companies. For example, the term "company" under Malaysia's Companies Act 1965 includes any corporate entity incorporated within or outside Malaysia, as well as foreign companies. Foreign companies operating in Malaysia must set up subsidiaries or register a number of branches, which is an internationally accepted practice. Similarly, when a foreign company conducts investment and business activities in China, it is also required to establish a joint venture, a cooperative enterprise or a foreign-funded enterprise, or approve the registration of its branch in accordance with Chinese law. However, in law, the subsidiary and the branch have different legal statuses.

(Ⅳ) States and international organizations. In addition to legal persons and natural persons, countries and international organizations are also important subjects of international investment law.

As a subject of international law, States have the ability to participate independently in international relations and directly bear rights and obligations under international law. Therefore, states have the right to conclude treaties on international investment with other countries.

Many intergovernmental international economic organizations have international legal personality according to the international treaties and documents established by them. They can conclude treaties with other legal entities, acquire and dispose of property, and protect their rights and interests through litigation or other legal means. These international economic organizations can also be the subject of international investment law.

V. Methods and Forms of Investment

(Ⅰ) New investment. New investment, also known as greenfield investment or new enterprises, refers to foreign investors exporting capital (including own capital or medium-and long-term credit capital) to the host country, directly establishing a new enterprise, and having management rights or control over the operation and management of the enterprise. New businesses formed in this way can be joint ventures, co-ops, or sole proprietor-ships. Its characteristics are: Large investment amount, long construction cycle, high investment risk.

A. Joint venture. Joint venture, referred to as a joint venture, is a form of enterprise in which two or more parties jointly invest, operate, share risks and share profits and losses in order to achieve specific commercial purposes. An international joint venture is an enterprise in which one or more foreign investors (legal person or natural person) and the government, legal person or natural person of the host country jointly contribute capital in accordance with the legal or agreed proportions, jointly operate a specific business, share profits and bear losses.

a. Equity joint venture. An equity joint venture is a legal entity formed by mutual agreement between the partners for the purpose of operating a common enterprise. This type of joint venture shall have independent legal personality; The capital contribution of a joint venture is divided into shares, and the parties exercise certain rights and assume certain obligations to the enterprise in proportion to their own capital contribution. The enterprise has a certain management organization. For example, Sino-foreign joint ventures in China, joint ventures in Belgium, and joint stock limited companies in Poland belong to this category. From the perspective of international practice, the joint venture formed as a company mainly takes two basic forms: Limited liability company and joint stock limited company.

A limited corporation, also known as a limited company, is an enterprise legal person established in accordance with the Company Law and composed of no more than a certain number of shareholders, each shareholder is liable to the company according to the amount of capital it has subscribed to, and the company is liable to the debts of the company with all its assets.

A joint stock company is a legal person in which all the capital is divided into equal shares, the shareholders are liable to the company to the extent of the shares they hold, and the company is liable to the debts of the company with all its assets. A stock limited company has organizational assets, the assets of the company itself are the total guarantee for the repayment of debts, and the credit of the company has nothing to do with the credit of its members. In the securitization of the capital of a joint stock limited company, the rights of the shareholders are transferred with the delivery of the shares, and the existence of the company has nothing to do with the change of shareholders and the increase or decrease of the number of shareholders.

b. contractual joint ventures. A contractual joint venture is an economic organization in which the parties to a joint venture are involved in a common undertaking under a joint contract. This type of joint venture usually does not have the status of a legal person, the parties to the joint venture do not make capital contributions in the form of shares, nor do they share risks, profits, and losses according to the shares, but enjoy certain rights and obligations to the enterprise according to the agreement of the joint venture contract, and retain their rights to the assets of the partnership. In other words, the contribution of the parties to a contractual joint venture may not be converted into a unified monetary unit, and the sharing of benefits, risks and losses between the parties may be carried out through the agreement of the joint venture contract.

B. Co-operative enterprises. Cooperative enterprises are also called cooperative enterprises. The partner shall provide funds, technology and equipment. An enterprise engaged in the operation of a specific project in which the other party provides the basic conditions such as site, existing plant and labor service. The parties to the cooperation shall not make capital contribution in the form of shares. still, they shall distribute the profits and losses according to the proportion of sharing as stipulated in the contract. It is commonly used in small cooperative projects with small scope, little investment, short cycle and quick effect. A contractual joint venture may form a legal person at the will of the parties, or it may not create a legal person, and representatives of the parties may form a joint organization to carry out operation, management and daily activities. A cooperative business relationship without a legal person is a partnership in which each partner is jointly and severally liable for the debts of the business.

C. Foreign enterprise. In international investment, foreign enterprise is a form of international investment enterprise compared with joint venture enterprise and cooperative enterprise. It is generally believed that foreign-funded enterprises mainly refer to enterprises established in the territory of the host country in accordance with the laws of the host country, and all or most of the capital is invested by foreign investors. However, at present, the laws of various countries have different provisions on the proportion of foreign capital in an enterprise before it can be regarded as a foreign-funded enterprise. The laws of some countries stipulate that all enterprises with the majority of foreign capital are foreign-funded enterprises. However, in some countries, the law strictly limits only those enterprises whose total capital is owned by foreign investors are foreign-owned enterprises, also known as wholly foreign-owned enterprises.

(Ⅱ) Enterprise merger and acquisition. In addition to the cross-border establishment of new enterprises, international investment can also be carried out through the merger or acquisition of existing enterprises in the host country. With the deepening of the reform of China's economic system and the continuous expansion of the field of opening up to the outside world, the Chinese law not only allows foreign investors to invest in the establishment of new enterprises in the territory, but also allows foreign investors to make direct investment through mergers and acquisitions.

The forms of mergers and acquisitions include new mergers, absorption mergers and acquisitions.

A. A new merger refers to the merger of two or more companies to create a new company, the establishment of a new company, and means the dissolution or disappearance of the parties involved in the merger.

B. A merger by absorption, also known as a merger, is when one company absorbs another company. The merger does not mean that all parties involved in the merger are dissolved, but that one party continues to exist as a surviving company, and the absorbed company is dissolved or disappears.

C. A takeover is an offer made by an acquiring company to purchase part or all of the equity or assets of a target company in order to control the company's actions.

Acquisitions can be divided into offers and agreements. Tender offer refers to the acquisition by the acquirer by issuing a tender offer to the shareholders of the target company. Acquisition by agreement is an acquisition made by the acquirer through reaching a purchase agreement with the shareholders of the acquired company.

(Ⅲ) Franchise①. Franchise refers to the agreement between a state and a foreign private investor that during a certain period, in a designated area, it is allowed to enjoy certain rights exclusive to the State under certain conditions to invest in special economic activities such as the construction of public utilities or the development of natural resources. The main models for acquiring franchises from host countries are BOT and PPP.

A. International cooperative development. International cooperative development is a form of international cooperation in which countries use foreign investment to jointly develop natural resources. Usually, governments or government companies of resource countries sign agreements with foreign investors, allowing foreign investors to cooperate with resource countries in exploration and exploitation of natural resources in the deve-

---

① 特许经营。

lopment zones designated by resource countries and within a certain period of time, and to jointly bear risks and share profits according to agreed proportions. It consists of four basic modes.

a. Concession agreement. Concession agreement refers to a legal agreement between a state and a foreign private investor, agreeing to allow them to enjoy certain rights exclusive to the state under certain conditions, to invest in special economic activities such as the construction of public utilities or the development of natural resources during a certain period in a designated area, and to grant special permission based on certain procedures.

b. The joint venture system. There are two kinds of joint ventures: One is equity joint venture in which a joint venture is established; The second is contractual joint venture or partnership. The former is an independent legal person, while the latter generally only reaches a joint agreement without forming a new independent legal person. The parties to the cooperation maintain their independence financially and legally, calculate their expenses and income separately, pay taxes separately, and assume legal responsibilities respectively.

c. Product-sharing contracts. The basic characteristics of this form of contract are: The resource country owns the ownership of the land and resources in the working area; The national company of the resource country shall be responsible for the operation and management of petroleum development operations; The foreign contractor is responsible for carrying out the oil operations and providing the costs and technology necessary for oil exploration, development and production; All petroleum products shall be shared between the national company and the foreign contractor in accordance with the provisions of the contract after the development costs are covered. This form of contract grants management responsibilities to national companies, gives the host country more significant control over resources and products, and provides more straightforward financial procedures.

d. Service contract. The characteristics of this form of contract are: The host country or other national companies have the right to oil exploration and exploitation, independent investment and operation; By signing service contracts with foreign companies, certain work in exploration and development is assigned to foreign contractors to complete the tasks; The oil product is acquired entirely by the host country or its national company, and the foreign contractor receives only the corresponding remuneration, usually a portion of the product. Service contracts can be divided risk service contracts and risk-free contracts.

B. BOT (Build-Operate-Transfer). BOT (Build-Operate-Transfer) means that the government grants a private enterprise a franchise for a certain period of time through a contract, allowing it to finance the construction and operation of a specific public infrastructure, and allowing it to repay loans by charging users or selling products to recover investment and earn profits. When the concession term expires, the infrastructure is handed over to the government free of charge. It has the following characteristics:

a. It's suitable for large-scale infrastructure projects with high investment risk, stable income source and monopolistic operation of the host country.

b. During the term of the concession, the private enterprise is responsible for financing, building and operating the infrastructure project, as well as repaying loans, recovering investments and making profits. The private enterprise that obtains the concession has the independent right to build and operate the specific project.

c. At the end of the concession period, the project company is required to hand over the infrastructure to the government without compensation.

BOT projects often involve large investment, long cycle and multi-stakeholder. For BOT projects to succeed, long-term and stable government support is essential, especially for developing countries. Government support takes many forms, mainly financial support, performance guarantees, tax incentives and protection from competition.

In the use of international and domestic private capital for public infrastructure construction in various countries around the world, BOT model is the most mature and widely used project financing model at present. Still, this model also has several shortcomings: Both the public sector and private enterprises often need to go through a long process of investigation, negotiation and consultation, resulting in too long a project stage and excessive bidding costs; Investors and lenders are too risky and have no way out, making financing difficult; The interest conflicts of the parties involved in the project investment cause obstacles to financing; The mechanism is not flexible, reducing the enthusiasm of private enterprises to introduce advanced technology and management experience; The government loses control of the project during the concession period.

C. PPP (Public-private-partnership). PPP model is the abbreviation of public-private-partnership, usually translated as "Public Private Partnership system", refers to the cooperation between the government and private organizations to build urban infrastructure projects. In order to provide certain public goods and services, a partnership is formed between each other based on the concession agreement, and the rights and obligations of both parties are clearly defined by the signing of the contract to ensure the smooth completion of the cooperation, and ultimately the cooperation parties achieve more favorable results than expected to act alone.

PPP model is an optimized project financing and implementation model developed in the construction of public infrastructure, which a modern is financing model based on the "win−win" or "multi−win" cooperation concept of all participants. It's typical structure is: Government departments or local governments sign franchise contracts with special purpose companies composed of winning bidders through government procurement, and the special purpose companies are responsible for financing, construction and operation. The government usually has a direct agreement with the financial institution providing the loan. This agreement is not an agreement to guarantee the project, but an agreement to promise the lending institution that it will pay the relevant fees according to the contract signed with the special purpose company. This agreement enables the special purpose company to obtain loans from the financial institution more smoothly. The essence of this form of financing is that the government grants long−term franchise rights and revenue rights to private companies in exchange for faster construction and efficient operation of infrastructure.

Section Ⅱ Administrative System for Admission of Foreign Capital

When foreign investors invest in a country, the first problem they encounter is what kind of investment the country is allowed to accept, which sectors they can invest in, and what conditions these investments should meet, which are generally clearly stipulated in foreign investment laws of various countries.

Ⅰ. Definition and Capital Composition of Foreign Investment

Generally speaking, foreign capital refers to any form of capital imported from outside the country, but different countries have different regulations on what constitutes foreign capital. Foreign capital as stipulated in the foreign capital legislation of most countries refers to the investment made by natural persons, legal persons or unincorporated entities with foreign nationality.

The capital composition of foreign investment, also known as the way of investment, generally includes foreign currency cash, machinery, equipment, raw materials and other physical goods, patent rights, trademarks and other industrial property rights and other rights, including both tangible assets and intangible assets.

(I) Cash. Cash is one of the most common forms of capital for foreign investment and is an indispensable and important part of foreign investment.

(II) Tangible assets. Foreign investment laws of all countries generally allow investment in tangible assets. The range of tangible assets is very wide. Such as machinery and equipment, raw materials, spare parts, buildings, plants, etc. Using tangible assets as capital contribution usually involves the conditions, ownership, pricing and other issues as capital contribution.

(III) Industrial property rights and know-how. Industrial property rights are collectively referred to as patent rights (including invention patents, utility model patents, design patents, etc.) and trademark rights (including commodity marks, service marks, etc.) . Proprietary technology (know-how) , also known as technical know-how or technical secrets, is a kind of transferable and imparted, the public does not know and do not obtain patent technical knowledge, its content mainly includes manufacturing process, material formula, and business management secrets. One of the important reasons why the capital importing country wants to attract foreign private investment and allow it to invest and set up factories in the host country is to absorb the industrial property rights and know-how that accompany the capital.

II. Investment Scope and Investment Proportion

The foreign investment laws of all countries generally specify the scope of foreign investment, and define the participation degree of foreign investment by the provision of the proportion of investment. Foreign investors must invest within these limited conditions and scope.

(I) Scope of foreign investment. The scope of foreign investment refers to the industrial sectors in which foreign investment is permitted. In order to ensure that foreign investment is beneficial to the economic development of the host country, the capital importing country must regulate the scope of foreign investment. On the one hand, the industries and departments related to national security and major interests, the national economy and the people's livelihood should be kept in the hands of the government and its nationals. On the other hand, foreign investment should be directed to industries and departments that are in urgent need of development in the country, so as to ensure that foreign investment is consistent with the country's economic development goals. There-fore, laws all over the world have provisions on the scope of investment, that is, the sectors that stipulate that foreign investment is prohibited①, restricted, permitted or en-couraged.

Due to different national conditions, the provisions on the scope of investment in foreign capital laws of different countries are also different. Some countries clearly stipu-late the industries that are not open to foreign investors, others stipulate the industries that allow and encourage foreign investment, some countries only make provisions in principle, and some list the relevant industries in detail. In addition, the regulations of developed countries and developing countries are also very different. Developed countries generally prohibit or restrict fewer industries, while developing countries do not open more sectors.

A. Industries that are off-limits to foreign investment. In both developed and deve-loping countries, some sectors are closed to the outside world. These sectors are usually critical to national security or affect People's Daily lives, and thus involve the public interest. From the perspective of developing countries, in general, public utilities, which are of strategic or vital importance and dominate the lifeblood of the national eco-nomy, sectors where domestic capacity or domestic production is considered to be suffi-cient.

B. Sectors in which foreign investment is restricted. Sectors where foreign invest-ment is restricted, mainly refers to the restriction on the proportion of foreign equity in certain sectors (accounting for minority equity), there are also restrictions on the na-tionality and domicile of board members. Some countries also have sector-specific stan-dards, institution-setting or regulatory approval requirements that are specific to or spe-cific to foreign investors.

Developed countries have different forms of restrictions on foreign investment in cer-tain sectors, particularly in the service sector which include banking, insurance, com-munications, national transportation, agriculture, natural resource development, etc.

C. Sectors in which foreign in permitted or encouraged. The foreign investment laws

---

① In China, the sectors that foreign investment are prohibited is stipulated by negative list, which for foreign investment access. The negative list for foreign investment access refers to the special management measures for foreign investment access stipulated by the state in specific fields. The State shall give national treatment to foreign investment not on the negative list.

of many countries stipulate the sectors in which foreign investment is allowed and encouraged, that is, they determine the key areas of foreign investment and guide foreign investment to flow to industries that are conducive to the economic development of the country.

From the practice of developing countries, there are two main approaches: One is to determine the focus or target, delineate a general scope, without specifying the industry, where in line with the statutory focus or target, are allowed or encouraged industries. The main objectives of foreign investment in developing countries are: Attracting funds for large-scale and complex projects beyond the domestic capacity, introducing advanced technologies, replacing imports, increasing foreign exchange earnings from exports, increasing employment opportunities and training nationals etc. all of which meet these objectives can be invested. Second. The sectors in which foreign investment is allowed and encouraged should be clearly defined in accordance with their own economic development goals.

（Ⅱ）Proportion of foreign investment. From a microcosmic point of view, the investment ratio between the foreign investor and the local joint venture in the host country only involves the sharing of the interests of the joint venture and the allocation of management rights. The parties to a joint venture have their own considerations on what proportion to choose for their cooperation.

From a macro point of view, the host country regulates the proportion of foreign investment in its foreign investment legislation, which essentially reflects the host country's control over the direction of foreign investment in its territory. This control is not to exclude foreigners completely in a certain industry, but to increase the participation of local capital in foreign-invested enterprises.

Ⅲ. Review and Approval of Foreign Investment

（Ⅰ）Scope of review. The establishment of the approval process does not mean that all foreign investments need to be approved. From the perspective of developing countries, some countries require mandatory approval and registration of all foreign investments on a case-by-case basis. However, some countries require government approval only for foreign investment projects applying for preferential treatment. Other countries require approval of projects with foreign investment exceeding a certain amount or proportion of investment.

（Ⅱ）Approval criteria. According to the provisions of foreign investment laws of various countries, the approval standards are divided into positive standards and negative standards. The positive standard refers to the standard that the examination and approval authority appraise the positive role of foreign capital. Foreign investments may be approved if they meet one or more of the positive criteria. Negative approval refers to the condition that foreign investment is not approved.

Some foreign investment laws combine positive and negative criteria to consider various factors of foreign investment in order to decide whether to approve it.

(III) National security review system for foreign mergers and acquisitions. The acquisition and merger of existing enterprises by foreign investors can quickly enter a certain industry in the host country. Foreign mergers and acquisitions may not only lead to monopoly, but also affect national security. Therefore, many countries have established a national security review system.

At present, national laws do not define or make specific provisions on national security, whether it affects national security, it is up to the discretion of the review organs according to the actual situation, which factors should be considered in the national security review, some countries have made comprehensive provisions, and some countries consider from the strategic or sensitive industries.

In addition, for foreign mergers and acquisitions, in addition to the general investment review and national security review, it will also involve the review of anti-monopoly law.

Section III Management of Foreign Capital Business Activities

Due to the different economic systems and levels of economic development of different countries, the control of the operating conditions of foreign-invested enterprises is also different. Generally speaking, most developed market economy countries tend to adopt national treatment, while developing countries generally have certain restrictions on this, such as requiring the use of local materials, product export and hiring of local personnel.

I . The Management of Purchasing and Marketing Activities

Material procurement and product sales of foreign-invested enterprises are very important links in the process of production and operation of enterprises. Therefore, many countries' foreign capital laws mostly regulate the purchasing and marketing activities of enterprises.

II. Labor Employment and Management

Regarding the employment and management of foreign-invested enterprises, some countries have adopted a single labor code and separate regulations to adjust, and some countries have adopted foreign investment laws to provide for labor employment issues.

Based on social, economic, labor policy and employment considerations, foreign capital legislation and labor legislation in most countries have made different provisions and restrictions on the employment of workers at home and abroad.

III. Technology Introduction and Management

One of the main purposes of utilizing foreign capital in the world is to introduce foreign advanced technology. Therefore, the foreign capital legislation of many countries has made clear provisions on technology introduction, and some countries have also formulated special legislation on technology transfer or technology import control.

IV. Environmental Protection

The government has the responsibility to take corresponding measures for environmental protection and sustainable development, including canceling subsidies for users who excessive or abuse natural resources, levying pollution taxes and other measures, setting emission and discharge standards, establishing responsibility and compensation systems, etc. Many developing countries have now established regulatory frameworks for environmental protection.

The host country can take corresponding environmental management measures, the most critical measure is at the stage of foreign investment access, review and assessment of the environmental impact of foreign investment projects, only in line with the requirements of the environmental law can be approved. After foreign investment access, the environmental impact of the business activities of foreign investment enterprises in the channel country also needs to be monitored. Its oversight measures include environmental impact assessments by independent, qualified bodies and accountability for violations of environmental law.

Section IV   Protection and Encouragement of Foreign Investment

In order to attract and utilize foreign capital, the foreign capital laws of various countries protect the security and interests of foreign investment, and even give various incentives and preferences, including the protection of nationalization and compensation, the guarantee of the remittance of foreign capital profits and investment principal, as well as tax incentives and other advantages and preferences.

I. Assurances on Expropriation and Nationalization

Nationalization refers to acquisition by a state of property previously held by private persons or companies usually in exchange for some consideration. In order to protect the security interests of foreign investment and improve the domestic investment environment, many countries take many measures to provide legal protection for foreign investors in terms of nationalization and compensation. The specific practices of various countries are different. Some countries provide guarantee through bilateral investment treaties, and many countries also provide guarantee through domestic legislation. India's constitution provides only that no person shall be deprived of his property cannot be expropriated except by the authority of law. The German constitution requires that a taking be in the public interest and pursuant to the law. Mexico's constitution says that private property cannot be expropriated except for public use and upon payment of compensation. The constitutions of Argentina, Iraq, Malaysia, the Philippines, the Sudan all say that a taking must be in the public interest, by means of a law or procedures established by law, and that fair, just, or adequate compensation must be provided.

Many countries guarantee the nationalization risk through constitutions or foreign capital legislation, and stipulate that expropriation or nationalization and compensation are only implemented under legally limited conditions, so as to maintain investment security, attractforeign capital and develop their own economy.

II. Guarantee on the Return of Foreign Investment Profits and Principal

In countries that implement foreign exchange control, foreign investment will have the risk that the investment profit and principal in the host country cannot be transferred out of the country, and this risk is not conducive to the host country to attract and utilize foreign capital. While implementing foreign exchange control, many capital importing countries provide guarantees for foreign investors through international treaties and domestic legislation.

Some foreign capital laws allow free remittance of investment profits without restrictions, and many foreign capital laws provide certain restrictions under the principle of allowing free remittance.

The implementation of foreign exchange control leads to the existence of foreign exchange risks. In order to reduce or avoid the foreign exchange risks of foreign investors, capital importing countries must provide guarantees for the remittance of foreign capital profits and principal. Most of the guarantees provided under the premise of foreign exchange control are conditional.

III. Incentives and Preferences for Foreign Investment

While focusing on protecting the security and interests of foreign investment, the foreign investment laws of various countries also take various measures to encourage foreign investment, such as granting tax incentives and other advantages to industries that focus on attracting foreign investment, and establishing special economic zones.

Tax preference is the tax relief and taxation from a low tax rate that a country legally grants to foreign investors.

In addition to tax incentives, many countries also offer different forms of incentives to foreign investment, such as financial subsidies, financial assistance, financing credit concessions and management convenience.

Chapter 14　Legal Rules on Overseas Investments

Section Ⅰ　Encouragement and Management of Overseas Investment

Ⅰ. Incentives for Overseas Investment

Private overseas investment has a positive effect on the country, helping to increase the country's fiscal revenue, conducive to the balance of international payments of the country, conducive to foreign raw materials and resources to drive and promote the development of the domestic economy and maintain its international competitive position. Therefore, all major capital exporting countries have taken measures to encourage overseas investment. These measures are mainly tax law provisions and other economic and administrative measures.

(Ⅰ) Tax incentives and protections. Investors who invest abroad are usually subject to dual jurisdiction for tax purposes, so that the overseas investor is liable for double taxation, even if he enjoys low tax rates and tax relief in host country; he still has to pay tax in his home country.

In order to solve this problem, capital exporting countries generally adopt two ways: One is tax credit, if the overseas investor has paid tax in the host country, it can be offset or deducted from the tax payable in the country; the other is tax exemption law, which recognizes the separate tax right of the capital importing country, and the country waives the tax. Most countries adopt the method of credit.

(Ⅱ) Government funding and services. Governments of capital exporting countries provide their private investors with information on the economic situation and investment opportunities in the host country through administrative agencies or embassies and consulates so that they can make investment choices.

Some countries provide full or partial financial support to investors. And train technical personnel for overseas investment enterprises. Some capital exporting countries have also set up special financial institutions to finance overseas investments by their private investors in the form of loans or guarantees, or the establishment of special funds.

II. Management Measures for Overseas Investment

In order to ensure that domestic private overseas investment is beneficial to the balance of payment and economic development of the country, capital exporting countries also have some regulatory measures on overseas investment.

(I) Require overseas investment companies to disclose information. In order to supervise the operation of overseas invested enterprises, the company law and securities law of various countries require listed companies to disclose information and release balance sheets and other important business information to the government and the public, which is helpful for the government to understand and supervise the operation of domestic overseas invested enterprises.

(II) Prevent overseas investment enterprises from evading taxes. If private overseas investors do not repatriate their profits in time, it will not only affect the balance of payments of the investor's home country, but also reduce the fiscal and tax revenue of the home country. Therefore, in addition to general tax evasion and avoidance measures, countries also take some special measures.

There are mainly two special measures. One is to prevent affiliated enterprises from abusing transfer pricing to evade tax. Many countries adopt the principle of normal transactions, and the business transactions between affiliated enterprises are calculated according to fair market transaction prices. Second, in order to prevent the use of tax havens to evade taxes, some major developed countries have taken different measures to prevent overseas investors from using companies with bases in tax havens to evade taxes. Britain passed laws to block the establishment of a Qaeda companies, and the United States scrapped tax deferrals.

Section Ⅱ   Overseas Investment Insurance System

Ⅰ. Definition and Characteristics of Overseas Investment Insurance System

(Ⅰ) Definition of overseas investment insurance system. The overseas investment insurance system is a system in which the governments of capital exporting countries provide guarantees or insurance for the political risks that their overseas investors may encounter abroad. If the investors apply for insurance from domestic investment insu-rance institutions, the domestic insurance institutions will compensate their losses if the insured political risks occur.

(Ⅱ) Characteristics of overseas investment insurance system.

A. Overseas investment insurance is limited to overseas private direct investment.

B. The scope of overseas investment insurance is limited to political risks, such as expropriation risks, foreign exchange risks, war risks, etc. , excluding general commercial risks.

C. Overseas investment insurance is written by a government agency or public corporation and is not intended to make a profit, but to protect the investment.

D. The task of overseas investment insurance is not only to compensate afterwards, but more importantly to prevent problems before they happen.

Ⅱ. The Insurer

According to the legislation and practice of each country, there are government agencies, government companies or public companies responsible for implementing overseas investment insurance business.

In the United States, government companies act as insurers, while in Japan, political risks of overseas investment are insured by government agencies. In Germany, the government and state-owned companies are jointly responsible for underwriting political risk in foreign investments.

China Export and Credit Insurance Corporation is a wholly state-owned insurance company engaged in policy-based export credit insurance business, arranged by the state budget.

III. Insurance Coverage

（ I ）Foreign exchange insurance. Foreign exchange insurance includes currency in-convertibility risks and transfer risks, some countries only cover prohibited risks, others cover all risks.

（ II ）Collection insurance. Collection insurance generally means that due to the implementation of collection or nationalization measures by the host government, the insured's investment property has suffered partial or total losses, and the insurer is responsible for compensation.

What is the act of expropriation, the provisions of different countries are different. The insurance covered by Chinese insurance institutions refers to the forced expropriation, confiscation, nationalization, seizure and other acts of the investment taken, approved, authorized or agreed by the government of the country where the investment is located. These acts must continue for a period of time and prevent the investor from establishing or operating the project enterprise, or deprive or hinder the investor's rights and interests.

（ III ）War and civil disorder insurance. War risk means damage to the investor's insured property in the host country as a result of war, revolution, insurrection, civil unrest, terrorism or sabotage, for which the insurer is liable.

IV. Insurance Object

This refers to eligible investments that can be insured against. To qualify an investment, not only the form of the investment and the host country of the investment must qualify, but also the investment itself must meet certain criteria.

Overseas investment must be in line with the interests of the investor's home country, to benefit the economic development of the host country, generally limited to new overseas investment.

V. The Insured

Qualified insured persons include the following situations:

（ I ）National refers to a natural person who acquires the nationality of the country under the laws of the country.

（ II ）National corporation, partnership or other association.

(Ⅲ) Foreign companies, partnerships, associations, generally have strict restrictions.

Section Ⅲ Foreign Investment Law of People's Republic of China

The Foreign Investment Law, which came into effect on January 1, 2020, replaces the Law on Sino-Foreign Joint Ventures promulgated in 1979, the Law on Foreign-Funded Enterprises and the Law on Chinese-Foreign Cooperative Ventures promulgated in 1986 and 1988, and is a new basic law in the field of foreign investment. It provides a more powerful institutional guarantee for further opening up to the outside world and actively and effectively utilizing foreign investment under the new situation. With unified provisions for the entry, promotion, protection and management of foreign investment, it is a new and fundamental law for China's foreign investment. The New Foreign Investment Law as a landmark in the legislative history of foreign investment in China aims to improve the transparency of foreign investment policies and ensure domestic and foreign enterprises are subject to a unified set of rules and compete on a level playing field. The new law shows China's will and determination to follow through with reform and opening up in a new historical context. It is a full testament to China's determination and confidence in opening wider to the outside world and promoting foreign investment in the new era.

The Foreign Investment Law marks the institutional opening of our country. The Foreign Investment Law has the following highlights and significance.

Ⅰ. Establishment of the Foreign Investment Promotion System

The purpose of the Foreign Investment Law is to further open up to the outside world, actively promote foreign investment, protect the legitimate rights and interests of foreign investment, promote the formation of a new pattern of all-round opening up, and promote the healthy development of the socialist market economy.

The foreign investment promotion system is mainly reflected in the following five aspects:

(Ⅰ) Established the pre-establishment national treatment and negative list system.

Quite a number of foreign and Chinese investment enterprises complain about the different treatment offered to investment enterprises even after China acceded to the WTO. The New Foreign Investment Law also aims to guarantee national treatment to all investment enterprises equally. Article 4 provides that the State maintains a system of pre-entry national treatment plus negative list management for foreign investment. The pre-entry national treatment mentioned in the preceding paragraph refers to the treatment given to foreign investors and their investment at the stage of investment admission no less than that to domestic investors and their investments; in other words, China will treat foreign investment no less favorably than domestic investment during the investment access stage including the "establishment, acquisition, expansion and such other stages of an enterprise" -unless the negative list provides otherwise. The so-called negative list refers to the special management measures that for the admission of foreign investment in special areas. The State gives national investment outside the negative list.

(Ⅱ) Improve the transparency of foreign investment policies.

(Ⅲ) Ensure that foreign-invested enterprises participate in market competition on an equal footing.

(Ⅳ) Strengthen services for foreign investment.

(Ⅴ) Encouraging and guiding foreign investment in accordance with laws and regulations.

Ⅱ. Establishment of the Foreign Investment Protection System

In order to strengthen the protection of the legitimate rights and interests of foreign investors, the general provisions of the Foreign Investment Law stipulate that the state protects the investment, income and other legitimate rights and interests of foreign investors in China in accordance with law. At the same time, a special chapter on "Investment Protection" has been set up to make provisions in four aspects to provide foreign investment with legal protection that keeps pace with The Times.

(Ⅰ) Strengthening property rights protection for foreign-invested enterprises. Article 20 of the *Foreign Investment Law* stipulates that the State shall not levy on the investment of foreign investors; under special circumstances, the State may, for the public interest, expropriate or requisition the investments of foreign investors in accordance with the provisions of the law. The expropriation or requisition shall be carried out in accordance with legal procedures and fair and reasonable compensation shall be given in a timely manner. Article 21 Foreign investors' capital contributions, profits, capital gains, assets disposal proceeds, intellectual property rights licensing fees, lawfully obtained compensation or compensation, liquidation proceeds, etc. within China may be freely remitted or remitted in RMB or foreign exchange according to law. Article 22 The State protects the intellectual property rights of foreign investors and foreign-invested enterprises and encourages technical cooperation based on voluntary principles and commercial rules.

(Ⅱ) Strengthen the constraints on the formulation of normative documents related to foreign investment.

Article 23 of the *Foreign Investment Law* stipulates that the people's governments at all levels and their relevant departments shall formulate normative documents concerning foreign investment in accordance with the provisions of laws and regulations. Without the basis of laws and administrative regulations, it shall not derogate from the legitimate rights and interests of foreign-invested enterprises or increase their obligations, shall not set conditions for market access and exit, and shall not interfere with the normal production and business activities of foreign-invested enterprises.

(Ⅲ) Encourage local governments to keep their commitments.

Article 24 of the Foreign Investment Law stipulates that the local people's governments at all levels and their relevant departments shall strictly fulfill the policy commitments made in accordance with the law and various types of contracts concluded in accordance with the law; Where it is necessary to change government commitments and contractual agreements due to national or public interests, such changes shall be made in strict accordance with legal authority and procedures, and compensation shall be made for the losses suffered by foreign investors and foreign-invested enterprises as a result.

(Ⅳ) Improve the complaint mechanism for foreign-invested enterprises.

Article 25 and 26 of the Foreign Investment Law provide that the state shall establish a complaint mechanism for foreign-invested enterprises, coordinate and improve major policies and measures in the complaint work of foreign-invested enterprises, and promptly solve problems reported by foreign-invested enterprises; Foreign investors and foreign-invested enterprises may establish and voluntarily join chambers of commerce and associations in accordance with law to safeguard their legitimate rights and interests.

Ⅲ. Establishment of the Foreign Investment Management System

In order to strengthen the administration of foreign investment, the Foreign Investment Law makes provisions in four aspects:

（Ⅰ） Implementation of the negative list management system for foreign investment.

（Ⅱ） Clarify the approval and record-keeping system for foreign investment projects.

（Ⅲ） The establishment of the national foreign investment information reporting system.

（Ⅳ） Establishing a foreign investment security review system.

Part Ⅶ   International Taxation Law

As we all know, taxation is the main source of national fiscal revenue, the economic basis of government organization and state machine operation, and the main form of national income distribution. In domestic tax law, the state is the only subject of tax collection in essence, and the right of tax collection is the embodiment of the supreme sovereign power of the state. In international tax law, the state, as the main body of international tax distribution, is the concrete embodiment of national sovereignty and external independence. Therefore, international tax law is the body of international legal rules and domestic legal norms that adjust the international tax distribution relationship between countries arising from the income of transnational taxpayers.

This part is International Tax Law, which includes from Chapter 15 to Chapter 17. Chapter 15 is about international tax law and international tax jurisdiction, including the concept, characteristics and legal sources of international tax law, as well as the concept, type of international tax jurisdiction and legal provisions of international tax treaties. Chapter 16 is international double taxation, including the concept and causes of international double taxation and the countermeasures to the problem of double taxation. Chapter 17 focuses on international tax avoidance and tax evasion, including the concept and means of international tax avoidance, the difference between international tax evasion and tax avoidance, the main ways of international tax evasion and the prevention of international tax evasion.

众所周知，税收是国家财政收入的主要来源，是政府组织和国家机器运转的经济基础，是国家参与国民收入分配的主要形式。在国内税法中，国家作为实质意义上的唯一征税主体，征税权是国家主权对内最高统治权的具体体现。而在国际税法中，国家作为国际税收的分配主体，则是国家主权对外独立权的具体体现。国际税法因而就是调整国家之间因跨国纳税人的所得而产生的国际税收分配关系的国际法与国内法律规范的总称。

本部分为国际税法，包括第 15 章至第 17 章。其中第 15 章是国际税法和国际税收管辖权，包括国际税法的概念、特征与法律渊源以及国际税收管辖权的概念、类型与国际税收协定。第 16 章是国际双重征税，包括国际双重征税的概念与致因、国际双重征税问题的应对之策。第 17 章是国际避税和逃税，包括国际避税的概念与避税手段、国际逃税和避税的区别、国际逃税方式与预防。

Chapter 15   International Tax Law and Tax Jurisdiction

Section Ⅰ   Introduction to International Tax Law

Ⅰ. Definition of International Tax Law

It refers to the totality of laws and regulations on international tax allocation relationships existing in the objects of transnational tax levy.

The new comprehensive tax law branch system that has gradually developed from the traditional domestic tax law. It is the product of the development of international economic exchanges to a certain historical stage, and it constantly develops and changes with the emergence and development of international tax relations.

Ⅱ. Characteristics of International Tax Law

(Ⅰ) International tax relations are the distribution of economic benefits between two or more countries and taxpayers on transnational tax objects, the distribution of tax rights and interests between relevant countries, and the unity of tax collection and payment relations between them and taxpayers.

(Ⅱ) The tax subjects in the international tax relationship are two countries, and they both have the right to collect tax on the transnational tax objects of taxpayers.

(Ⅲ) The object of international tax relations is the transnational income or transnational property value of taxpayers, which is usually governed by the tax jurisdiction of two countries.

Ⅲ. Sources of International Tax Law

International tax law is a comprehensive legal system composed of domestic law norms and international law norms. The legal sources of international tax law include domestic law norms and international law norms.

The source of domestic law is mainly the domestic tax law formulated by the governments of various countries. In common law countries, in addition to the enactment law on tax, due to the influence of the tradition of case law, the source of international tax law includes the tax cases of the court, whose main function and role in adjusting international tax relations is to determine the tax jurisdiction of the state over the object of transnational tax collection, the scope and degree of tax collection, and the way and procedure of tax collection.

The source of international tax law is mainly the bilateral or multilateral international tax treaties signed by countries to coordinate the taxation of transnational tax objects, as well as the international tax conventions generally followed by countries in international tax practice. Their main role is to coordinate the conflicts between tax jurisdictions of different countries to avoid international double taxation. And establish the international tax administrative assistance relationship.

In practice, the sources of domestic law and international law of international tax law cooperate with each other, complement and penetrate each other, and adjust the international tax relationship together.

Section II   Introduction to International Tax Jurisdiction

I . Definition of International Tax Jurisdiction

Tax jurisdiction is the power of a government to collect taxes, which is the embodiment of national sovereignty in the tax field. Countries always assert their tax jurisdiction based on the personal and territorial effects of sovereignty.

II . Types of International Tax Jurisdiction

(I) Resident tax jurisdiction. Resident tax jurisdiction[①] is the right of taxation that the tax collecting state asserts to exercise based on the legal fact that there is a resident status relationship between the taxpayer and the tax collecting state.

---

① 居民税收管辖权。

The taxpayer under this tax jurisdiction is subject to unlimited tax liability, and the taxing country taxes the taxpayer on all worldwide income or property value.

As for the recognition of the resident status of taxpayers, there is no unified standard in the world, and governments of various countries basically stipulate the identification standards of resident taxpayers in their domestic tax laws, so as to confirm the identity of resident taxpayers.

In the practice of tax law in various countries, there are mainly the following standards for the confirmation of the resident status of natural persons:

A. Domicile standards. The domicile criterion determines the resident or non-resident taxpayer status of a natural person based on the legal fact that he or she has a domicile in the territory of the taxing State.

B. Standard of accommodation. Residence generally refers to the place where a person regularly lives in a certain period of time, and does not have the nature of permanent residence.

C. Time of residence standard. Due to the uncertainty in the actual implementation of the residence standard, more and more countries now adopt the residence time standard to determine the identity of an individual as a resident taxpayer, that is, whether a person stays in the territory of the tax country for a certain period or more, as a standard to classify its residents or non-residents, regardless of whether an individual owns property or a residence in the territory of the country.

According to Article 1 (1) of the newly amended Individual Income Tax Law of China in 2018, individuals who have a domicile in China or have no domicile and have resided in China for a cumulative period of 183 days in a tax year are resident individuals. Residents shall pay individual income tax in accordance with the provisions of this Law on their income derived from sources within and outside China.

The identification of tax resident status of legal persons in various countries mainly includes the standard of the place of registration, the standard of the actual control center or the standard of the location of the head office. China adopts both the standard of the place of registration and the standard of the location of the head office. Article 2, paragraph 2, of the Enterprise Income Tax Law of China stipulates that the term "resident enterprise" as used in this Law refers to an enterprise lawfully established within the territory of China, or an enterprise legally established under the laws of a foreign country, but whose actual management organ is within the territory of China.

(Ⅱ) Citizen tax jurisdiction. The tax jurisdiction of citizens[①] is the tax right claimed by the tax collecting state on the basis of the nationality legal relationship between the taxpayer and the tax collecting state.

Under this tax jurisdiction, the taxing State taxes all worldwide income or property value of a taxpayer who is a national of the taxing State, regardless of whether he or she has an actual economic or property interest with the taxing State. Taxpayers are also subject to unlimited tax liability under this tax jurisdiction.

(Ⅲ) Tax jurisdiction in the source of income. Based on the fact that the income or property subject to taxation originates from or exists in its own territory, the taxing power claimed by the taxing state is called the jurisdiction of the source of income tax law and the jurisdiction of the location of property tax law. Under this type of tax jurisdiction, the taxpayer has limited liability to the government of the taxing state for the portion of his income that originates in the territory of the taxing State or for the portion of the value of his property that exists in territory of the taxing State, while his income and property in territory of his country of residence and other countries fall outside the jurisdiction of taxing State.

It generally comes from four kinds of income tax in the country, including business income, investment income, service income and property income.

At present, the principle of permanent establishment is widely used in the taxation of non-resident business income. The principle of Permanent establishment refers to the principle of taxation of commercial and industrial profits obtained by a non-resident taxpayer through a permanent establishment in the territory.

Individual non-resident income from services includes income from individual independent services and income from non-individual independent services. The former refers to the income obtained by individuals engaged in independent professional activities, such as doctors, lawyers, accountants, etc. The way to establish the source of independent labor income generally adopts the "fixed base principle" or the "183-day rule"; The latter refers to income earned by non-residents in the employment of others, which is generally taxed at source by the country of origin.

For investment income and property income, countries generally adopt the way of withholding from the source of taxation. However, in order to avoid double taxation, countries generally divide taxation rights through bilateral agreements.

---

① 公民税收管辖权。

III. International Tax Treaties

An international tax treaty is a bilateral or multilateral written document signed by two or more sovereign states to coordinate their tax distribution relations and deal with tax issues.

At present, there are two kinds of international tax treaty format documents which are more influential in the world: OECD model and United Nations model.

The full name of the OECD Model is *Model Agreement on the Avoidance of Double Taxation on Income and Property*, which was formulated and published by the Organization for Economic Cooperation and Development in 1977. The model emphasizes that the tax jurisdiction of residents is limited to the tax jurisdiction of the source of income, which is more favorable to capital exporting countries, so it is mostly adopted by developed countries. The United Nations Model is called the *Model Agreement on the Avoidance of Double Taxation between Developed and Developing Countries*, which was formulated and adopted by the Economic and Social Council of the United Nations in 1979. The model focuses on the jurisdiction of source tax, which is more favorable to capital importing countries, so it is mostly adopted by developing countries.

Bilateral tax treaties are the main means to solve the conflict of tax jurisdiction between countries in the international tax law.

Chapter 16　International Double Taxation

Section I　General Introduction to Double Taxation

I. Definition of International Double Taxation

International double taxation is also known as "international duplicate taxation". It means that two or more countries, based on the tax jurisdiction of residents and the tax jurisdiction of income sources, tax the same object of the same tax on the same taxpayer in the same tax period.

Arising on the basis that taxpayers, including natural and legal persons, simultaneously receive income or own property in one or more States other than their State of residence or nationality. It will have a negative impact on international investment activities, cause fiscal and tax conflicts between countries, and hinder the development of international economic and technological cooperation. How to avoid and eliminate international double taxation is one of the most serious problems in international tax law.

II. Causes of International Double Taxation

(I) Positive conflict of jurisdiction. Different countries exercise resident tax jurisdiction and source tax jurisdiction at the same time, so that taxpayers with transnational income, on the one hand, as resident taxpayers, bear tax obligations to their countries of residence on worldwide income; On the other hand, as a non-resident taxpayer, he is liable to pay tax to the source of income on the income obtained in that country, which results in international double taxation.

(II) Positive conflict of resident identification criteria. The different standards for the identification of resident status make the same transnational taxpayer recognized as a resident in different countries, and all have to bear unlimited tax obligation which also produces international double taxation.

(Ⅲ) Positive conflicting criteria for identifying sources of income. The different recognition standards of the source of income make the same transnational income belong to two different countries at the same time, and bear tax obligations to both countries, which results in double taxation.

Section Ⅱ　Resolution of International Double Taxation

Internationally, the principle that the tax jurisdiction of the source country has priority has been widely recognized. Therefore, when the source country has priority tax collection, the country of residence must take corresponding measures to avoid or alleviate international double taxation. At present, the resident country to avoid or mitigate international double taxation methods mainly include tax exemption, credit system, deduction system and tax reduction.

Ⅰ. Tax Exemption

Tax exemption means that one party of the country of residence gives up the jurisdiction of resident tax on the transnational income of its residents from the country of origin that has been taxed in the country of origin under certain conditions.

Ⅱ. Credit System

The credit system is a method adopted by most countries to avoid international double taxation. When this method is adopted, the country of residence calculates the tax payable on the basis of the full amount of the resident taxpayer's foreign income or general property value, but the income tax or property tax already paid by the resident taxpayer in the country of origin is allowed to be deducted from the tax payable in the country of residence. The credit system is often adopted in the bilateral tax treaties signed by our country.

Ⅲ. Deduction System and Tax Deduction

The deduction system means that the country of residence allows the tax paid in the country of origin to be deducted from the total taxable income when the resident taxpayer is taxed. Tax reduction means that the country of residence gives certain reduced care to its residents' income from abroad. Both the deduction system and the deduction system can only reduce the tax burden of taxpayers to a certain extent and alleviate international double taxation, but neither can completely eliminate international double taxation like the tax exemption system and the credit system.

IV. Differences between International Double and Overlapping Taxation[①]

International double taxation means that two or more countries levy the same or similar taxes on the same taxpayer for the same object of taxation at the same time. For example, in 2016, Peter, who settled in Country A, was sent to work in Country B for 10 months and was paid $300000 for his labor. According to the tax laws of both countries, Peter is a tax resident of Country A, not Country B. For Peter's $300000 of labor income, State A can exercise resident tax jurisdiction, and State B can exercise source tax jurisdiction. If both countries tax Peter's $300000 labor income, it constitutes international double taxation.

International overlapping taxation refers to the phenomenon that two or more countries levy tax once on the same income in the hands of different taxpayers with certain economic ties, which usually occurs between companies and shareholders. For example, if company A in Country A invests in wholly owned company B in country B, according to the tax laws of both countries, Company A is a tax resident in Country A and company B is a tax resident in Country B. In 2016, Company B generated a profit of US $1 million, and Country B levied corporate income tax on Company B. Company B distributes $750000 of after-tax profit to Company A as A dividend, and State A taxes Company A's $750000 dividend income. In this case, the act that country B taxes Company B first, and then country A taxes shareholder Company A, constitutes international overlapping taxation.

The main difference between the two is the difference of tax subjects: International double taxation is the same income of the same taxpayer; International overlapping taxation is the imposition of multiple taxes on the same income of different taxpayers.

Companies are increasingly operating worldwide, but tax systems are still primarily organized on a national level. For international companies this means on the one hand

---

① 双重征税与重叠征税的区别。

double taxation and an increased administrative burden, but on the other hand the opportunity to use differences between national tax rules in order to reduce their tax burden. In order to reverse this trend, States all over the world are considering to adapt their national tax rules and bilateral tax agreements.

Chapter 17　International Tax Avoidance and Tax Evasion

Section Ⅰ　International Tax Avoidance

Ⅰ. Definition of International Tax Avoidance

International Tax Avoidance is an act of evading the law, which means that transnational taxpayers make use of the loopholes and differences in tax laws of various countries or the defects in international tax agreements in a lawful way, the act of arranging one's own economic affairs by changing one's place of business, mode of business and the movement and non-movement of persons and property across tax borders in order to minimize or avoid the tax burden.

Ⅱ. The Main Ways of International Tax Avoidance

International tax avoidance is mainly through the international transfer of tax subjects or tax objects to achieve the purpose of tax avoidance.

The transnational movement of tax payers is one of the most common ways of international tax avoidance for natural persons. Since countries generally take legal facts such as the existence of residence, residence or residence within the territory of an individual for a certain period of time as the basis for exercising resident tax jurisdiction, taxpayers often resort to ways such as emigrating abroad or reducing the time of residence in a country to avoid the purpose of resident taxpayer obligations in a country. There are two main ways of international tax avoidance through the transfer of tax objects: The first is the transfer pricing of transnational affiliated enterprises, that is, transnational affiliated enterprises do not according to the general market price standards when conducting transactions, but based on the purpose of avoiding the tax of the relevant countries to determine the transaction price between each other, or artificially raise the transaction price or lower the transaction price, so that profits from high-tax countries to low-tax countries to avoid tax. Second, by setting up a base company in a tax haven, the income and property outside the tax haven are pooled under the account of the base company, so as to achieve the purpose of tax evasion.

Section II　International Tax Evasion

I. Definition of International Tax Evasion

International tax evasion refers to the behavior of transnational taxpayers taking certain means or measures in violation of tax law to reduce or evade their transnational tax obligations.

II. The Differences between International Tax Evasion and Tax Avoidance

(I) In nature, international tax evasion is an illegal act explicitly prohibited by law, while international tax avoidance is just an immoral act, not obviously illegal in nature.

(II) Because of the direct illegality of international tax evasion, the means of its realization are often hidden. Although international tax avoidance is also from the subjective intention of taxpayers, but there is no violation of the law, so the means of its realization can be public.

(III) International tax evasion not only needs to be prevented, but also sanctions, taxpayers should bear the corresponding administrative, civil and criminal legal responsibilities. For international tax avoidance, tax-collecting countries can't hold taxpayers legally responsible. They can only modify or make corresponding supplementary provisions for the imperfections in domestic tax laws or tax agreements, root out loopholes in the tax law to prevent tax avoidance.

III. The Main Ways of International Tax Evasion

There are a variety of ways for taxpayers to engage in international tax evasion, and the more common ways are: Failing to submit tax information to tax authorities, falsely reporting income, fabricating or oversharing deduction items such as costs, expenses and depreciation, and forging account books and receipts and expenditures vouchers.

Ⅳ. Prevention of International Tax Evasion

International tax evasion can be prevented through the enactment of domestic legislation and the strengthening of international cooperation.

(Ⅰ) Domestic legislation. The general legal measures adopted by various countries to control international tax evasion by taxpayers are mainly to strengthen the international tax declaration system, strengthen the tax examination of transnational transaction activities, and implement the taxation of assessed income or consolidated profits.

In view of transnational taxpayers' behavior of avoiding tax through internal transactions, transfer pricing and unreasonable allocation of costs and expenses, countries mainly adopt the principle of normal transactions and the principle of total profit to make adjustments. If a phenomenon that does not conform to this principle occurs, such as the price being raised or lowered for the land, the tax authorities of the countries concerned can readjust their due income and expenses according to this fair market price. The principle of total profit refers to the distribution of the total profit of a multinational company to its affiliates according to a certain standard. It does not require the tax department of the relevant country to review every income and expense incurred between the affiliates directly, but allows them to distribute it according to the transfer price established internally.

In view of the behavior of transnational taxpayers using international tax havens to evade tax, the legal control measures implemented by various countries can be divided into three types:

A. Pass laws to prohibit taxpayers from setting up base companies in tax havens.

B. Prohibit improper profit shifting.

C. The deferral of tax treatment for domestic shareholders on undistributed dividend income in the base company is abolished, thus discouraging taxpayers from setting up base companies in tax havens to accumulate profits.

(Ⅱ) International cooperation. It is difficult to combat the increasingly serious international tax evasion and tax avoidance by relying solely on domestic legal measures. Only through international cooperation and comprehensive application of domestic and international legal measures can we effectively curb the phenomenon of international tax evasion. At present, countries mainly assist each other in tax collection by establishing an international tax information exchange system. In order to prevent international tax evasion, international cooperation methods such as anti – arbitrage agreement clauses should be added to international tax treaties.

Part Ⅷ International Economic Dispute Settlement Law

With the deepening of economic globalization, transnational economic and trade activities between countries are becoming more and more frequent. Due to the diversification of interest subjects, contract disputes and economic contradictions between different national interest subjects are unavoidable, which are characterized by various types of disputes, complex dispute subjects, and diverse legal norms and business habits involved. Objectively, it is necessary to provide diversified solutions for disputes in cross-border trade, investment, finance, project contracting and other fields between countries.

This part is the legal system for settlement of international economic disputes, including from Chapter 18 to Chapter 21. Chapter 18 focuses on major approaches for the settlement of international economic disputes, including overview, the legal ways and the legal rules to deal with the international economic disputes. Chapter 19 is the dispute settlement through diplomacy, including the concept and characteristics of diplomatic settlement and the actual methods of diplomatic settlement. Chapter 20 is dispute settlement in municipal courts, consisted of the jurisdiction of domestic courts, choice of forum clause and choice of law clause. Chapter 21 focuses on international tribunal, including the dispute settlement mechanisms of not only the International Court of Justice, but also the WTO and the International Centre for Settlement of Investment Disputes.

随着经济全球化程度的不断加深，各国之间的跨国经济贸易活动日益频繁。由于利益主体的多元化，不同国家利益主体之间的合同纠纷与经济矛盾难以避免，且呈现出争端类型多样、纠纷主体复杂、关涉的法律规范和商业习惯多样等特点，客观上需要针对国家间跨境贸易、投资、金融、工程承包等领域的纠纷提供多元化的解决途径。

本部分是国际经济争端解决法律制度，包括第 18 章至第 21 章。其中第 18 章是国际经济争端的主要解决途径，包括概述、国际经济争端处理的法律途径与法律规则。第 19 章是国际经济争端的外交解决途径，包括外交解决途径的概念和特点以及具体方法。第 20 章是国际经济争端的国内司法解决途径，包括国内法院的管辖权、法院的选择条款和法律适用的选择条款。第 21 章是国际经济争端的国际法解决途径，包括国际法院争端解决机制、WTO 争端解决机制及国际投资争端解决中心争端解决机制。

Chapter 18   Major Approaches for the Settlement of Regulation-Related International Economic Disputes

Section I   Introduction of International Economic Dispute Settlement Law

International economic dispute refers to the legal dispute between international economic law subjects in international economic exchanges. Since the subject of international economic law includes private individuals, states and international economic organizations, international economic disputes include legal disputes arising from economic exchanges between private individuals of different nationalities, between countries, between international economic organizations, between private individuals of countries and other countries, between international economic organizations and private individuals, and between countries and international economic organizations.

Section II   Legal Ways for Handling International Economic Disputes

The resolution of international economic disputes among people who are citizens of different countries, with business deals that span continents and cultures, can be fraught with difficulty and uncertainty due to the significant differences in legal systems, cultures politics, and national policies of economic development. In addition, these problems also make resolution more time-consuming and costly. The legal ways to deal with international economic disputes are judicial settlement and arbitration settlement.

I . Judicial Settlement Methods

(I) International judicial solutions. International judicial settlement refers to the parties that refer international economic disputes to the International Court of Justice for settlement The International Court of Justice is one of the principal statutory bodies of the United Nations. Parties to proceedings in the International Court of Justice are limited to States and no organization, group or individual may become a party. The Court's jurisdiction includes, all cases submitted by States parties: all matters specified in the Charter of the United Nations or existing treaties and agreements; The four categories of disputes concerning the interpretation of treaties, any question of international law, the existence of any fact which, if established, constitutes a breach of an international obligation, and the nature and scope of reparation due to a breach of an international obligation are premised on the declaration of acceptance of compulsory jurisdiction by the parties. It follows that the Court's functions in dealing with international economic disputes are very limited.

(II) Domestic judicial solutions. Domestic judicial settlement means that international economic disputes are submitted to national courts for settlement. National courts mainly hear economic disputes between private individuals of different nationalities. In view of the fact that the determination of jurisdiction is a prerequisite for the acceptance of a particular case and the conduct of litigation, and is often closely related to the application of law, thus directly affecting the outcome of the trial of the case, the relevant laws of some countries clearly specify the jurisdiction of their courts over such disputes. Since there are currently no generally accepted rules regulating the jurisdiction of national courts over such disputes, such disputes inevitably fall within the jurisdiction of several national courts, which gives rise to the issue of conflict of jurisdiction of domestic courts.

National courts may also hear economic disputes between States and private individuals in other States. A number of countries, particularly in Latin America, have established through domestic legislation the exclusive jurisdiction of their courts to hear economic disputes between private individuals in their own countries and those in other countries. In the event of an economic dispute between a State and a private individual of another State, the private individual of another State may also seek relief in the courts of his or her State or in the courts of a third State, but the question of the immunity of the State and its property may then arise.

Ⅱ. International Arbitration

Arbitration means that the parties voluntarily submit the dispute to a third party for adjudication. In the settlement of an international investment dispute, a third party shall be a relevant institution of a third country or an international institution other than the parties. The main feature of arbitration is that the arbitrator makes a decision on the dispute as a judge. Such an award shall generally be final and binding on both parties. If one party fails to automatically enforce the award, the other party has the right to apply to the court for enforcement. Arbitration institutions are non-governmental organizations with no legal jurisdiction. Arbitration institutions accept relevant cases according to the arbitration agreement between the two parties. The judicial settlement method is difficult to apply to disputes between states or between states and private individuals due to the limitation of jurisdiction. However, the arbitration method is generally applicable to all kinds of international disputes with the consent of the parties to the dispute.

Arbitration settlement methods include AD hoc arbitration tribunal and permanent arbitration tribunal. The AD hoc arbitral tribunal shall be formed according to the consent of the parties to the dispute and in accordance with certain procedures, and shall be dissolved upon completion of the trial. Permanent arbitration institutions are established according to international treaties or domestic laws, which can be divided into three types: global permanent arbitration institutions, regional permanent arbitration institutions and national permanent arbitration institutions. In general, a permanent arbitral institution is conducive to the settlement of disputes because it can provide the parties to the dispute with the necessary conditions for the conduct of arbitration, including arbitration venues and services, and it can facilitate the rendering of awards and make technical assessments as to whether the awards are binding.

Although there are many similarities between the permanent arbitration institutions handling international economic disputes, they have their own characteristics in terms of jurisdiction, application of law and arbitration awards. Therefore, when looking for a suitable arbitration institution for dispute settlement, the relevant situation should be fully understood in order to choose a more suitable arbitration institution to safeguard the interests of the party effectively.

Section Ⅲ　Legal Norms for Handling International Economic Disputes

The legal norms for dealing with international economic disputes are composed of the relevant norms of international law and domestic law.

Ⅰ. Relevant Norms of International Law

The international community has concluded a series of international treaties to deal with disputes, particularly economic disputes, between States and private individuals or between individuals of different nationalities. Such treaties fall broadly into three categories:

(Ⅰ) International treaties on administration of justice and arbitration. In judicial terms, such treaties include the Statute of the International Court of Justice, 1945, the Convention on Civil Procedure, 1954, the Convention on Service Abroad of Litigation and Non-Litigation Instruments in Civil and Commercial Cases, 1965, and the Convention on the Recognition and Enforcement of Foreign Judgments in Civil and Commercial Cases, 1970.

(Ⅱ) International treaties dealing specifically with international economic disputes. International treaties dealing with international economic disputes, such as the Convention on the Settlement of Investment Disputes between States and Private Parties (hereinafter referred to as the Washington Convention) and the Understanding on Rules and Procedures for the Settlement of Disputes (DSU) in Annex Ⅱ to the WTO Agreement, provide specific provisions on the methods of mediation, arbitration or other special settlement of international economic disputes. The Washington Convention is a major achievement of the international community in adjusting international investment relations and improving the international investment environment by means of multilateral investment treaties. It plays an increasingly important role in resolving international investment disputes. The Convention entered into force in October 1966. Under the Convention, the International Centre for the Settlement of Investment Disputes (ICSID) was established as an international specialized body for the settlement of investment disputes between a Contracting State and nationals of another Contracting State. The DSU establishes the WTO's basic system of dispute settlement. It provides for the scope of application of the WTO dispute settlement mechanism, the governing body, the strengt-hening of the multilateral system of dispute settlement procedures, and special procedures involving the least developed members.

The innovation of the WTO dispute settlement mechanism is to set up a special "Dispute Settlement Body" (DSB), whose main functions include the establishment of panels, the adoption of panels and appellate body reports, the maintenance of the supervision of decisions and recommendations, and the authorization to suspend concessions and other obligations under the covered agreement. The main procedures of the mechanism include consultation, good offices mediation, conciliation and arbitration, panels of experts, appellate bodies, and enforcement of awards. Compared with the GATT dispute settlement procedure, the WTO dispute settlement mechanism has strengthened its distinctive features as a means of judicial settlement, mainly in the aspects of sound dispute settlement organization, quasi−automation of dispute settlement procedure, setting of dispute settlement schedule and strengthening of enforcement procedure. On December 11, 2001, China joined the WTO and accepted the WTO dispute settlement system.

(Ⅲ) Relevant norms of bilateral economic treaties. A large number of bilateral economic and trade treaties have made specific provisions on mediation, arbitration or other special settlement methods for dealing with international economic disputes. China has signed a series of bilateral investment treaties since 1980, most of which provide for AD hoc arbitration of international economic disputes.

Ⅱ. Relevant Norms of Domestic Law

National legislation generally advocates jurisdiction over international economic disputes within national territory. Some countries have also adopted foreign−related economic legislation and civil procedure laws, specifically stipulating ways of mediation, arbitration or judicial settlement of international economic disputes.

Chapter 19   Dispute Settlement Through Diplomacy

Section I   Definition and Features of Diplomatic Methods

I. Definition of Diplomatic Methods

Diplomatic settlement of disputes refers to the settlement of disputes by diplomatic means by the States concerned, which applies to any type of dispute settlement and does not affect the adoption by the parties of other means of dispute settlement at the same time or in the future.

II. Features of Diplomatic Methods

Diplomatic methods are characterized by: Not adhering to legal provisions, but trying to clarify facts and fully express views, and trying to reach a compromise solution acceptable to all parties to the dispute, with great flexibility. From the initiation of dispute settlement to the end of dispute settlement and the implementation of dispute settlement results, the will and wishes of the parties to the dispute are fully respected and are not mandatory.

Section II   Type of Diplomatic Methods

I. Negotiation and Consultations

Negotiation refers to the method by which two or more subjects of international law negotiate and reach an agreement on the issues they dispute in order to settle the dispute.

Consultations are similar to negotiations, but they can be expanded to include a number of neutral countries and essentially adopt a consensus voting procedure. In general, States parties to negotiations or consultations are not obliged to enter into binding agreements.

The most important feature of negotiations and consultations is the direct exchange of views between the parties or their negotiators, often directly and face—to—face. There is some debate as to whether a discussion of a dispute within an international organization can be considered a negotiation. In the South West Africa case, South Africa submitted a preliminary objection that the discussions on South West Africa at the United Nations did not indicate that the dispute was beyond a negotiated settlement, and that the fact that the discussions in which the parties had participated had ended in an impasse showed that the dispute was beyond a negotiated settlement. In their dissenting opinion, Judges Spencer and Fitzmaurice held that discussions in international organizations were no substitute for direct negotiations between the parties.

The advantage of negotiation and consultation is that the parties have the greatest degree of direct control over the principles, methods, advances and choices of dispute settlement, which is conducive to the parties directly safeguarding their own rights and interests, and is most likely to reach a satisfactory settlement between the parties. The limitations of negotiation and consultation, however, lie in the obvious impossibility of negotiation if the parties to the dispute refuse to make any representations with each other. If one party does not recognize the other party as a subject of international law, it is impossible to negotiate. Negotiations will be fruitless if the two sides' positions are opposite and there is no common interest to bridge the gap. In addition, negotiations are more likely to be influenced by the balance of power between the parties than third-party independent arbitration or judicial proceedings.

II. Good Offices and Mediation

Good offices and mediation are methods by which a third party assists the parties to resolve a dispute. Mediation refers to the activities taken by a third party at the request of the parties concerned or on its own initiative to promote the settlement of disputes through direct negotiations between the two parties, but the mediating country does not participate in the negotiations between the parties concerned and does not propose a dispute settlement solution. For example, if there is a dispute between two countries, the Secretary-General of the United Nations comes forward to persuade the two countries to settle the dispute through negotiations, but the Secretary-General of the United Nations does not participate in the negotiations between the two countries, and the behavior of the Secretary-General of the United Nations is a good office.

Mediation means that a third party, at the request of the parties concerned or with the consent of both parties, puts forward substantive proposals as the basis for negotiations as a mediator, and organizes and directly participates in negotiations between the parties concerned. For example, in the event of A dispute between two countries, the United Nations Secretary-General not only persuades the two countries to settle the dispute through negotiations, but also participates in the negotiations between the two countries and ultimately helps to reach a settlement of the dispute. The conciliator's proposal is not binding in itself, and the conciliator assumes no legal obligation or consequence for the conduct of the conciliation or its success or failure. There is also generally no obligation to monitor and guarantee the outcome of mediation.

The fundamental difference between good offices and mediation is whether a third party is directly involved in the negotiations between the disputing States.

III. Inquiry and Conciliation

Inquiry means that in a dispute involving only factual issues, where the dispute has not been resolved through negotiation and consultation, the parties to the dispute agree to establish an international commission of inquiry to find out the facts through investigation, so as to facilitate the settlement of the dispute. It mainly applies to disputes where the basic facts are unclear. The aim is to establish the facts and prepare the ground for negotiations, without necessarily making special proposals. The inquiry was first established in 1899 under the Convention for the Peaceful Settlement of International Disputes. Article 9 of the Convention recommends that States parties, in cases of international disputes which do not involve national honor or fundamental interests but arise solely from differences of opinion on the facts, should, if the parties to the dispute are unable to resolve them by diplomatic means, establish international commissions of inquiry, as far as the circumstances permit, to resolve the factual issues on the basis of an impartial investigation in order to facilitate the settlement of the dispute. The Second Hague Peace Conference in 1907 drew on the practical and successful experience of international investigations during the two conferences and provided for more detailed investigation procedures in the revised Convention. In particular, article 35 emphasizes that the mandate of the international Commission of Inquiry is to investigate the circumstances of the case and to issue a report that is "limited to stating the facts" and in no way "of the nature of an arbitral award", placing in the hands of the parties to the dispute the right to determine the validity of the report. The purposes of the United Nations include the "settlement of international disputes by peaceful means", and the Security Council (UNSC) mainly adopts this approach. After 1913, the United States and more than 30 countries in Latin America and Europe signed a series of bilateral treaties called "Bryan Treaties" (named after the then US Secretary of State Bryan), creating a permanent international Commission of inquiry system, placing more emphasis on submitting disputes that have not been settled through negotiations to the Commission of Inquiry, expanding the scope of disputes applicable to the Commission of Inquiry. It also stipulates that the parties to the dispute shall not commence war operations until the report of the Commission of Inquiry has been published.

Conciliation, also known as mediation, refers to the submission of a dispute to a neutral international conciliation commission, which establishes the facts and makes reports and recommendations to bring the parties to an agreement to resolve the dispute. By its nature, conciliation seems to be a system between the methods of investigation and arbitration. The main purpose of the investigation is to clarify the facts, and it does not involve recommendations or judgments on the settlement of the dispute. For reconciliation, finding out the facts through investigation is only the first step. More importantly, it is necessary to make reports and recommendations on the basis of facts and actively help the parties to reach an agreement. Both arbitration and judicial methods emphasize the basis of law, and the award is legally binding, while the settlement report is not legally binding, although it must respect the facts and strive to be fair, but it does not necessarily need to be based on law.

Like the inquiry system, conciliation was gradually established on the basis of the Hague Convention for the Peaceful Settlement of International Disputes of 1899 and, after 1913, the Blaine Peace Treaty system. The General Protocol for the Peaceful Settlement of International Disputes (1928) and the Revised General Agreement for the Peaceful Settlement of International Disputes (1949) further formed an independent system of reconciliation.

In international disputes, due to the unclear basic facts so that the disputing parties cannot unified understanding, usually by the two parties to the dispute through an agreement, the establishment of an investigation committee or conciliation committee to investigate the facts of the dispute and submit a report, by the parties themselves to resolve the dispute. Investigation only solves factual issues, and conciliation is to further propose substantive solutions to disputes on the basis of investigation.

In practice, once a dispute occurs, the parties generally first seek to resolve the dispute through direct negotiation and consultation, and only when the dispute cannot be resolved through direct negotiation and consultation will they seek mediation, mediation, mediation, arbitration or court litigation and other third-party dispute settlement methods. Many treaties make negotiation and consultation the first obligation to resort to, and many make negotiation and consultation a prerequisite for further initiation of arbitration or court proceedings to settle disputes. However, there is no general obligation for the parties to settle their disputes through negotiation and consultation, unless specific obligations are specified in other express agreements. Once negotiations and consultations have become treaty obligations, then the parties must negotiate in good faith, which does not require the parties to reach an agreement, nor does it imply the appearance of formality through negotiation, but rather requires the parties to make good faith efforts to reach an agreement.

Chapter 20   Dispute Settlement in
Municipal Courts

Domestic judicial settlement means that international economic disputes are submitted to national courts for settlement. National courts mainly hear economic disputes between private individuals of different nationalities. Usually, a lawsuit will not proceed if the court does not have jurisdiction.

I . Jurisdiction

In view of the fact that the determination of jurisdiction is a prerequisite for the acceptance of a particular case and the conduct of litigation, and is often closely related to the application of law, thus directly affecting the outcome of the trial of the case, the relevant laws of some countries clearly specify the jurisdiction of their courts over such disputes.

Since there are currently no generally accepted rules regulating the jurisdiction of national courts over such disputes, such disputes inevitably fall within the jurisdiction of several national courts, which gives rise to the issue of conflict of jurisdiction of domestic courts.

II . Choice of Forum Clauses

Even in the absence of the issue of conflict of jurisdiction in domestic courts, difficulties arise when parties to a dispute of different nationalities choose the court to administer their dispute. In practice, parties wish to choose their national courts for the settlement of disputes because they are more familiar with their national legal system and can expect the benefits of their national courts. In economic disputes between private individuals from developed and developing countries, the issue of choosing a court is further complicated by the possibility that they are not familiar with each other and do not trust each other's legal systems. One way to solve such problems is to choose a court in a third country. In making this choice, there is also the flexibility to choose the substantive law, including the national law of the party concerned or the law of a third State. To seek a more just and reasonable settlement of disputes, the parties may also choose a court specialized in hearing such disputes.

National courts may also hear economic disputes between States and private individuals in other States. A number of countries, particularly in Latin America, have established through domestic legislation the exclusive jurisdiction of their courts to hear economic disputes between private individuals in their own countries and those in other countries.

In the event of an economic dispute between a State and a private individual of another State, the private individual of another State may also seek relief in the courts of his or her State or in the courts of a third State, but the question of the immunity of the State and its property may then arise. In the practice of most States, if a foreign private person has the host State as the defendant in a complaint against the court of his or her home State or a third State, the relevant action can only proceed with the consent of the host State.

National courts cannot settle economic disputes between States, between or between international economic organizations because, in accordance with generally accepted principles of international law and international practice, States and international economic organizations enjoy judicial immunity unless they waive that right. In practice, there is no precedent in which both parties to a dispute are States, international economic organizations, or one party is a state and the other is an international economic organization. Both voluntarily waive their judicial immunity and submit to the jurisdiction of the domestic courts of a third country.

(I) Forum non convenience. This doctrine refers to an appropriate forum－even though competent under the law—may divest itself of jurisdiction if, for the convenience of the litigants and the witnesses, it appears that the action should proceed in another forum n which the action might originally have been brought. Forum non convenience allows a court to exercise its discretion to avoid the oppression or vexation that might result from automatically honoring plaintiff's forum choice. However, dismissal on the basis of forum non—convenience also requires that there be an alternative forum in which the suit can be prosecuted. It must appear that jurisdiction over all parties can be secured and that complete relief can be obtained in the supposedly more convenient court. Further, in at least some states, it has been held that the doctrine cannot be successfully invoked when the plaintiff is resident of the forum state since, effectively, one of the functions of the state courts is to provide a tribunal in which their residents can obtain an adjudication of their grievances. But in most instances a balancing of the convenience to all the parties will be considered and no one factor will preclude a forum non convenience dismissal, as long as another forum is available.

(II) Minimum contacts. This legal doctrine requires that before a person or a company is brought before a court, it must have had minimum contacts with the forum. This requirement is based on the premise that bringing an individual or corporation before a court when the person has never had legal contract with that place would be unfair. This concept has important implications as to when a company has had sufficient contracts that it can be brought before a particular court on a tort, contract, or statutory claim.

III. Choice of Law Clauses

Because the validity of a contractual forum selection clause may turn on its validity under the law which governs the contract, the validity of the Choice of Law Clause assumes an added importance. Generally, in common law and European civil law jurisdictions, parties may choose the law which they wish to govern their contract relationship, as long as the law chosen is that of a place which has a substantial relationship to the parties and to the international business transaction, and is not contrary to a strong public policy of the place where a suit is brought.

Chapter 21   International Tribunal

Section I   International Court of Justice

Court settlement of international disputes means that the parties to the dispute submit the dispute to the International Court of Justice or a special international tribunal for trial and make a legally binding judgment in accordance with international law. As one of the principal organs of the United Nations, the International Court of Justice is the most representative international judicial body in the international community.

I. Composition of the International Court of Justice

The International Court of Justice is the principal judicial organ of the United Nations established under the Charter of the United Nations. The Statute of the International Court of Justice is an integral part of the Charter, and the States Members of the United Nations are ex officio parties[①] to the Statute. The International Court of Justice was formally established on 6 February 1946.

In accordance with the provisions of the Charter of the United Nations and the Statute of the International Court of Justice, the International Court of Justice shall consist of 15 judges, of whom no two shall be nationals of the same State. Judges are nominated by groups of States to the Permanent Court of Arbitration, with no more than four members from each group, on the basis of which the Secretary–General of the United Nations submits the nominations to the General Assembly and the Security Council. Candidates can only be elected if they obtain an absolute majority of votes in both the General Assembly and the Security Council. When the Security Council votes, the permanent members cannot exercise their veto power. It is customary for permanent

---

① 当然当事人。

members of the Security Council to be elected to the Court. Judges serve nine-year terms and are eligible for re-election.

For example, on 28 May 2010, Shi Jiuyong, a Chinese member of the International Court of Justice, resigned, leaving the seat of the Court vacant. The UN General Assembly and the UN Security Council held the by-election of judges on June 29, the same year. Jiang Hanqin, a senior Chinese diplomat, was elected as an international judge by a large number of votes, with 15 votes in the UN Security Council and 150 votes in the UN General Assembly respectively.

In cases involving the judge's own country, the judge has the right to participate in the recusal system① does not apply, unless he or she participated in the case before assuming office② as an international judge. In a case before the Court, if the Court has judges of the nationality of one of the parties, the other party shall have the right to appoint one of the judges to sit in the trial of the case. If neither party has a judge of its own nationality, each party may select a judge to sit in the trial of the case③. Such AD hoc judges are called AD litem judges. ④ They are on a full equal footing with other judges in their participation in the adjudication process⑤, but are not entitled to participate in other International Court Justice trials and therefore become AD hoc judges.

For example, when a dispute arises between two countries, they jointly agree to submit the dispute to the International Court of Justice of the United Nations. If State A finds that one of the 15 current judges of the International Court of Justice is a judge of State B, State A has no right to ask the judge of State B to recue himself on the grounds of nationality, unless there is evidence that the judge participated in the dispute on behalf of State B before becoming an international judge. However, A State has the right to select one of its own to participate in the trial of the case as a judge AD hoc before the International Court of Justice, and to participate in the judgment of the case with exactly the same rights and obligations as other judges.

II. Jurisdiction of the International Court of Justice

(I) Contentious jurisdiction. In exercising its jurisdiction, the International

---

① The recusal system: 回避制度。
② Assuming office: 就职。
③ To sit in the trial of the case: 参加案件的审理。
④ 这种专案法官被称为诉讼法官。
⑤ In the adjudication process: 在裁决过程中。

Court of Justice involves two aspects: Jurisdiction in person and jurisdiction in matter.

A. Jurisdiction personae. That is, who can be a party to proceedings before the Court. According to the Statute of the International Court of Justice, there are three categories of States that may be parties to proceedings before the Court: (i) Member States of the United Nations; (ii) States that are not Members of the United Nations but are parties to the Statute of the International Court of Justice; (iii) A State that is not a Member of the United Nations or a party to the Statute may also become a party to proceedings before the Court if, in accordance with Article 35 of the Charter of the United Nations, it deposits in advance with the Registry of the Court a declaration indicating its willingness to submit to the jurisdiction of the Court in accordance with the Charter and the Statute and its rules, and undertakes to earnestly implement the judgments of the Court. These three categories of States are on a fully equal footing in the proceedings of the International Court of Justice. No international organization, legal person or individual may be a party to proceedings before the Court.

B. Jurisdiction over matters, which can be subject to the jurisdiction of the International Court of Justice. In accordance with article 36 of the Statute of the International Court of Justice, the scope of the jurisdiction of the International Court of Justice has three aspects: (i) Voluntary jurisdiction means all cases voluntarily submitted by agreement between the parties after the outbreak of a dispute; (ii) Jurisdictional agreement refers to the referral of a particular dispute or matter to the jurisdiction of the International Court of Justice by the parties to the dispute in accordance with the provisions of the Charter of the United Nations and treaties binding on them; (iii) Optional compulsory jurisdiction means that a State party to the Statute may at any time declare that certain legal disputes recognize the compulsory jurisdiction of the International Court of Justice in respect of any other State that accepts the same obligation, without the need to enter into a special agreement. My country has made no declaration of acceptance of the optional compulsory jurisdiction of the International Court of Justice.

(II) Advisory jurisdiction. Advisory jurisdiction means that the International Court of Justice, as the judicial organ of the United Nations, provides authoritative opinions on legal questions. Under the provisions of the Charter, United Nations bodies, including the General Assembly and its Interim Committee, the Security Council, the Economic and Social Council, the Trusteeship Council, committees requesting review of judgment of the Administrative Tribunal, and specialized or other United Nations agencies authorized by the General Assembly, may request an advisory opinion from the

Court on any legal question relating to the performance of their functions. No other state, group or individual has the right to request an advisory opinion from the Court. Although advisory opinions issued by the Court are not legally binding, they have an important impact on the settlement of relevant issues and the development of international law.

III. Judgment of the International Court of Justice

In all cases before the Court, except in cases of suspension of proceedings, the Court rendered its judgment. After written and oral proceedings, the judges of the Court hold private deliberations and draft judgments vote on them. The judges may not abstain from voting, and the judgment is passed by a majority of the judges. Any judge, whether or not he or she agrees with the majority opinion, may attach his or her personal opinion to the judgment. There are actually two kinds of personal opinions: agreeing with the conclusion of the judgment, but not agreeing with the reasons on which the judgment is based, called individual opinions; Disagreeing with neither the conclusion nor the grounds on which the judgment is based is called an objection. The judgment shall be read at the session of the Court and shall be binding on the parties from the date of its announcement.

The judgment of the International Court of Justice is final. Once the judgment is made, it will have a binding force on the case and the State concerned, and the State concerned must comply with it. If a party refuses to comply with the judgment, he may appeal to the Security Council, which may make relevant recommendations or decide to take measures to enforce the judgment. There has never been a case in which a judgment has been rejected since the court was established. In the event of a dispute as to the meaning or scope of a judgment, the parties may request an interpretation from the International Court of Justice. If, after the judgment has been rendered, new facts have been discovered that may affect the judgment and could not be known during the course of the proceedings, the parties may apply to the court for a review of the judgment, the review procedure is the same as the proceedings. An application for review should be made no later than 6 months after the discovery of new facts and no more than 10 years from the date of the judgment.

Section II   WTO Dispute Settlement Mechanism

I. Overview of the World Trade Organization

The predecessor of the World Trade Organization (WTO) was the General Agreement on Tariffs and Trade (GATT). The General Agreement on Tariffs and Trade has two meanings: first, it is an international agreement, the General Agreement on Tariffs and Trade, signed in 1947 and provisionally applied on January 1, 1948; Secondly, it also refers to the international body that governs the agreement, because the General Agreement on Tariffs and Trade has no organizational provisions, no organizational structure, personnel and budget, the General Agreement on Tariffs and Trade does not have the status of an international organization in the strict sense of international law.

The General Agreement on Tariffs and Trade presided over eight rounds of trade negotiations, in the eighth round, the Uruguay Round, negotiators decided to establish a formal trade organization, the World Trade Organization. In accordance with the Agreement Establishing the World Trade Organization reached in the Uruguay Round of the General Agreement on Tariffs and Trade (GATT), the World Trade Organization was formally established and began to operate on January 1, 1995, with its headquarters in Geneva, Switzerland. The World Trade Organization (WTO) is a permanent international organization established by WTO agreements ratified by the legislatures of its members and has the status of an international organization under international law.

The World Trade Organization replaced the General Agreement on Tariffs and Trade, and since then, the General Agreement on Tariffs and Trade as an organization has ceased to exist. However, the General Agreement on Tariffs and Trade (GATT) remained as a rule, modified and supplemented as part of the World Trade Organization (WTO) Agreement in the form of GATT 1994. Parties to the General Agreement on Tariffs and Trade became founding members of the World Trade Organization.

II. WTO Membership and Legal Framework

(I) WTO membership. WTO members include governments and governments of separate customs territories. A separate customs territory is a territory that does not have independent and complete national sovereignty but has full sovereignty in the conduct of foreign trade relations and other matters stipulated in the WTO agreement, such as Hong Kong, Macao and Taiwan of China.

(II) The legal framework of the WTO. The legal system of the WTO is a unified multilateral trade legal system with the Agreement establishing the WTO as its core.

Annexes I, II and III are collectively referred to as multilateral trade agreements, which are binding on all members and must be complied with by all members. Annex IV, known as plurilateral trade agreements, applies only to WTO members who have specifically expressed their acceptance of their binding, and is not binding on those who do not.

III. WTO Dispute Settlement Mechanism

(I) Scope of application of the dispute settlement mechanism. The WTO's dispute settlement mechanism is characterized by uniformity and applies to disputes arising from any WTO agreement between any member and is based on the Understanding on Dispute Settlement Rules and Procedures, which forms part of the WTO's multilateral trading system.

(II) Types of disputes to be settled by the dispute settlement body. The types of disputes settled by the Dispute Settlement Body of the World Trade Organization mainly include the three types specified in Article 23 of the General Agreement on Tariffs and Trade:

A. Violation complaint. This is the main type of dispute. The complaining party must prove that the accused party breached the terms of the agreement. The determination of such disputes often requires the respondent to repeal or modify the measures in question. For example, in 2007, the United States sued China that Article 4 of the Copyright Law violated the WTO Agreement on Trade-Related Aspects of Intellectual Property Rights (TRIPs), which was a violation complaint, and China lost the lawsuit and amended Article 4 of the Copyright Law in 2010.

B. Non-violation complaint. The review of such a complaint does not investigate whether the accused party has violated the terms of the relevant agreement, but only deals with whether the accused party's measures are impaired or lost the benefits enjoyed by the complaining party under the relevant agreement. For the determination of such disputes, the accused party has no obligation to cancel the relevant measures, only to make compensation. For example, if country A sues country B for adopting a series of promotion and protection measures for a certain product in its territory, which makes it difficult for the related products of Country A to enter the market of Country B, and Country A thus suffers certain losses in the market of Country B, this complaint is a non-violation complaint. If Country A succeeds in its appeal, Country B does not need to cancel or modify its domestic promotion and protection measures. However, compensation should be made for the loss of interests of A State.

C. Other circumstances. So far, there have been no disputes of any kind other than those mentioned above.

(Ⅲ) The basic procedures for dispute settlement. The basic procedures of WTO dispute settlement include consultation procedures, panel procedures, Appellate body review procedures, procedures for the adoption of panel and appellate body reports, and procedures for the supervision and implementation of awards and recommendations. In addition to the above basic procedures, the WTO dispute settlement procedures also include good offices, mediation, arbitration and other non-essential procedures.

A. Consultation. Consultation is a prerequisite for the application for the establishment of a panel, but the matters of consultation and the adequacy of the consultation have nothing to do with the application for the establishment of a panel and the ruling to be made by the panel. Consultation is a necessary procedure in the basic procedure of WTO dispute settlement.

Under Article 4 of DSU, each Member undertakes to accord sympathetic consideration' to and afford adequate opportunity for consultation regarding any representations made by another Member concerning measures affecting the operation of any covered agreement taken within the territory of the former. In other words, each member is obligated to undertake consultation to settle their dispute rather than direct panel.

This Article further states that if a request for consultations is made pursuant to a covered agreement, the Member to which the request is made shall, unless otherwise mutually agreed, reply to the request within 10 days after the date of its receipt and shall enter into consultations in good faith within a period of no more than 30 days after the date of receipt of the request, with a view to reaching a mutually satisfactory solution. If the Member does not respond within 10 days after the date of receipt of the request, or does not enter into consultations within a period of no more than 30 days, or a period otherwise mutually agreed, after the date of receipt of the request, then the Member that requested the holding of consultations may proceed directly to request the establishment of a panel.

B. Panel procedure. Panel procedure is the core procedure of the WTO dispute settlement mechanism. If the consultation has not resolved the dispute within 60 days from the date of the request for consultation, the complainant may apply for the establishment of a panel, which is a non-permanent body to settle the dispute. The panel is generally composed of three members, or five members if the parties agree. The members of the panel are generally selected after consultation between the parties to the dispute from the list of expert panels existing in the WTO Secretariat. They are appointed by the Director-General of the WTO only if the parties cannot reach agreement.

Both the complaining party and the accused party shall bear the corresponding burden of proof for their claims or claims. After one party initially proves the authenticity of its claims or claims, the other party shall refute them. Finally, the expert group shall decide which evidence to accept and make a ruling based on its assessment of the relevant evidence. The Panel hears cases within the limits of its competence established by the Complainant in its application for the establishment of the Panel. It does not have the authority to listen to and decide on claims not made by the disputing parties. The Panel may, on the basis of the necessity for an effective settlement of the dispute, refrain from reviewing some of the claims brought by the complainant under different rules, if it considers that the dispute has been effectively resolved, which is called the principle of judicial economy.

The final report of the Panel, which shall normally be submitted to the parties to the dispute within six months, shall set out the findings of the facts, the application of the relevant World Trade Organization rules, and the underlying reasons for the findings and recommendations.

C. The appellate body review procedure. The appellate review system is a major feature of the WTO dispute settlement mechanism. Within 60 days of the publication of the panel's report, any disputing party can appeal to the Appellate Body. The appellate Body is a permanent body in the dispute settlement body, and appeals cases are heard by a collegiate panel composed of three of the seven members of the Appellate Body, but the final report of the appellate body is collectively reviewed and discussed.

The Appellate Body may overturn, modify or rescind the findings and conclusions of the Panel. When overturning the relevant decisions and conclusions, in order to achieve an effective settlement of the dispute, if the facts determined by the Panel and the facts recorded in the proceedings of the panel that the parties to the dispute have no objection are sufficient, The appellate body may continue to examine the disputes between the two parties and make rulings and conclusions on the issues in dispute.

D. Procedures for the adoption of Panel and Appellate Body reports. The reports of both the Panel and the Appellate Body must be discussed and adopted by the Dispute Settlement Body to form the decisions and recommendations of the Dispute Settlement Body. In contrast to the GATT dispute settlement mechanism, the WTO Dispute Settlement Body has made a major breakthrough in the procedure for adopting panel and Appellate body reports, replacing the previous consensus principle with the reverse consensus principle, which means that a panel or appellate body report can be rejected only if all members of the dispute Settlement Body disapprove it. The principle of reverse consensus has greatly strengthened the binding force of the WTO dispute settlement mechanism, and also endowed the panel and appellate body with the maximum independent trial power, which reflects the independence of the WTO dispute settlement mechanism.

E. Procedure for supervising the implementation of rulings and recommendations. The party found to have violated the relevant agreement shall implement the ruling and recommendations of the dispute Settlement Body within a reasonable time. If the accused party fails to perform the award and recommendation within a reasonable period of time, the original complaining party may, in cross-retaliation authorized by the dispute Settlement Body, suspend concessions or other obligations to the accused party, provided that the level and scope of such suspension or suspension of other obligations shall be equal to the damage suffered. The so-called cross retaliation means that retaliation should be carried out in the same industrial sector, and when the same industrial sector is not enough to achieve the level of retaliation, it can be retaliated across industrial sectors, and finally it can be retaliated across the scope of the agreement.

For example, if country A's illegal measures hindered the import of textiles from country B, country A was sued and lost, and the WTO ruling required country A to cancel its illegal measures within a time limit. If State A fails to comply with the judgment, State B may retaliate against State A with the authorization of the dispute Settlement Body. If country A's exports of textiles to country B are limited, Country B can retaliate against other products that country A exports to country B. If Country A exports goods to Country B is limited, country B can retaliate against Country A in the field of trade in services and intellectual property rights, whether with industrial sectors, cross-industry sectors or cross-agreement retaliation. The level of retaliation shall be comparable to the damage suffered by State B as a result of State A's contravention.

Section Ⅲ ICSID Dispute Settlement Mechanism

Ⅰ. International Center for the Settlement of Investment Disputes (ICSID)

Investment disputes between countries can be settled by traditional dispute settlement methods in public international law such as negotiation, good offices, mediation or the jurisdiction of the International Court, while disputes between private investors of different nationalities can be settled by traditional methods in domestic law such as negotiation, mediation, commercial arbitration or judicial proceedings. However, these traditional dispute settlement methods are insufficient to resolve investment disputes between countries and nationals of other countries. Thus, in 1965, the World Bank sponsored the conclusion of the Convention on the Settlement of Investment Disputes between States and Nationals of Other States, which provided a convenient means for the settlement of such disputes.

The Convention on the Settlement of Investment Disputes between States and Nationals of Other States entered into force in 1966 because it was adopted in Washington, USA, and is also known as the Washington Convention. Our country signed the Convention on 9 February 1990 and submitted its instrument of ratification on 7 January 1993.

The purpose of the Convention is to establish an international center for the settlement of investment disputes, hereafter known as the Centre or ICSID, to facilitate mediation or arbitration for the settlement of investment disputes between Contracting States and nationals of other Contracting States.

Ⅱ. Conditions of the Center's Jurisdiction

(Ⅰ) In respect of the principal part. The admissibility of disputes is limited to disputes between the Government of one Contracting State (the host State) and nationals of another Contracting State (foreign investors), but disputes between the host State and legal persons of the host State controlled by the foreign investor are also admissible if both parties to the dispute agree. For example, Company A in country A sets up company B solely in Country B, and Country B imposes the property of Company B, resulting in the loss of Company B and Company A. 1. If A dispute is brought by Company A of

Country A and Country B, the Center may accept the dispute if other conditions are met. If a dispute is brought by Company B and Country B established in Country B, the Center may also accept the dispute if both parties agree.

(II) The nature of the dispute. The accepted dispute must be a legal dispute directly arising from the international investment.

(III) Subjective conditions. Both parties to the dispute need to issue a written document agreeing to the jurisdiction of the Center.

III. The Legal Consequences of the Center's Jurisdiction

Unless otherwise stated, submission to the Centre for arbitration shall be deemed to be an agreement by the parties to exclude any other remedy, provided that the host country may require the investor to exhaust all local administrative or judicial remedies as a condition of its agreement to submit to the Centre for arbitration.

IV. Law Applicable to Settlement of Investment Disputes

In accordance with the provisions of the Convention, the Central Tribunal shall decide the dispute in accordance with the rules of law agreed by the parties to the dispute. If the parties to the dispute do not agree on the applicable rules of law, the arbitral tribunal shall apply the domestic law of the Contracting State that is a party to the dispute and the applicable rules of international law. In addition, the arbitral tribunal may decide the dispute in accordance with the principles of fairness and good faith when the parties to the dispute agree.

(I) Law on the application of consent of the parties. According to Article 42, paragraph 1, of the Convention, the arbitral tribunal must first apply the rules of law agreed to by the parties, which explicitly recognizes the principle of autonomy of the parties' choice of law.

The Convention does not limit what law the parties choose to apply. It is generally accepted that the parties have absolute freedom of choice of law, and may choose domestic law, international law, or both; The domestic law chosen may be the law of the host country or the domestic law of the investor, or the law of a third country. The chosen international law can govern the whole investment relationship or it can govern part of the relationship. Whatever law the parties choose, the Central tribunal is obliged to respect the choice of the parties. In practice, most investment agreements between foreign investors and the host country are governed by the laws of the host country.

The choice of the parties shall be limited to their express consent. If the domestic law of a State to which the parties have agreed has subsequently changed, should the arbitral tribunal apply the law as it was at the time of the agreement or should it apply the law as it changed at the time of the arbitration? In this regard, it has been argued that the law at the time of arbitration (including the limitation rules therein) should apply. Still, the Convention also allows the parties to agree that the law at the time of contracting should apply, and if there is such agreement, the law of such agreement should apply.

(Ⅱ) Supplementary rules for the application of law in the absence of agreement between the parties.

A. Application of the law of the host country. There should be no doubt that the arbitral tribunal should apply the law of the host country when the parties have no choice of law. Since investment activities are carried out in the territory of the host country, they should be subject to the territorial jurisdiction of the host country. In addition, the place where the investment contract is concluded and the place where the contract is performed is usually in the territory of the host country and has the closest connection with the host country. The application of the law of the host country mainly refers to the application of the substantive law of the host country, and the conflict rules are only applicable in special circumstances. In the event of a change in the law of the host country, the arbitral tribunal shall, in general, apply the law at the time of the arbitration.

B. Application of international law. As to whether international law should be applied, there was a debate between developing and developed countries in the process of formulating the Convention. Many representatives of developing countries oppose the application of international law, arguing that investment relations in disputes are governed by the domestic law of the host country and never by international law, and international law does not reflect the interests of newly independent countries, but is mainly used to protect the interests of industrial powers or nationalists. The application of international law is harmful to the interests of developing countries. The representatives of the developed countries were in favor of providing for the application of international law, arguing that domestic law would usually always be applied, but above all including the possibility of applying international law, which provided additional protections for private foreign investors. Domestic courts in many countries must apply not only domestic law, but also international law, etc. The Convention's provision that international law is applicable is the result of a compromise between developing and developed countries.

（Ⅲ）Concerning the application of the law established by the rules prohibiting refusal of judgment. The provisions of Article 42, paragraph 2, of the Convention are referred to as the rule prohibiting refusal of judgment. Under this rule, the arbitral tribunal must decide a dispute referred to it even if the applicable law lacks a norm applicable to the case or if the relevant provisions are vague. In addition, Article 48, paragraph 3, provides that: "The award shall address each issue brought before the Tribunal and state the grounds on which it was based. In this way, Article 42, paragraph 2, might be interpreted as permitting the tribunal to apply general principles of law, that is, to draw appropriate general principles and rules from the systems of domestic law and international law of other States and apply them.

（Ⅳ）On the application of the principle of fairness and good will with the special consent of the parties. According to Article 42, paragraph 3, of the Convention, the parties may authorize the arbitral tribunal to make an award on the basis of the principle of public good, regardless of whether the law is applicable or not, or whether the law is unclear. The so-called fair and good principle means that the arbitrator, with the consent of both parties, can make a binding award based on other fair and reasonable criteria, rather than in accordance with legal provisions. Therefore, some people call it non-legal standard. In practice, the so-called friendship arbitration and the principle of fairness and kindness are often shared.

V. Recognition and Enforcement of Awards

In accordance with Article 53 of the Convention, the arbitral award of the Centre shall be binding on the parties to the investment dispute, and neither party shall raise any such objection to the arbitral award or resort to any remedy other than that provided for in the Convention. Except in cases of suspension under the Convention, the parties and the courts of each State Party concerned shall comply with and enforce the arbitral award of the Centre.

参考文献

一、英文文献

（一）英文专著

［1］Aaditya Mattoo, Robert M. Stern, Gianni Zanini. A Handbook of International Trade in Services ［M］. Oxford：Oxford University Press, 2007.

［2］Correa, Carlos María. Trade Related Aspects of Intellectual Property Rights：A Commentary on the TRIPS Agreement ［M］. Oxford：Oxford University Press, 2007.

［3］Debashis Chakraborty, Oindrila Dey. Influence of WTO and Global Dynamics on Trade Flows ［M］. Singapore：Springer Singapore, 2024.

［4］Eun Sup Lee. A Guide to International Trading ［M］. Cham：Springer Cham, 2023.

［5］EUN SUP LEE. World Trade Regulation International Trade under the WTO Mechanism ［M］. Cham：Springer, 2012.

［6］Jarrod Hepburn. Domestic Law in International Investment Arbitration ［M］. New York：Oxford University Press, 2017.

［7］J. Bradford Jensen. Global Trade in Services：Fear, Facts and Offshoring ［M］. Washington D C：Peterson Institute for International Economics, 2011.

［8］Marc Bungenberg, August Reinisch. From Bilateral Arbitral Tribunals and Investment Courts to a Multilateral Investment Courts：Options Regarding the Institutionalization of Investor-State Dispute Settlement ［M］. New York：Spinger International Publishing, 2018.

［9］Michiel Spanjaart. Multimodal Transport Law ［M］. London：Routledge, 2017.

［10］Nicolas F. Diebold. Non-Discrimination in International Trade in Services："Likeness" in WTO/GATS ［M］. Cambridge：Cambridge University Press, 2010.

［11］Norman A. Martinez Gutiérrez. Serving the Rule of International Maritime Law ［M］. London：Routledge, 2009.

［12］Petros C. Mavroidis. Trade in Goods：The GATT and the Other WTO Agreements Regulating Trade in Goods ［M］. Oxford: Oxford University Press, 2012.

［13］ Rudolf Dolzer, Christoph Schreuer. Principles of International Investment Law ［M］. New York: Oxford University Press, 2008.

［14］ Stephen Girvin. Carriage of Goods by Sea ［M］. Oxford: Oxford University Press, 2011.

［15］ Stephen Schill. The Multilateralization of International Investment Law ［M］. Cambridge: Cambridge University Press, 2015.

［16］ Van Harten, Gus. Investment Treaty Arbitration and Public Law ［M］. New York: Oxford University Press, 2017.

［17］ WTO Secretariat. Guide to the GATS: An Overview of Issues for Further Liberalization of Trade in Services ［M］. The Hague: Kluwer Law International, 2001.

（二）英文期刊

［1］ Anthea Roberts. Investment Treaties: The Reform Matrix ［J］. American Journal of International Law, 2018, 112: 191-196.

［2］ Ghosh, Atish Rex, Stanley, Andrew. The Evolving IMF ［J］. Finance and Development, 2024, 61 (2): 16-17.

［3］ Henrique Sachetim, Rafael Codeco. The Investor-State Dispute Settlement System Amidst Crisis, Collapse, and Reform ［J］. Arbitration Brief, 2019, 6 (1): 20-59.

［4］ Kendra Leite. The Fair and Equitable Treatment Standard: A Search for a Better Balance in International Investment Agreements ［J］. American University International Law Review, 2016, 32 (1): 363-401.

［5］ Kristine Kruma. Sustainable Development in World Trade Law ［J］. European Law Journal, 2008, 14 (3): 387-388.

［6］ Malcolm Langford, Daniel Behn, Runar Hilleren Lie. The Revolving Door in International Investment Arbitration ［J］. Journal of International Economic Law, 2017, 20 (2): 301-332.

［7］ Marceau, Gabrielle Z. Silence in WTO ［J］. Journal of World Trade, 2022, 56 (2): 187-214.

［8］ McGuirk K. Intellectual Property and Information Wealth: Issues and Practices in the Digital Age ［J］.? Online Information Review, 2008, 32 (4): 543-544.

［9］ Michael Faure, Wanli Ma. Investor-State Arbitration: Economic and Empirical Perspectives ［J］. Michigan Journal of International Law, 2020, 41 (1): 1-62.

［10］ Mira Burri. Intellectual Property, Public Policy, and International Trade ［J］. European Journal of International Law, 2009, 20 (3)：923-925.

　　［11］ Peter Muchlinski. Caveat Investor? the Relevance of the Conduct of the Investor under the Fair and Equitable Treatment Standard ［J］. International & Comparative Law Quaterly, 2006, 3 (55)：527-558.

　　［12］ Ruto, William. A Consensus is Forming for IMF Reform ［J］. Finance and Development, 2024, 61 (2)：42-44.

　　［13］ Te-Cheng Lu, Jin-Li Hu, Yan-Shu Lin. Coordination of Trade and Intellectual Property Rights Policies Additional Contact Information ［J］. The Singapore Economic Review (SER), 2023, 68 (5)：1771-1785.

二、中文文献

（一）中文专著

　　［1］ 查尔斯·希尔，托马斯·霍特. 国际商务（英文版）［M］. 北京：中国人民大学出版社，2018.

　　［2］ 陈安. 陈安论国际经济法学 ［M］. 上海：复旦大学出版社，2008.

　　［3］ 陈安. 中国特色话语：陈安论国际经济法学（四卷本）［M］. 北京：北京大学出版社，2018.

　　［4］ 陈安. 国际经济法学 ［M］. 北京：北京大学出版社，2024.

　　［5］ 东村仁. 知识产权贸易论 ［M］. 北京：中国政法大学出版社，2024.

　　［6］ 法国商法典 ［M］. 金邦贵译. 北京：中国法制出版社，2000.

　　［7］ 范健. 德国商法：传统框架与新规则 ［M］. 北京：法律出版社，2003.

　　［8］ 高祥. 《国际贸易术语解释通则2020》理解与适用 ［M］. 北京：北京对外经济贸易大学出版社，2021.

　　［9］ 国际商会. 国际贸易术语解释通则·2020 ［M］. 中国国际商会/国际商会中国国家委员会组织译. 北京：对外经济贸易大学出版社，2020.

　　［10］ 国际商会中国国家委员会. 2000年国际贸易术语解释通则 ［M］. 曲鹏程译. 北京：中信出版社，2000.

　　［11］ 韩立余. 世界贸易组织法 ［M］. 北京：中国人民大学出版社，2014.

　　［12］ 姜作利. 国际贸易法（英文版）［M］. 北京：中国人民大学出版社，2015.

　　［13］ 姜作利. 国际商法（双语版）［M］. 北京：法律出版社，2020.

　　［14］ 李贺. 报检与报关实务 ［M］. 上海：上海财经大学出版社，2022.

　　［15］ 刘剑文. 国际税法学 ［M］. 北京：北京大学出版社，2020.

［16］美国法学会，美国统一州法委员会．美国《统一商法典》及其正式评述［M］．孙新强译．北京：中国人民大学出版社，2004.

［17］Ray August．国际商法（影印本）［M］．北京：高等教育出版社，2007.

［18］上海国际经济贸易仲裁委员会．中国企业 RCEP 国家经贸风险防范和争端解决指引［M］．上海：上海人民出版社，2023.

［19］石静霞，陈卫东．WTO 国际服务贸易成案研究［M］．北京：北京大学出版社，2005.

［20］石静霞，韩天竹，杨幸幸．WTO 服务贸易法［M］．北京：北京大学出版社，2021.

［21］王贵国．国际投资法：中国视角［M］．北京：法律出版社，2022.

［22］王贵国．国际货币金融法［M］．北京：法律出版社，2007.

［23］姚梅镇．国际经济法概论［M］．武汉：武汉大学出版社，2004.

［24］银红武．ICSID 公约理论与实践问题研究［M］．北京：中国政法大学出版社，2016.

［25］张建．国际投资法原理［M］．北京：首都经济贸易大学出版社，2023.

［26］张乃根．WTO 与贸易有关的知识产权协定［M］．北京：北京大学出版社，2018.

［27］张晓君．国际服务贸易救济法律制度研究［M］．厦门：厦门大学出版社，2012.

［28］中国国际商会，国际商会中国国家委员会．国际商会指南运输业与《国际贸易术语解释通则·2010》［M］．北京：对外经济贸易大学出版社，2019.

［29］朱金生．国际贸易理论与实务［M］．北京：人民邮电出版社，2011.

（二）中文期刊

［1］戴艺晗．WTO 数字贸易政策与区域主义多边化进程［J］．国际贸易，2021（11）：16-23.

［2］方乐．中国海外投资保险制度的反思与重构——以政策性与商业性的融合为切入口［J］．金融与经济，2023（7）：18-27.

［3］高祥．《国际贸易术语解释通则》的使用方式与适用范围［J］．中国外汇，2023（22）：42-45.

［4］郭萍，许凯婷．《国际贸易术语解释通则2020》内容演进及其对国际贸易之影响［J］．法治论坛，2020（2）：82-100.

［5］韩爽，韩露．平衡安全与发展：中国出口管制的发展路径［J］．经济体制改革，2021（5）：34-40.

［6］洪晓东．世贸组织的变化、挑战和未来［J］．国际经济评论，2022

（1）：21-25.

　　［7］胡绪雨．国际海上班轮货物运输合同中强制性规则的适当性［J］．中国法学，2016（6）：198-213.

　　［8］胡正良．《海牙规则》之回顾与启示［J］．中国海商法研究，2024（3）：19-31.

　　［9］靳也．国际投资争端解决中条约解释的一致性：实践冲突、价值反思与改革目标［J］．环球法律评论，2020（5）：178-182.

　　［10］瞿霞，葛顺奇．多边投资担保机制的价值及中国企业的应用建议［J］．国际贸易，2021（10）：88-95.

　　［11］李俊久，姜默竹．人民币"入篮"与国际货币体系未来走向［J］．现代国际关系，2016（6）：5-12.

　　［12］李阳．论《汉堡规则》对传统海运强国的影响［J］．宁夏社会科学，2014（3）：38-44.

　　［13］刘慧芝．国际贸易术语对信用证实务的影响［J］．中国外汇，2023（22）：58-59.

　　［14］刘楠，郭萍．承运人之履行辅助人责任问题研究［J］．甘肃社会科学，2015（2）：149-152.

　　［15］潘灿君．美国337条款对我国海外知识产权纠纷援助机制的启示［J］．电子知识产权，2011（5）：56-60.

　　［16］唐海霞，王德高．人民币"入篮"对我国经济的影响［J］．中国管理信息化，2017（14）：117-118.

　　［17］郑玲丽．国家安全视域下美国出口管制法嬗变及中国应对方案——以WTO中美出口管制案为例［J］．武大国际法评论，2023（6）：138-157.

　　［18］朱文龙．投资者与东道国争端解决机制中的调解及我国的因应［J］．国际经济法学刊，2023（2）：107-121.